POLITICISING PARENTHOOD IN SCANDINAVIA

Gender relations in welfare states

Edited by Anne Lise Ellingsæter and Arnlaug Leira

Published in Great Britain in June 2006 by

The Policy Press
University of Bristol
Fourth Floor
Beacon House
Queen's Road
Bristol BS8 1QU
UK

Tel +44 (0)117 331 4054
Fax +44 (0)117 331 4093
email tppinfo@bristol.ac.uk
www.policypress.org.uk

Reprinted 2007

British Library Cataloguing in Publication Data
A catalogue record for this book is available from the British Library.

Library of Congress Cataloging-in-Publication Data
A catalog record for this book has been requested.

ISBN13 978 1 86134 645 2 (paperback)
ISBN-13 978 1 86134 646 9 (hardcover)

Cover design by Qube Design Associates, Bristol
Front cover: photograph supplied by kind permission of www.samfoto.com
Printed and bound in Great Britain by Athenaeum Press, Gateshead

Contents

List of boxes, figures and tables

Boxes

Figures

Tables

Acknowledgements

For the past two years, the contributors to this volume have provided a stimulating sharing of ideas – a great pleasure and challenge. During the early stages, the work was much encouraged by the generous support of Professor Jane Lewis, London School of Economics and Political Science, and Professor Annemette Sørensen, Harvard University. We gratefully acknowledge the financial support of the Norwegian Research Council's Welfare State Programme. The project has been based at the Institute for Social Research in Oslo, and as always the Institute has provided excellent services. Our warm thanks also to the editors at The Policy Press for their competent and patient assistance during the process.

List of contributors

Thomas P. Boje, Professor, Department of Social Sciences, Roskilde University, Denmark.

Anette Borchorst, Associate Professor, Department of History, International and Social Studies, Aalborg University, Denmark.

Anne Lise Ellingsæter, Professor, Department of Sociology and Human Geography, University of Oslo, and Senior Research Fellow, Institute for Social Research, Oslo, Norway.

Anita Haataja, Senior Researcher, Government Institute for Economic Research (VATT), Helsinki, Finland.

Heikki Hiilamo, Kirkkohallitus/KDY (The Church Council, Department of Diaconia and Social Responsibility), Helsinki, Finland.

Johanna Lammi-Taskula, Senior Researcher, STAKES (National Research and Development Centre for Welfare and Health), Helsinki, Finland.

Arnlaug Leira, Professor, Department of Sociology and Human Geography, University of Oslo, Norway.

Anita Nyberg, Professor, Department of Labour Law, Labour Market and Citizenship, The National Institute for Working Life, Stockholm, Sweden.

Marit Rønsen, Senior Research Fellow, Division for Social and Demographic Research, Statistics Norway, Oslo, Norway.

Minna Salmi, STAKES (National Research and Development Centre for Welfare and Health), Helsinki, Finland.

Anne Skevik, Research Fellow, NOVA (Norwegian Social Research), Oslo, Norway.

Kari Skrede, Director of Research, Division for Social and Demographic Research, Statistics Norway, Norway.

ONE

Introduction: politicising parenthood in Scandinavia

Anne Lise Ellingsæter and Arnlaug Leira

During an historically short time span, family forms and family practices have been profoundly transformed throughout Western Europe. Falling birth rates, ageing populations, rising employment rates of mothers and increasing divorce and parental separation have all prompted questions about the future of the family institution. Demographic, economic and cultural change necessitates welfare state restructuring. Changing patterns of welfare needs and risks are giving impetus to a rethinking of the relationship between the welfare state and parents with young children. The 'politicisation of parenthood' forms part of wide-ranging, controversial political processes in which gender relationships in parenting and family obligations are redesigned. While there are many commonalities in these trends, there are significant differences among countries (see, for example, Millar and Warman, 1996; Bettio and Prechal, 1998; Esping-Andersen, 1999; Lewis, 2002; Michel and Mahon, 2002; Hantrais, 2004; Saraceno, 2005). How to respond to the needs of working parents has become a pressing social policy issue in contemporary European welfare states.

This book is a critical assessment of the Scandinavian experience of balancing work and childcare, providing a unique updated documentation and synthesis of the politicising of parenthood in Scandinavia since the 1990s. Drawing upon studies from Denmark, Finland, Norway and Sweden, the main questions addressed are: What typifies the Nordic welfare state approach to work/family balance during this period of economic fluctuations and ideological shifts? What are the effects of policy interventions, as evidenced for example in their reception among mothers and fathers? Of particular interest is the influence of the policy rationale of 'free choice' in childcare reform and parental response; are the Scandinavian welfare states facing the end of gender equality as a central aim of work/family policy? For convenience the terms 'Scandinavia' and 'Nordic countries' are used interchangeably in this book, although 'Scandinavia' in a strict sense usually refers to Denmark, Norway and Sweden, and 'the Nordic countries' often includes Finland and Iceland.

Why consider the Scandinavian model – again?

Today, as all Western industrialised societies are destined to grapple with an upheaval of gender relations similar to the one experienced since the 1960s and 1970s in the Nordic region, the Scandinavian endeavour meets with renewed interest. Gender equality, facilitated by generous work/family policy, is increasingly being considered a prerequisite of a productive society (Esping-Andersen et al, 2002). In a European policy context, the mobilisation of women's labour market reserves and the maintenance of reasonable fertility rates have emerged as major policy ambitions (for example the European Union's European Employment Strategy). In a period of profound family change, reform aimed at supporting/changing the work/ family arrangements of parents with young children has attained new dimensions. Ambitious targets for childcare provision set at the European Council in Barcelona in 2002 state that, by 2010, such provision has to be in place for one in three of the under-threes and for 90% of children between three years and mandatory school age. The Scandinavian countries are the only ones expected to reach the targets (European Communities, 2004).

The Scandinavian welfare states pioneered the transformation of parenthood into political issues. As employment of women, including the mothers of young children, was gaining ground from the 1960s, the position of women in society was increasingly debated. The inequalities women faced – in the educational system, in access to the labour market and in wages, politics and public life – were redefined as political concerns and coincided with the larger societal project of welfare state expansion and institutionalisation of social rights. The politicisation of parenthood and gender equality were closely linked. From the 1970s, politically, gender equality was an important part of the welfare state model, and legislation facilitating the reconciliation of work and family was passed to this end. The dual-earner/dual-carer family model set new standards for gender relations in families with young children. Apparently, welfare state intervention in gender and family arrangements has been more widely accepted, indeed *expected* in social democratic Scandinavia than in states of a liberal or conservative bent (Leira, 2002).

In the 1990s parenthood policy redesign took place in a context of the rapidly changing economic and cultural environments of the Scandinavian welfare states. Economic recession, increased pressures from globalising economies, and the deregulation of labour markets were interpreted as forewarnings of a demise of the Scandinavian model. External constraints necessitated a rethinking and 'recasting' of the welfare state. The revival of neoliberal ideological currents has further challenged the traditional set-up and values of the Scandinavian welfare states, adding to the pressure to restructure social benefits and services. The sustainability of a high-cost, universally oriented, egalitarian welfare state is increasingly in question. The value base is challenged by changing welfare risk patterns in regard to economic provision and care, and by increasing individualisation, flexibilisation and diversification and emphasising consumers' choice vis-à-vis the welfare state. The dynamics of the welfare state response to changing external and internal tension is moulded in the interplay of policies, economic structures, cultural norms and historic trajectories.

In many ways, the Scandinavian approach to gender and family modernisation has been successful. The Nordic countries have the highest scores on United Nations' gender equality indexes – the Gender Development Index (GDI) and the Gender Empowerment Measure (GEM) – which measure the gender distribution of welfare and access to economic/power resources, respectively. Nordic fertility rates are among the highest in Europe (Rønsen and Skrede, this volume), as are the employment rates of mothers – a combination often taken as an indicator of the impact of parenthood policies facilitating the reconciliation of work and childcare for both mothers and fathers. The Scandinavian 'parenthood policy experiments' – extensive policy packages addressing the parents of young children – are clearly receiving wider interest in the ongoing European debates. In a recent contribution, Ulrich Beck and Anthony Giddens (2005) express the more general renewal of interest in Scandinavia this way: 'The most egalitarian and solidary societies in Europe (indeed, in the world), the Scandinavian countries, have also been the most reformist.... How much can the rest of Europe ... learn from these more successful countries? Many say, not much, because they are mostly small and have distinctive welfare systems that can't be copied elsewhere. But we say: a lot. We can't all become Scandinavians. But we can profit from examples of best practice'.

Politicising parenthood

In contemporary welfare states parenthood is increasingly attracting public interest and concern, and projected as a matter for political intervention and investment. Issues of parenting, childcare and gender equality take centre stage in often heated public and political debates. The question of which family forms, if any, the welfare state should support reflects on what a family *is* and *should* be today – who and what should constitute a family and moral conceptions about what families are for (Silva and Smart, 1999; Beck-Gernsheim, 2002; Ellingsæter and Leira, 2004). Experienced at the individual level, post-industrial parenthood displays conflicts associated with the transition to post-industrial societies to do with the social organisation and value foundations of society. New arrangements and norms governing the relationship between parents, labour markets and welfare states are confronting the institutional order and traditions of the industrial era.

The concept 'politicising parenthood' in this book is used in a broad sense, referring to the complex processes shaping policies of parenthood. 'Politicising parenthood' centres on the relationship between parents and the state and its transformation in the ongoing renegotiation of boundaries between the public and the private. As applied in the book, 'politicising parenthood' includes the public motivation and mobilisation for reform of policies of parenthood; the political processes in which these policies are formulated, legislated and enacted; and, finally, the public and parental response to policy interventions, that may in turn feed back into public debate and political mobilisation, policy formulation and so on. The various chapters highlight one or more of these processes.

Politicising parenthood is nothing new, as family history has amply demonstrated. Indeed, it has been argued that 'family' and 'parenthood' like all social institutions and practices are politicised – at least implicitly. Some illustrations: in the 1970s Zillah Eisenstein (1981) argued the analytical distinction between 'biological' and 'political' motherhood. Jacques Donzelot (1980) examined the 'policing of families' in the history of France. The necessity of 'politicising the private sphere' to undermine the 'patriarchal' family order was an influential idea in Scandinavian feminism. Helga Hernes (1987) introduced the 'woman-friendly' welfare state in her analysis of welfare states and woman power in Scandinavia.

The discussions of the Scandinavian experience in this book focus on the changing assumptions of motherhood, fatherhood and parenthood in policy-making and legislation central to the work/family and gender equality policies of the 1990s and early 2000s. Of special interest in this context is the politicising of parenthood evidenced in policy reforms regarding childcare and working hours: legislation of paid parental leave and cash benefits for child care; and expansion of state-sponsored early childhood education and care. Analyses of policy reforms are followed up by examinations of their reception among working mothers and fathers of young children.

It is increasingly acknowledged that the causal relationship between family policies and family change can be quite complex. The politicising of parenthood confronts changes in family values and norms as family forms in the early 2000s have 'recovered their complexity', to use Göran Therborn's (2004) expression. Policy interventions may play different roles in different historic periods, and the timing of policy reform needs consideration. Welfare state policies may react or adapt to changing circumstances, or may sometimes be proactive (Kautto et al, 2001). Some family policies respond to family change, some aim at conserving a traditional family pattern, while others aim to induce family change (Leira, 2002). Not all family change becomes the subject of policy reform. Policies instituted to close gaps that have developed between policy regulations and social practices in effect support ongoing social transformations, and thus can be expected to be more successful than reforms trying to reverse family trends (Ellingsæter, 2003).

Moreover, as will be demonstrated in the contributions to this volume, the meaning of seemingly similar national policies can be quite different (for example, Lammi-Taskula; Hiilamo; Boje; Skevik). Often the motivation behind such policies differs, and the context into which they are inserted is often different (Daly and Lewis, 2000). For instance, Bruning and Plantenga's (1999) comparative study of European parental leave regulations concludes that those regulations have a fairly broad range of policy aims embedded in their particular national policy mixes. Also, policy ambiguity and inconsistency are common (Daly, 2000; Daly and Lewis, 2000; Ellingsæter, 2003; this volume), and need to be taken into account.

The active role of parents in generating change in parenthood practices and policies should not be underestimated. Mothers' and fathers' practices are generated in the interplay of policies, economic structures, cultural norms and historic trajectories. The employment of mothers and the rearranging of the economic provider aspects of parenthood were well advanced before large-scale welfare state support was established, in Scandinavia as elsewhere (Leira, 1992). The conclusion of a comparative analysis of 16 countries from the early

1960s to the late 1980s actually suggests a relationship the other way around (Huber and Stephens, 2000): women's employment is an important determinant of expansion in welfare state services, after controlling for other social, political and historical factors. The hypothesis is that employed women need better welfare services to relieve their care work, and women's chances of success in making these claims increase with their increasing numbers. Distinct for Scandinavia is the considerable extent to which the state has adjusted policies according to women's changing needs, processes in which the presence of social democratic governments has been a vital factor.

Gender equality – the Scandinavian way

The politicisation of parenthood of the 1970s was strongly influenced by *universalism* and *egalitarianism*, that is, what welfare state analysis commonly takes as the core values in the constitution of the so-called 'social democratic Nordic model' (Esping-Andersen, 1990, 1999). The Nordic welfare state model is usually classified as institutional in that it provides a wide range of services and benefits that are commonly universalist in orientation, often redistributive in aim, and often perceived as entitlements of citizens. In his well-known typology of welfare states, Gøsta Esping-Andersen (1990, pp 27-8) points to the importance of universalism and egalitarianism as principles of legitimisation in the formative years of the Nordic social democratic welfare state model. In sum: 'This model crowds out the market, and consequently constructs an essential universal solidarity in favour of the welfare state. All benefit, all are dependent; and all will presumably feel obliged to pay' (Esping-Andersen, 1990, p 28). According to Joakim Palme (1999, p 9), the Nordic welfare state model is a distinctive development of social protection in Europe, having 'established a universal model of social protection, where benefits and services based on residence are combined with earnings-related social insurance programmes'.

The redistributive aspects of the Scandinavian welfare state are often underlined, and the welfare state model is interpreted as an expression of commitment to egalitarian values (see Siim, 1993; Sainsbury, 1996; Kautto et al, 1999). For example, 'the passion for equality' has been noted as a main characteristic of the welfare states in the region (Graubard, 1986). The welfare state is commonly expected to address inequalities in economic resources, political power and influence between social classes and regions. In the 1970s, the situation of women in society entered the political agenda. The egalitarian tradition was broadened to include sexual or gender inequality (Leira, 1993).

In the Nordic tradition, gender equality is about more than equality of opportunity; equality of outcome is an important part of policy thinking. Ideologically, the promotion of gender equality policies is legitimated as central to the promotion of the continuing processes of democratisation. Summarising the view of the Nordic Council of Ministers (1995, pp 10-12): Nordic politics commonly acknowledge that gender equality is crucial to democratic progress in the Nordic societies. Gender equality is integral to Scandinavian citizenship and represents a central element of the Nordic welfare state model. Further, equality between women and men is not only about labour market participation and economic independence, but also about work/family arrangements. If gender equality is to be realised, 'the distribution of the workload between women and men in the family and in society must be changed' (Nordic Council of Ministers, 1995, p 10).

In accordance with the views expressed, Nordic reproduction policies, and particularly the care of young children, have been reformulated as central to the promotion of gender equality. Policies aimed at the reconciliation of work and family emphasise the importance of improving opportunities for working motherhood, and, increasingly, for caring fatherhood. Welfare state investment (or intervention) in the care of children entails not just *defamilisation*, but also *refamilisation*, and provides a basis from which parents are entitled to make claims on the welfare state (Leira, 2002; this volume).

The gender equality model presented as predominant in Nordic parenthood policies promotes the parental sharing of both paid and unpaid work and care, and the dual-earner/dual-carer family. This is mainly a model supported by social democracy and the left. An alternative family model, often supported by the centre-right, is also evident in policy discourse. This model is formally gender-neutral, valorises unpaid work and care, and advocates making care 'costless' for the carer, for example by the use of cash grants for childcare and establishing social rights and benefits for unpaid carers. Generally, the policies endorsed are perceived as support for a traditional family model with mothers at home. In the mid-2000s, as parenthood policies targeting gender equality are challenged by the idea of parental choice, it may well be asked if the importance of gender equality policies and ideology, in particular the ambition of gender equality in outcome, is giving way to parental choice.

Families, gender equality and welfare states – research and politics

Theoretically, this book is influenced by Scandinavian research on the relationship between the welfare state and the family, by developments in international research on the family and family policy change and by the ongoing discussion of welfare state regimes and their different characteristics. Particularly important is the emphasis on integrating the study of family, gender, parenthood and social reproduction into welfare state analysis.

The relationship between research and politics has been closer in Scandinavia than in many other regions. The expanding welfare state increasingly made use of social research inputs. Criticising the overall positive functions commonly ascribed to the gender-differentiated nuclear family by traditional family sociology, Scandinavian scholars early on argued the advantages of less specialisation of the parental roles of mothers and fathers. Various 'shared role' family models were proposed in this research tradition, emphasising the benefits of mothers' employment and the participation of fathers at home. More attention was paid to the family as a site of conflicting interests. Throughout the 1970s radical gender-role thinking was influential in the politicising and legislation of gender equality. Advocating a more active involvement of the welfare state in supporting new family forms, policy proposals of social scientists included public support for extra-parental childcare, part-time work for mothers and fathers and part-time day care for the children.

In the following decades, the Scandinavian feminist strand of welfare state research developed a considerable body of knowledge about the relationship between the welfare state, families and gendered citizens. This tradition has introduced analytical perspectives and concepts that have caused debate. Changes in the relations between the labour market, family and welfare state were main issues (see, for example, Ruggie, 1984; Hernes, 1987). In particular, Helga Hernes' (1987) concept of the *woman-friendly* welfare state has received wide attention. She emphasised the 'woman-friendly' potentialities of the Nordic democracies, envisaging a state form in which 'injustice on the basis of gender would be largely eliminated' (1987, p 15) (for a recent discussion of this concept, see Borchorst and Siim, 2002). Pictured as a mix of grassroots activities interacting with initiatives from women in elite politics (Hernes, 1987), *state feminism* places women not only as policy-takers but also highly influential as policy-makers. Scandinavian studies show a continuing interaction of research and policy interests. Feminist research also pointed to the *collectivisation of social care* as one of the particular features of Nordic welfare policies. In the terms of the time, social reproduction was 'going public'. Analyses of the relationship of welfare states to working mothers demonstrated gender differences in the social rights of citizens as earners and carers (Borchorst and Siim, 1987; Hernes, 1987; Leira, 1992). As will be reflected in the contributions to this volume, a considerable body of research has accumulated since the 1990s on the relationship between the family, state and labour market. Among the most important additions in recent years is the integration of the labour market and the workplace, and the role of fathers, in particular the caring father, into the analysis.

A growing interest in the family institution, as defined in family law and welfare policies, and in the gendering of family responsibilities is noted in comparative European studies (see, for example, Anttonen and Sipilä, 1996; Millar and Warman, 1996; Bettio and Prechal, 1998; Hantrais, 2004). More recently, 'woman-friendliness' of policies and the need to 'update the gender contract' is also acknowledged in mainstream welfare state research (for example, Korpi, 2000; Esping-Andersen et al, 2002). As shown in a number of studies, the significance of the family institution and of gender relations is increasingly being integrated in comparative welfare research.

The context of policy reform

The period of policy redesign under study took place in a context of changing economic and cultural environments of the Scandinavian welfare states. Increased pressures from internationalised finance and product markets, and a revival of an ideology of the downscaling of welfare states and of labour market deregulation clearly challenge crucial features of the Scandinavian models (Ellingsæter, 2000). The 1990s was a period of unprecedented economic and employment problems in the Nordic region, most notably in Finland and Sweden (see Kautto et al, 1999; also Haataja and Nyberg, and Hiilamo, this volume). Unemployment levels reached a dramatic high of 16.8% in Finland in 1994, while for Sweden the highest rate registered in decades (9.9%) was noted in 1996 (OECD, 2004, p 293). Sweden's employment problems have since diminished, and unemployment has dropped to about 5% in recent years. Finland, however, is still experiencing high unemployment rates of around 9%. Norway's economic recession was over by 1993, when unemployment was at an historical high of 6.6%. Later, the level stabilised at around 4%. Unemployment levels in Denmark, historically in the Scandinavian context comparatively high, have fallen since the early 1990s, and in recent years have been commensurate with levels in Norway.

Women's labour market integration has been a robust feature of the Scandinavian models in the turbulence of the 1990s (Ellingsæter, 2000). Today the Scandinavian welfare states still have the highest activity rates among women in the industrialised world. In the age group 25-34, women's labour force rate was about 80% in all the four countries in 2004 (Nordic Council of Ministers, 2004). The gender difference was largest in Finland and Denmark, where men had activity rates 13 and 11 percentage points higher than women, while the rates of Norwegian and Swedish men were seven and six percentage points above women's.

Mothers' employment patterns also differ in the region. While the economic activity rate of mothers with children under six was 78% in Sweden and 73% in Norway in 2000, the corresponding rate in Finland was significantly lower, 59% (OECD, 2001). The prevalence of women's part-time work has been quite different, with Norway at the high and Finland at the low end, although differences have been declining in recent years.

High economic activity among young women goes together with relatively high fertility levels. While the fertility decline that started in the 1960s has continued in the rest of Europe, this trend reversed in the Nordic countries in the 1980s. Sweden has had a rather volatile development, however. During the recession period, fertility dropped drastically, from 2.13 in 1990, to 1.54 in 2000, but has since been increasing slowly. In 2002, the fertility rate was lowest in Sweden (1.65) and highest in Norway (1.75), with Denmark and Finland in between (1.72) (www.scb.se/BE0701).

Data – cases and comparisons

The different contributions in this volume in toto provide a comprehensive study of the multifaceted experience of childcare reforms since the 1990s in Denmark, Finland, Norway and Sweden. From a variety of analytical perspectives, a range of policies targeting parents is examined, including the expansion of childcare services as a social right of parents and children, the legislation of parental leave with a special leave for fathers, and the institution of cash benefits for childcare. Based on comparative statistical data and studies of the political history of gender equality and childcare, the similarities and differences among the Nordic countries are highlighted. Some chapters provide overviews of trends in Scandinavian demographic development, work/family and gender equality policies. Others take form as in-depth national case studies of parenthood policies. Some compare different policies aimed at reconciling work and family in two or more countries dealing mainly with the reception of reforms as measured in the take-up and use among mothers and fathers. The various chapters draw upon data from one or more of the Nordic countries. For an overview of current childcare policies, parental leave take-up rates among fathers, and day care coverage rates in the four countries, see Box 1.1 and Tables 1.1 and 1.2 in the appendix to this chapter.

The economic recession and post-recession development serve as a strategic case for examining the sustainability of the gender equality policy ambition. How did the economic downturns of the 1990s affect restructuring of policies of parenthood? In what ways have shifts in policy discourse emphasising flexibility, individualisation and freedom of choice influenced the universalist, regulationist and egalitarian traditions of the Scandinavian welfare model?

The contributions

The book is organised in three main parts. Part One, 'Politicising parenthood – legacies and challenges' (Chapters Two and Three), provides an outline of the main trends in the recent political history of work/family policies, gender equality and childcare, and of the demographic developments associated with these policies since the early 1970s.

Welfare state support for the reconciliation of work and family is widely regarded as a trademark of the Scandinavian welfare states. In Chapter Two, 'Parenthood change and policy reform: Scandinavia 1970s–2000s', Arnlaug Leira outlines the main trends in the social and political redesign of motherhood and fatherhood in Scandinavia from the early 1970s to the early 2000s. How has the welfare state addressed the two basic aspects of parenthood, that is, the *economic provider* and, in particular, the *caring, nurturing and upbringing* aspects? The focus is on the far-reaching policy reforms of setting parents free for paid work with the provision of extra-family childcare services, and the liberation of parents from paid work to be carers for their children. Examining the interplay of parenthood change and policy reform, the chapter highlights a dominant shift in 'parenthood thinking', namely the translation of parental responsibility for children's care into social rights of mothers and fathers.

Based on recent comparative studies, Marit Rønsen and Kari Skrede in Chapter Three, 'Nordic fertility patterns: compatible with gender equality?', examine the connection between policies of parenthood and fertility levels. The fertility development of the Nordic countries and the possible effects of the 'Nordic model of family welfare' have received considerable attention. The Nordic combination of high levels of female labour force participation with relatively high levels of fertility may suggest that a sustainable level of fertility is compatible with gender equality, and that family policies play an important role in generating this fortunate situation. However, there are reasons to take a critical look at these assumptions. In order to understand fertility dynamics, one needs to go beyond crude fertility rates. A diversification in fertility patterns characterises recent trends, with an increasing polarisation between those not having children and those having many children. It is argued that the role of family policies in maintaining high fertility levels is often overstated, and that the present Nordic fertility patterns indicate that a sustainable level of fertility in the long run is dependent on parenthood policies with stronger incentives for gender equality.

Part Two, 'Gender equality and parental choice in welfare state redesign' (Chapters Four to Seven), illuminates the responses of mothers and fathers to policy reforms, and analyses divergent influences of individualisation and choice in Scandinavian policy reforms in the 1990s. Special attention is paid to the politicising of fatherhood, and the different take-up and use of father-specific entitlements and entitlements framed as parental choice. Based on survey data and in-depth studies, the contributions take the 'daddy quota' of the parental leave schemes and cash grants for childcare as main policy cases.

Johanna Lammi–Taskula's 'Nordic men on parental leave: can the welfare state change gender relations' (Chapter Four) raises the crucial question: what is the likelihood of changing gender relations with the help of welfare policies such as parental leave? It was not until the 1990s that the working father came to be conceptualised as a social problem, and a period earmarked for fathers (the daddy quota) was introduced in parental leave schemes to promote the father's role as a parent. Focusing on the politicising of fatherhood, this chapter compares the current entitlements of fathers for taking parental leave in five Nordic countries: Sweden, Norway, Denmark,

Iceland and Finland. Based on a review of Nordic studies, the chapter further examines the socioeconomic and cultural conditions affecting the take-up of leave possibilities, and considers, in particular, negotiations of gender relations in the everyday life of families and workplaces.

Anette Borchorst explores the Danish case of politicising fatherhood in more detail in Chapter Five, 'The public–private split rearticulated: abolishment of the Danish daddy leave'. While the notion of men as carers has become an integral part of policies of gender equality in all the other Nordic countries, it has played a minor role in Denmark, where the right-wing government in 2002 *abolished* the daddy quota. This chapter focuses on the background for this decision. As part of the analysis, the timing of different policies influencing changes in the position of women from the 1960s onwards is addressed more generally, and childcare policies and policies of gender equality are dealt with more particularly. A long historical perspective on parliamentary negotiations on maternity and paternity leave from 1901 until the late 1990s is provided. How the decisions to adopt a daddy leave in 1997 and abolish it in 2001 illuminate Danish gender equality paradoxes is discussed.

The Scandinavian countries are usually associated with the dual-earner family model. However, in a historical perspective, Norway has been more of a hybrid: a dual-earner/traditional-breadwinner mix, combining policies classified as dual-earner support with generous cash transfers to families. It can be argued that the policy dualism has been reproduced in recent years. In Chapter Six, 'The Norwegian childcare regime and its paradoxes', Anne Lise Ellingsæter explores the current Norwegian childcare regime, focusing on regulations of parents' right to work versus care in the early stages of parenthood – the central contemporary battlefield for these issues. It is argued that a multi-causal, contextual approach is needed in the study of parenthood policies, and that approaching childcare policies as a 'regime' – examining parental leave, cash-for-care benefits and day care services *jointly* – adds to our insights about policy dynamics and uncovers contradictions inherent in the Norwegian childcare regime.

Based on survey data from 5,000 Finnish parents of young children, Minna Salmi analyses the outcome of the 1990s family policy reforms from a gender equality perspective in 'Parental choice and the passion for equality in Finland' (Chapter Seven). Two policy reforms are examined: first, parents' views on the arrangement of parental leave and how it should be shared between parents, and second, the issue of parents' choice of day care or a cash grant for care. A main question is whether childcare policy arrangements have actually worked for gender equality. The analysis further suggests that the new ways of developing family leave arrangements – presented by politicians and social partners – are in disharmony with the wishes of men and women who presently live in families with young children. And, there is a gap between general opinions about equality issues, such as men's role in parenting, and opinions at the more concrete level of sharing parental leave.

Part Three, 'Work, family and the welfare state: redefining family models' (Chapters Eight to Eleven), concentrates on the labour market–family interaction. Labour market transformations, such as underemployment and increasing labour market flexibility, provide an important structural context for policy reform and changing gender relations. As mentioned earlier, the Nordic countries ran into grave economic problems in the 1990s. The existence of a model based on full employment was in jeopardy because of soaring unemployment and dramatic increases in social expenditure.

In 'Woman-friendliness and economic depression: Finland and Sweden in the 1990s' (Chapter Eight), Heikki Hiilamo takes economic recession and recovery as a strategic case for examining the sustainability of the gender equality ambition of the two countries. The analysis focuses on the implications of family and parenthood policy reform in terms of economic gender equality, or more specifically the implication for women's economic autonomy. The study deals with policy developments during the 1990s, considering changes in the allocation of income transfers within families, taxation and services. How did family and parenthood policies in Finland and Sweden respond to recession and recovery? How did the aim of economic equality between women and men fare? In short, despite harsh economic conditions, may Sweden and Finland still be labelled as women-friendly welfare states?

Chapter Nine, 'Working time and caring strategies: parenthood in different welfare states' by Thomas P. Boje, compares two rather similar Scandinavian countries, Denmark and Sweden, with two other countries, the Netherlands and the United Kingdom (UK), with different work cultures and family policy systems. The variation in the level of employment and working-time strategies among mothers and fathers discloses social differences among groups of women. The chapter discusses how the choices of work/care strategies can be explained by the different childcare policies. Moreover, parents' subjective experience of work/family conflicts, and discrepancies between actual and preferred working time, are explored. Finally the implications for gender equality of different strategies in organising working time and care are elaborated.

In 'Diverging paths? The dual-earner/dual-carer model in Finland and Sweden in the 1990s' (Chapter Ten), Anita Haataja and Anita Nyberg compare the policy developments in the two countries. They argue that any analysis of change in policy models and their outcomes needs to be interpreted in relation to labour market developments and macro-economic conditions more generally. These are important premises for parents' opportunities of choice. The 1990s are particularly interesting in this respect since economic growth was negative at the beginning of the decade. The main analytical focus is on the response to or effects of policy interventions in combination with economic development, in terms of changes in mothers' and fathers' employment, unemployment and incomes. The analysis emphasises the need to analyse partnered and lone mothers separately, since parental response to and/or effects of the policies and economic development might differ.

In the course of the 1990s, an explicit policy goal of many countries has been to increase the labour market participation of lone mothers. The Nordic countries have sometimes been seen as pioneers in this respect, because all have had relatively high employment rates among lone mothers over long periods. What happened to the employment of this group after the economic depression and the institutional restructuring in the 1990s is discussed by Anne Skevik in 'Lone motherhood in the Nordic countries: sole providers in dual-breadwinner regimes' (Chapter Eleven). It is argued that the Nordic countries can be seen as 'natural laboratories' for lone mothers' employment: they are similar in many ways, but there are also crucial differences. They have faced different challenges and chosen different responses in the 1990s.

The Epilogue, Chapter 12, summarises main trends in the Nordic welfare states' approach to work/family balance since the 1990s, and returns to consider one of the main questions addressed: in what directions are parenthood policies taking gender relations?

References

Anttonen, A. and Sipilä, J. (1996) 'European social care services: is it possible to identify models?', *Journal of European Social Policy*, vol 6, no 2, pp 87-100.

Beck, U. and Giddens, A. (2005) 'Discovering Real Europe: a Cosmopolitan Vision'(www.policy-network.net/php/print_preview.php?aid=471).

Beck-Gernsheim, E. (2002) *Reinventing the Family*, Cambridge: Polity Press.

Bettio, F. and Prechal, S. (1998) *Care in Europe*, Joint report of the 'Gender and Employment' and the 'Gender and Law' Groups of Experts, Brussels: European Commission, DGV, Employment and Social Affairs.

Borchorst, A. and Siim, B. (1987) 'Women and the advanced welfare state: a new kind of patriarchal power', in A.S. Sassoon (ed) *Women and the State*, London: Hutchinson, pp 128-57.

Borchorst, A. and Siim, B. (2002) 'The woman friendly welfare states revisited', *NORA Nordic Journal of Women's Studies*, vol 10, no 2, pp 90-8.

Bruning, G. and Plantenga, J. (1999) 'Parental leave and equal opportunities: experiences in eight European countries', *Journal of European Social Policy*, vol 9, no 3, pp 195-209.

Daly, M. (2000) 'A fine balance: women's labor market participation in international comparison', in F.W. Scharpf and V.A. Schmid (eds), *Welfare and Work in the Open Economy*, Volume II, Oxford: Oxford University Press, pp 467-510.

Daly, M. and Lewis, J. (2000) 'The concept of social care and the analysis of contemporary welfare states', *British Journal of Sociology*, vol 51, pp 281-98.

Donzelot, J. (1980) *The Policing of Families*, London: Hutchinson.

Eisenstein, Z. (1981) *The Radical Future of Liberal Feminism*, New York, NY: Longman.

Ellingsæter, A.L. (2000) 'Scandinavian transformations: labour markets, politics and gender divisions', *Economic and Industrial Democracy*, vol 21, no 3, pp 335-59.

Ellingsæter, A.L. (2003) 'The complexity of family policy reform: the case of Norway', *European Societies*, vol 5, no 4, pp 419-43.

Ellingsæter, A.L. and Leira, A. (2004) *Velferdsstaten og familien: Utfordringer og dilemmaer*, Oslo: Gyldendal Akademisk.

Esping-Andersen, G. (1990) *The Three Worlds of Welfare Capitalism*, Cambridge: Polity Press.

Esping-Andersen, G. (1999) *Social Foundations of Postindustrial Economies*, Oxford: Oxford University Press.

Esping-Andersen, G. with Gallie, D., Hemerijck, A. and Myles, J. (eds) (2002) *Why We Need a New Welfare State*, Oxford: Oxford University Press.

European Communities (2004) *Jobs, Jobs, Jobs: Creating More Employment in Europe*, Report of the Employment Taskforce chaired by Wim Kok, Luxembourg: Office for Official Publications of the European Communities.

Graubard, S. (1986) *Norden – The Passion for Equality*, Oslo: Norwegian University Press.

Hantrais, L. (2004) *Family Policy Matters: Responding to Family Change in Europe*, Bristol: The Policy Press.

Hernes, H. (1987) *Welfare State and Woman Power*, Oslo: Norwegian University Press.

Huber, E. and Stephens, J.D. (2000) 'Partisan governance, women's employment, and the social democratic service state', *American Sociological Review*, vol 65, pp 323-42.

Kautto, M., Fritzell, J., Hvinden, B., Kvist, J. and Uusitalo, H. (2001) *Nordic Welfare States in the European Context*, London: Routledge.

Kautto, M., Heikkilä, M., Hvinden, B., Marklund, S. and Ploug, N. (1999) *Nordic Social Policy, Changing Welfare States*, London: Routledge.

Korpi, W. (2000) 'Faces of inequality: gender, class and patterns of inequalities in different types of welfare states', *Social Politics*, vol 7, no 2, pp 127-91.

Leira, A. (1992) *Welfare States and Working Mothers: The Scandinavian Experience*, Cambridge: Cambridge University Press.

Leira, A. (2002) *Working Parents and the Welfare State*, Cambridge: Cambridge University Press.

Lewis, J. (2002) 'Gender and welfare state change', *European Societies*, vol 4, no 4, pp 331-57.

Michel, S. and Mahon, R. (eds) (2002) *Child Care Policy at the Crossroads: Gender and Welfare State Restructuring*, New York, NY: Routledge.

Millar, J. and Warman, A. (1996) *Family Obligations in Europe*, London: Family Policy Studies Centre.

Nordic Council of Ministers (1995) *Gender Equality – the Nordic Model*, Copenhagen: Nordic Council of Ministers.

Nordic Council of Ministers (2004) *Nordic Statistical Yearbook 2004*, Copenhagen: Nordic Council of Ministers.

OECD (Organisation for Economic Co-operation and Development) (2001) *Employment Outlook 2001*, Paris: OECD.

OECD (2004) *Employment Outlook 2004*, Paris: OECD.

Palme, J. (1999) *The Nordic Model and the Modernisation of Social Protection in Europe*, Copenhagen: Nordic Council of Ministers.

Ruggie, M. (1984) *The State and Working Women*, Princeton, NJ: Princeton University Press.

Sainsbury, D. (1996) *Gender, Equality and Welfare States*, Cambridge: Cambridge University Press.

Saraceno, C. (2005) 'Family: from a specific and marginal subfield to a core issue both in social research and in policy discourses', Plenary lecture, ESA Research Network meeting ICS, University of Lisbon, 3-4 March.

Siim, B. (1993) 'The gendered Scandinavian welfare states: the interplay between women's roles as mothers, workers and citizens in Denmark', in J. Lewis (ed) *Women and Social Policies in Europe*, Aldershot: Edward Elgar, pp 25-48.

Silva, E.B. and Smart, C. (1999) 'The 'new' practices and politics of family life', in E.B. Silva and C. Smart (eds) *The New Family?*, London: Sage Publications, pp 1-30.

Therborn, G. (2004) *Between Sex and Power: Family in the World 1900–2000*, London and New York, NY: Routledge.

Appendix

Box 1.1: Leave for parents and childcare arrangements in Denmark, Finland, Norway and Sweden (2005)

Denmark

Leave for parents

Maternity leave: 18 weeks. The amount of the benefit is calculated on the basis of the income the worker/employee would have received if he/she had not been on maternity/paternity or parental leave. There is a maximum on the benefit paid by the municipality of 3,267 DKR per week, that is, approximately 435 euros per week. If the person receiving benefit is a member of an unemployment benefit scheme – which is voluntary in Denmark – the maternity/paternity or parental leave benefit amounts to the same sum as that person would receive in the case of unemployment. There is a combination of a general maximum which is 654 DKR per day, approximately 87 euros per day (for full-time workers), and a maximum of 90% of wages.

Paternity leave: A father is entitled to two weeks' paternity leave with unemployment benefit during the first 14 weeks after the birth of a child – normally immediately after.

Parental leave: 32 weeks following maternity leave to be shared by parents. There are some possibilities to prolong the parental leave period by accepting reduced benefit, and some possibilities to postpone the leave until later. Each parent is entitled to 32 weeks' leave following maternity leave (or in the father's case, during or following maternity leave). Subject to the employer's agreement, this leave can be taken until the child is nine years old. Wage compensation is 90% for a total of 32 weeks, which can be shared between the parents. Under collective agreements, up to 80% of parents have their unemployment benefit supplemented to full pay up to 24 weeks after the birth (including 18 weeks' maternity leave).

Childcare services

From July 2005 all municipalities have to offer a guarantee of childcare for children from the age of nine months until the school age of six years.

If the municipality fails, parents are entitled to economic compensation corresponding to private care with a maximum of the costs of day care facilities for children in the age group. Parents' fees are income related and are free for parents on a low income. A maximum is set at 30% of the costs (33% from July 2005).

Finland

Leave for parents

Maternity leave: 105 weekdays (Monday to Saturday). Maternity benefit, of 43% to 82% of earnings, is inversely proportional to earnings (66% average). Nearly half of all mothers with an employment contract receive full pay, with employers making up the difference. There is a minimum flat-rate allowance for those not employed before the birth; since 2005 this is 15.20 euros per weekday.

Paternity leave: Fathers are entitled to a total of 18 weekdays of leave, to be taken up during maternity leave or the mother's parental allowance period. Since 2003, it has been possible to extend the paternity leave by a 'bonus' of one to 12 weekdays if the father also takes the last 12 days of the parental allowance period. The extension must be taken in a single period immediately following the parental leave period. For wage compensation, see maternity leave. Full pay during the leave is not negotiated for fathers in collective agreements.

Parental leave: 158 weekdays (Monday to Saturday) between the parents. Parents can both take partial parental leave and work part time, provided that they each work 40% to 60% of their normal working hours. For wage compensation, see maternity leave. The incentive for high-income group fathers may be small due to the fact that the benefit is inversely proportional to earnings. Benefit during partial parental leave is half of full benefit.

Home care leave: Applies after parental leave until the child is three years of age. For benefit, see home care allowance.

Home care allowance

This benefit is paid for children whose parents do not use the entitlement to public day care services. The current benefit for one child is 294.28 euros per month, with an additional 84.09 euros for every other child under three, and 50.46 euros for every other child over three but under seven years of age. Benefit can be complemented by an additional sum of a maximum of 168.19 euros per month, the level depending on the size and income of the family.

The municipalities are obliged to arrange day care for a child at the end of maternal, paternal and parental leave, but if the entitlement is not used, the parents are entitled to home care allowance. Depending on the political interest and the cost of offering municipal day care, some municipalities pay extra home care allowance for parents who do not use their entitlement to day care. Thus, the actual level of home care benefits varies.

Childcare services

Since 1990 all children under the age of three are guaranteed a municipal childcare place irrespective of the labour market status of the parents. In 1996, this subjective right to day care was extended to cover all children under school age (seven years). Parents' fees amount to 15% of the costs.

Norway

Leave for parents

Maternity leave (included in legislation on parental leave): Three weeks before and six weeks after delivery.

Paternity leave: Two unpaid 'daddy weeks' around the time of birth, with wage compensation subject to collective agreements (in addition to the 44/54 weeks of parental leave).

Paternal leave: Daddy quota of six weeks (from 1 July 2006).

Parental leave: In total (including maternity leave and daddy quota), 44 weeks at 100% wage compensation or 54 weeks at 80% (duration/ payment is the choice of the parents) (from 1 July 2006). A time account scheme allows a flexible uptake of leave up to when the child is two years old.

Unpaid parental leave: Following paid parental leave, each parent is entitled to one year of unpaid leave, receiving a flat-rate cash benefit if the child does not attend state-sponsored day care.

Cash-for-care benefit

Parents with children of one to two years old who do not attend publicly subsidised childcare are entitled to a cash benefit of NOK 3,657 per month (about 430 euros) (2005). Parents with children who have part-time places in publicly supported services receive benefits proportional to the use of services, ranging from 80% benefit for eight weekly hours to 20% benefit for 25-32 hours.

Childcare services

Full coverage for childcare services is the political goal, implying the provision of places to all parents who want a place for their children. The last estimate of full coverage is 80% (children aged one to five) in 2005. Demand for places already exceeded 80% in 2002. Maximum payment for a full-time place was lowered from approximately 330 euros to 210 euros from 1 January 2006. About one in three institutions have income-graded payments.

Sweden

Leave for parents

Maternity leave (included in legislation on parental leave): 60 days.

Paternity leave: Statutory leave of 10 days in connection with the birth of the child, to be taken within 60 days after the child comes home from hospital. Daddy quota (included in legislation on parental leave) of 60 days.

Parental leave: Paid leave for 480 days. With the exception of 60 days per parent, leave can be transferred to the other parent. Mothers are entitled to draw parental benefit 60 days before the expected date of birth. Parental benefit can be drawn until the child reaches the age of eight, or until the end of the child's first year at school. Parents can choose part-time leave with reduced benefits. Compensation is subject to qualification criteria – 390 out of the 480 days are paid at sickness benefit level when relevant – otherwise at basic benefit level (180 SEK per day). 90 days are paid at minimum benefit level (60 SEK per day).

Childcare services

Municipalities have an obligation to provide day care for children whose parents work or study, or for children with a particular need for preschool activities. This obligation extends also to children of unemployed persons or persons on parental leave, for a minimum of three hours per day or 15 hours per week. A child will be offered a place without unreasonable delay, that is, normally within three to four months of the parents having requested a need for a place. A place will be offered as near to the child's home as possible. In addition, all children will be offered free pre-schooling for at least 525 hours per year from the autumn term of the year they reach their fourth birthday (general preschool). The municipalities are also required to provide childcare for school-aged children (until the child is 12 years old) whose parents work or study, or for children with a particular need for this form of care. Municipalities may apply a maximum fee for pre-school activities and childcare for schoolchildren. For pre-schools, families are charged a maximum of 3%, 2% or 1% of the combined household income for the household's first, second and third child, respectively. The monthly fee must, however, not exceed 1260 SEK for the first child, 840 SEK for the second, and 420 SEK for the third child in pre-school activities.

Sources: Information provided by contributors to this volume.

Table 1.1 Father's uptake of total leave days with benefit in the event of pregnancy, childbirth or adoption (%)

	Denmark	Finland	Iceland	Norway	Sweden
1990	4.1	2.4	..	..	8.8
2003	5.1	5.3	27.6	8.6	18.3

Source: Nordic Statistical Yearbook 2005.

Table 1.2 Children in day care as percentage of age group 2004[a]

Age of children	Denmark	Finland	Norway	Sweden
Total 0–5	77	45	58	69
0 years	12	1	2	0
1 years	78	28	33	45
2 years	87	45	54	87
3 years	94	62	79	92
4 years	94	69	87	96
5 years	97	73	89	97

Notes: [a] Includes children in publicly funded day care.

Denmark: Data for 2004 cannot be compared with 2003 and earlier due to new data collection.

Norway: 2003 data; children in open kindergartens are not included.

Source: Nordic Statistical Yearbook 2005.

Part One
Politicising parenthood –
legacies and challenges

TWO

Parenthood change and policy reform in Scandinavia, 1970s-2000s

Arnlaug Leira

Work/family policies to promote gender equality are widely regarded as a Scandinavian trademark,[1] and the institutional, universally oriented, social democratic welfare state is commonly presented as the driving force behind family change (Hernes, 1987; Esping-Andersen, 1999; Korpi, 2000). In the 1980s, the Nordic family was pictured as 'going public', the outcome of a grand political experiment to support new family arrangements. Mothers and fathers of the public family were both in paid work, while the 'caring state' provided day care services for children. Critical voices claimed that the welfare state was disrupting traditional family values and family solidarity (for example, Popenoe, 1988; Wolfe, 1989). In Helga Hernes' interpretation, however, work/family policies illustrated the 'woman-friendly' potentialities of the Nordic social democracies, enabling women 'to have a natural relationship to their children, their work and public life' (1987, p 15).

Welfare state typologies of the 1990s have added to the interventionist picture, placing social democratic Scandinavia as the more 'defamilising' (Esping-Andersen, 1999; Korpi, 2000). In Gøsta Esping-Andersen's analysis, social democracies differ from liberal and conservative welfare states in providing more services and benefits for families and households, and therefore in lessening the burdens on families. Unlike the conservative model, in which childcare arrangements are the responsibility of the family, and the liberal, which opts for a marketisation of services, the social democratic welfare state is sponsoring defamilised social, welfare and care services that facilitate the employment of women. Esping-Andersen (2002, p 20) further endorses Hernes' assessment of the qualities of Scandinavian reproduction policies, and takes woman-friendliness and gender equality as the main challenges for welfare state reform.

Implicit in the terms 'public family' and 'defamilising welfare state' is the assumption that it is the state that initiates the redesign of motherhood and childhood (fatherhood change is less noticed). However, the interplay of family change and policy reform deserves more attention (Leira, 2002). It is important to keep in mind that social and cultural redesign of parental practices, on the one hand, and on the other, political reconceptualisation of the mother–child and father–child relationship are not always synchronised. Family change has often preceded policy reform (Leira, 2002). The stated aims of parenthood policies do not always come to fruition, or policies may conflict. Unintended effects do occur. Furthermore, as I shall go on to demonstrate, in Scandinavian parenthood policies since the early 1970s defamilisation of the care for young children is but one characteristic. Less noticed are policies of refamilisation, in long periods of leave, with the welfare state promoting the caring father as the companion parent of the working mother.

This chapter outlines main trends in the social and political redesign of motherhood and fatherhood in Scandinavia from the early 1970s to the early 2000s, a period witnessing a dramatic change in family forms. How has the welfare state addressed the two basic aspects of parenthood, that is, the *economic provider* and, in particular, the *caring, nurturing and upbringing* (caring, for short) aspects? Is there a Nordic model of parenthood policies? The focus is on the pivotal – and potentially far-reaching – policy reforms about setting parents free for paid work with the provision of extra-family childcare services, and the liberation of parents from paid work to be carers for their children. Taking a special interest in the interplay of parenthood change and policy reform, the chapter highlights a dominant shift in 'parenthood thinking', namely the translation of parental responsibility for children's care into social rights of mothers and fathers. Three sets of work/family policies are discussed: the state-sponsoring of early childhood education and care; national legislation of paid parental leave, and cash benefits for parental childcare.

Parenthood policies and family models

The three policies mentioned are particularly interesting because they demonstrate two distinctly different approaches to mothers and fathers as breadwinners and carers. Commonly, the policies are also linked with family models central in work/family policy discourse. One implies a strengthening of the traditional gender-differentiated family, the other aims at challenging and changing it.

The gender-differentiated family model presumes a *specialisation* of parental roles, taking the domestication of women for granted, as 'natural' and leaving the breadwinning for the male head of household. Often referred to as the 'model family of industrialism', this model is known in social analysis, particularly as developed in functionalist family analysis (Parsons, 1955). The gender division of labour is seen as positive for the family, the occupational system and society at large. Cash benefits for parental childcare assume a main breadwinner who is not the carer, and this is generally interpreted as furthering a traditional, male-breadwinner/female-carer family.

The dual-earner/dual-carer family challenges the gender-typing of parental practices and presumes a more egalitarian partnership between mothers and fathers. As formulated by Rita Liljeström (1978) the model presents two adult persons, both of whom combine social roles as parents, workers, citizens and individuals with time for leisure. Fathers as well as mothers are presumed to be capable of balancing employment and the care of children. Public policies for childcare support the work/family commitment of both parents: State-sponsoring of childcare services facilitates the employment of both mothers and fathers, and the institution of paid parental leave advances care-sharing parenthood. In combination, the two policies support families in which mothers and fathers share responsibility for economic provision and childcare more equally (see also Fraser, 1994; Sainsbury, 1996, for a different discussion of the policies).

Each of the models is a blend of empirical observations and normative positions. As normative statements concerning the arrangement of 'good' motherhood and fatherhood, the models point to conflicting social and cultural values and political interests when it comes to politicising fatherhood and especially motherhood (see also Rønsen and Skrede, this volume).

The dual-earner/dual-carer family model came to dominate Scandinavian parenthood politics of the latter half of the 20th century, integrated in the expanding social democratic welfare state. Support for more traditional family forms remained pronounced in parts of the population and in some political parties in Norway and Sweden, and especially in Finland (see the section on cash grants below). Since the early 1970s, social democrats and parties to the left have advocated policies for the more equal sharing of economic provision and caring, while parties to the centre and right have been the main supporters of more traditional family forms.

The models and policies discussed are not special to Scandinavia. A long-term increase in the economic activity rates of mothers has transformed the European family and posed new demands on public policies. By the mid-1990s, in the European Union about half of the mothers of pre-school children were gainfully employed (Moss and Deven, 1999). Families with young children were converging towards dual-earner parenthood. The time had come to 'update the gender contract' (OECD, 1994, p 19; see also Esping-Andersen, 2002).

The timing of mothers' entry into the labour market has differed, as has the policy response of welfare states to new family practices (for example, Lewis, 1993; Drew et al, 1998; Boje and Leira, 2000; Gerhard et al, 2005). In Italy and Spain the rise in mothers' economic activity rates was gaining ground in the 1990s, at a time when the second and third generation of working mothers were registered as employed in Scandinavia (Leira et al, 2005). Increasingly, the conciliation of work and family has been acknowledged as a major challenge for European welfare states, and some common policy approaches to motherhood and fatherhood change have been instituted, for example the European Union's 1996 Parental Leave Directive and the European Council's 1992 Recommendation on Childcare (see also Hantrais, 2004). Yet, in the early 2000s, the welfare state/family arrangements still differ, and the ways in which 'fatherhood' and 'motherhood' are politically institutionalised also vary.

Changing parenthood – a Scandinavian backdrop

In the Scandinavia of the 1970s, processes of profound societal change contributed to the rethinking of the state–parent relationship. Of special importance was the redesign of the welfare state as a service-provider state (Sipilä, 1997), even a caring state (Leira, 1992), and the 'motherhood revolution', the entering of mothers into modernity.

A 'caring' state

From the 1960s – when, largely, the national insurance systems were in place – the Scandinavian welfare state entered a second stage (Siim, 1987; Kautto et al, 1999). Public funding and provisioning of a wide repertoire of services was expanded, in education and health care, and in welfare and social care for the very young, dependent adults and the frail elderly. Traditional boundaries between the state and family were redrawn. The responsibility of the state and local government for welfare and social care services increased, while for the family it declined. In this process, individual needs for care were redefined to form a basis for social rights (see Marshall, 1965). According to Jorma Sipilä (1997), the public funding of social care services is the key to understanding the Nordic welfare states. State-sponsoring of social care services served to maintain the form of institutional welfare state developed in Scandinavia, and facilitated women's gainful employment. Public services for childcare were to be made universally available, thus attaining the character of social rights.

The 1970s marked a watershed in Scandinavian work/family policy. Framed within the vocabulary of social rights, to which was added a profound political commitment to gender equality, parenthood policies promoted defamilisation as well as refamilisation of childcare, a moving out of the home of mothers, and a returning home of fathers.

Setting new standards for the distribution of childcare responsibilities was central to this project. First, responsibility for childcare was to be redistributed between parents and the state: early childhood education and care, once defined as a primary responsibility of parents, was redesigned as an interest common to – or a joint venture between – the parents and the welfare state. Next, parenthood policies were to promote a redistribution of childcare within the family, between mothers and fathers. Policy reforms were to include support for both working motherhood and caring fatherhood. State funding of early childhood education and care facilitated the employment of mothers as well as fathers. Parental leave legislation redefined the care for infants and sick children as a responsibility and right of fathers as well as of mothers. Legislation furthering gender equality marked a democratisation of economic and caring opportunities, and encouraged a de-specialisation of parental practices (see Table 2.1).

The motherhood revolution

From the 1950s and 1960s, motherhood and family change signalled a break with traditional family arrangements. From early on, 'full employment' in Scandinavia came to include the commodification of women's labour – even the employment of mothers of young children. Expectations were rising for every adult person to be able to provide economically for themselves and their children via participation in the labour market. Paid work enabled the economic provider aspects of motherhood and at the same time furthered the contribution of mothers to the common good via their payment of taxes. Increasingly, women gained more 'property in their persons', to use Carole Pateman's (1987) formulation. Oral contraception (from the 1960s) and abortion on demand (from the 1970s) made it easier for women to control

Table 2.1: Gender equality: legal reforms

	Denmark	Finland	Norway	Sweden
Family planning				
Contraceptive pill approved	Mid-1960s	1961	1967	1964
Women's right to abortion on demand	1973	a	1978	1975
Parental leave				
Parents granted paid parental leave after a child is born	1984	1978	1978	1974
Part of parental leave is reserved for the father	1997 (abolished 2002)	2003	1993	1994
Right to six-hour working day for parents of small children	–	1988	–	1979
Equal opportunities				
Act on equal opportunities at work	1978	–	–	1980
Act on gender equality	–	1987	1979	–

Note: [a] Abortion legislation 1970, on social and medico-social grounds.
Sources: Nordic Council of Ministers (1994: 3, p 14); contributors to this volume

fertility and childbearing (see Table 2.1; Rønsen and Skrede, this volume). Rising levels of education and smaller families smoothed the way for employment outside the home. The altering of traditional gender roles was hotly debated. From the 1970s, the feminist movement and mobilisation of women to political participation and representation in all levels of government helped to put women's issues on the political agenda.

The shift away from the traditional gender-differentiated family model towards employed-mother families started in Finland, then in Sweden and Denmark with Norway to follow. By the mid-1970s, close to half of all mothers of pre-school children were gainfully employed. In the late 1990s, approximately three out of four Swedish and Norwegian mothers with children under six years of age were economically active, as were six out of 10 of the Finnish mothers (Nordic Council of Ministers, 1999: 514, table 12, p 45). (Data for Danish mothers is not available.)

The expansion of the welfare state as provider of services, often in local labour markets, meant increased demand for women's labour. Job segregation may have facilitated high employment rates. Entering a strongly gender-segregated labour market, Scandinavian women – and mothers – were recruited to the expanding services sector, often as the wage workers of the welfare state, in the public provision of social, health and care services, in education and administration. In Finland and Denmark, the majority of mothers entered employment on 'standard conditions', that is, as full-time workers. In Sweden and Norway, part-time work was more common.

The coexistence of strongly gender-segregated labour markets and high participation rates of mothers of young children is a characteristic of Nordic labour markets, where the vertical and horizontal gender segregation reported in the 1970s has been persistent. In the late 1990s, of 27 Organisation for Economic Co-operation and Development (OECD) countries ranked by occupational gender segregation (as measured by the percentage of female employees who would have had to change occupation for the proportions of women and men to be equal), Finland and Norway were placed 24th and 23rd, respectively, Sweden 21st and Denmark 17th (OECD, 2000).

Post-industrial families, characterised by the decline of the male-breadwinner norm, are regarded by some as necessitating the intervention of the welfare state to harmonise work and family obligations. However, this is far from the general experience, because the shift from the single-earner to the dual-earner family has generally preceded policy reform in Europe (see, for example, Leira, 1992; Lewis, 1993; European Commission Childcare Network, 1996; Drew et al, 1998). Demand for mothers' labour increased demand for extra-family day care services for children. However, nowhere in Scandinavia did the *first* generation of mothers heading for employment in the 1960s and early 1970s enjoy generous state-sponsoring of services or benefits for childcare. Motherhood change preceded large-scale policy reform. Reports of fathers' returning home to replace mothers in childcare and domestic work are few and far between (Leira, 1992). The early stages of mothers' employment were not premised on sharing the caring.

Later on, the mass entry of mothers into the labour market did generate a politicisation of childcare on an unprecedented scale. In the 1980s, Danish scholars argued that an alliance had been formed, a partnership established between the Danish welfare state and mothers, in which the state acknowledged the dual role of women in production and social reproduction (Borchorst and Siim, 1987). Accepting that the economy needed mothers' labour, the policies of Denmark and Sweden provided publicly funded childcare to this end. Childcare and employment policies were more closely coordinated, and policies were more successful with regard to meeting the demand of working parents (Leira, 1992, 2002). Until the early 1990s, in Norway, the rising labour market participation of mothers made only modest impact on the provision of childcare services for the under-threes (see Table 2.2).

Further family change – increasingly reported since the 1970s – such as rising divorce rates, a growing acceptance of extra-marital cohabitation, a growth in extra-nuptial births and an increase in lone-parent families also meant that formal marriage was weakening as the framework for family formation and fostering. Among Scandinavian children, the parents breaking up was becoming a common risk (Jensen, 1999; Skevik, this volume). Greater instability and fragility of parental relationships added emphasis to the need to improve the opportunities of mothers to provide economically and of fathers to establish and keep up a caring relationship with their children. Increasing multi-ethnicity among Scandinavian families with young children has added to the public and political debates about which family values and parenthood models should be given political priority.

Childcare policy packages: 1970s-2000s

The 1970s were the formative years of Nordic welfare state childcare.[2] Family matters were translated into political concerns. The politicisation of parenthood took a new turn as welfare state policies were opening up for an undermining of the conventional gendered division of breadwinning and caring. A rapid politicising of parental relations and early childhood was taking place, processes that were to make a profound imprint on the everyday organisation of families with young children.

Parenthood policy packages of the 1970s were constructed around time, services and money. Two sets of reforms were of special importance for parenthood change. First, there was national legislation for the early childhood years, putting on record the responsibility of the state and local government in sponsoring and/ or provisioning early childhood education and care. In principle, as a long-term aim, publicly funded day care services were to be made available for all children whose parents wished for it, thus facilitating the employment of mothers. Second – internationally a real innovation in work/family policy – there was the welfare state inviting fathercare for babies. Via the institution of parental leave legislation, fathers were included among those entitled to paid leave to care for a new-born child. Extending caring rights to fathers was coupled with parental choice, that is, the leave period could now be shared by the parents at their discretion. Increasingly, the early childhood years were being redesigned as an area for welfare state investment, regulation and control.

Public investment in families with young children was widely accepted in Scandinavia, by the 1970s, but since then, controversy has remained over which family forms to support: the ones in which mothers were employed, or, the ones in which they stayed at home.

Childcare defamilised: state-sponsored childcare services

By the 1970s, in all the Nordic countries national legislation laid down the responsibilities of the state and local government in the planning, provision, funding and quality control of day care for pre-school children. Preceding legislation, state and local authority involvement in the early childhood years had long been contested politically. Objections were numerous, inter alia, because the sponsoring of childcare services was interpreted by some as challenging parental authority in the upbringing of children. Demands on the public purse would rise as provisioning was cost-intensive. Perceived as support for working mothers, public funding of childcare services was also opposed by those who preferred the mother's place to be in the home. However, support for public funding and provisioning of childcare was motivated by the rapid growth of new family forms, and especially the rising employment of mothers. Advocated as educationally and socially advantageous for young children, state-sponsoring of childcare was also presented as being in the best interests of the child, and as a means of overcoming social inequalities among children (Bergqvist et al, 1999).

In several respects the frameworks and structures of the national day care policies and provisions are similar. Influences of similar childcare philosophies are also evident in the interlinking of the traditions of the early children's asylums and the Froebel kindergarten, and in the early merging of care and educational concerns (*'småbarnspedagogikk'*). Variations in national legislation, regulations and priorities are also evidenced (Mikkola, 1991; Leira, 1992; OECD, 2001a).

The countries have taken somewhat different paths in their quest to meet demand. Since the early 1970s differences are reported, for example, in the forms of services offered, for instance as family day care or centre-based services; full time or part time; and in the proportion of children accommodated (for overviews, see NOSOSCO, 1990: 51; 2004: 23). The countries also differ with respect to parental choice of cash grants for childcare or publicly funded day care services (see below), and, as noted previously, with respect to the importance attributed to meeting the demand of working parents.

Forms of care

Publicly funded day care services for pre-school children come in two main forms, as centre-based (or institutional care) and family day care, offered full time or part time. For all age groups, there is an increase in full-time, centre-based care. In all the countries except Norway, publicly funded family day care (extra-parental care of children in private homes, publicly sponsored and under public auspices) was from early on integrated into the day care services for children, and has occupied a considerable share of the supply of childcare services. In the 1970s and 1980s, for the under-threes in Denmark and Finland, family day care was more common than centre-based care. Family day care has made up only a negligible part of state-sponsored childcare services in Norway (NOSOSCO, 1990: 11, 1999: 11).

Private childminding – outside of public control, regulation and funding – has been in use throughout Scandinavia, and was especially common in the 1970s and early 1980s. In Norway, largely due to shortage of public day care, until the late 1980s, private childminding remained a major source of the total extra-parental childcare supply for working parents (Leira, 1992).

Demand and supply

Since the 1970s, the age group for which public day care services are used has been narrowed, due to expansion of the parental leave period and/or lowering of the age of entry into school. Following the introduction of cash grants, for some years demand for day care services declined in Finland, but not so in Norway (see this volume, Ellingsæter; Salmi; see also Box 1.1, Chapter One, and Table 8.1, Chapter Eight). Following the introduction of maximum parental fees, demand has risen in Sweden and Norway.

Denmark took the lead in provision of public childcare services, and was for a long time in a league of its own with respect to providing for the under-threes. In 1975, Denmark accommodated 18% of the under-threes, and 27% of the older pre-schoolers; Sweden provided for 13% of younger and for 19% of the older children, while Finland and Norway provided for less than 5% of the under-threes, and for less than 10% of the older age group (see Table 2.2). In 2002, for children under the age of one year, in Denmark only, public day care services were used for 12% of the age group. For the older children, attending public day care is no longer an experience of the few. Denmark

Table 2.2: Children in publicly funded childcare, 1975, 1987, 1990, 1995 and 2002 (% of all children in the age group)[a]

Year/age of child	Denmark	Finland	Norway	Sweden
1975				
0-2	18	4	3	13
3-6	27	9	6	19
1987				
0-2	45	22	8	31
3-6	65	52	50	79
1990				
0-2	48	31	11	29
3-6	73	58	57	64
Total 0-6	61	44	33	48
1995				
0-2	48	18	22	37
3-6	83	55	61	74
Total 0-6	68	39	44	59
2002				
1-2	78	36	40	65
3-5	94	67	82	91

Note:

[a] Children in childcare centres and family day care.

Sources:

1975, 1987: NOSOSCO (1990: 51, table 5.3.1.1, pp 92-3, 220, table 5.3.3.1, p 96)

1995: NOSOSCO (1999: 11, table 4.11, p 53)

2002: NOSOSCO (2004: 23, table 4.12, p 58)

accommodated 78% and Sweden 65% of children aged one to two years, Norway offered places to 40% and Finland met demand at 36%. Of the older pre-schoolers in Denmark and Sweden, more than 90% of the age group attended public day care, as did more than 80% in Norway, while Finland was meeting demand at 67% (Table 2.2; see also Box 1.1, Chapter One).

From the 1970s, the provision of high-quality day care for children was integrated into the expanding publicly funded service systems of the four countries. Universal coverage was the aim: services were to be made available at affordable costs for all children whose parents wanted it, and not just for the children of employed people and students. During the 1970s and 1980s, as a social right of parents and children, access to state-sponsored childcare services remained incomplete, supply-conditioned, but on its way. In the early 2000s, except for Norway, access to high-quality, publicly funded day care services is no longer an incomplete right. Finland has instituted the right of all pre-schoolers to attend state-sponsored services, or, alternatively, parents may receive a cash grant for childcare. In Denmark and Sweden demand for childcare services is to be met with a minimum of delay, accommodation thus attaining the character of an entitlement. Norway's plan for coverage of demand by 2005 has proved too optimistic; demand for publicly funded services still exceeds supply in several regions, but is expected to be met some few years into the future.

Childcare refamilised 1: parental leave

The Nordic countries were the first to institute the right of fathers to care for their infant children, in a remarkable reformulation of the arrangement between the welfare state, the labour market and parents. Parental leave legislation of the 1970s was advancing the universal carer-parent model, emphasising the importance of both fathercare and mothercare during the first months of the child's life. Legislation applied to the general framework for employment in both the private and the public sector of the labour market. For fathers as well as for mothers the entitlement to paid leave with job security meant precedence to parental care over the demands of the job. Providing entitlements to fathercare for babies was a very radical approach to changing the gender division of childcare, a new approach to work/family policies and a noteworthy illustration of a policy-induced framework for change. Symbolically it was highly important, projecting as it did the notion of the employed male as carer for children. Legislation was not a response to any large-scale change or demand reported among fathers (Leira, 2002; Lammi-Taskula; Borchorst, this volume), but rather a follow-up of the political commitments to gender equality.

The notion of a special 'daddy quota', a spectacular proposal for policy intervention, was first aired in the 1970s. In Sweden, social democratic women Members of Parliament demanded earmarking of some of the total leave period for fathers, but it did not gain the support of the party leadership (Karlsson, 1996).

Expanding the leave schemes

In 1974, Sweden took the lead in instituting paid parental leave by transforming the traditional maternity leave entitlements at the birth of a child into an entitlement of parents. The leave schemes included entitlements for individual parents, and for the parents in common, as some of the leave was to be used according to parental choice. Norway and Finland followed in 1978, Denmark in 1984 (see Table 2.1). Fathers gained entitlements to time off work around the time of confinement, the so-called 'daddy days'. Sweden's scheme was – and still is – the longest (69 weeks in 2002) and most flexible. By the early 2000s, Finland and Norway were providing approximately one year of leave with wage compensation at different levels. Denmark's period of paid leave was for a long time the shortest in the region, and not until the early 2000s did Danish parents obtain a paid leave period comparable to that of its neighbours (expanded to 52 weeks) (NOSOSCO, 2004: 23; Lammi-Taskula, this volume).

Daddy quota – fatherhood by gentle force

The parental choice of the 1970s did not prove very efficient in making fathers into carers. In the 1980s, fewer than 5% of Danish, Finnish and Norwegian fathers made use of the leave. The exception was Sweden, where one in four fathers made some use of the leave available (OECD, 1995). In work/family policy, a new deal was called for.

In the early 1990s, Norway and Sweden strengthened entitlements to fathercare by earmarking special periods of parental leave, with a four-week daddy quota provided on a use-or-lose basis. In contrast to the emphasis on parental choice instituted in the 1970s, in the 1990s, fathercare was to be promoted by the use of gentle force. In 2002, Sweden extended the quota to two months; Norway added a fifth week in 2005 and a sixth in 2006. A daddy quota of two weeks was legislated in 1997 in Denmark, but withdrawn in 2002 when the government changed (Rostgaard, 2002; Borchorst, this volume). Finland has set special conditions for fathers' entitlement to a two-week quota (Lammi-Taskula, this volume).

Legislation on the daddy quota was premised on the sameness or perhaps rather the equal value of fathercare and mothercare. As carers for young children, mothers and fathers were generally assumed to be equally capable, although the ways in which they carry out childcare may differ (Leira, 1998). In Norway and Sweden, the shift in approach to furthering fathercare was argued as in everyone's best interests. The daddy quota provided opportunities for 'early bonding' between fathers and children, and was also regarded as a means of overcoming the obstacles fathers met with at work, and facilitating negotiations at home. Promotion of gender equality was an issue, too. Objections to the earmarking of fathers' leave, more pronounced in Denmark and Finland than in Norway and Sweden, came from some political parties, employers and parents who did not want state interference with parental choice (see Lammi-Taskula; Borchorst, this volume).

Take-up and use

In 2005, in all the Nordic countries, the majority of employed parents are entitled to paid leave of absence while retaining job security in connection with the birth or adoption of a child. (Non-employed mothers are entitled to cash grants.) All the countries reserve part of the leave for mothers, all offer special leave for fathers at the time of the birth of a child, and all provide a period for the parents to use according to parental choice. Excepting Denmark, all have earmarked periods of the total leave for fathers.

Entitlements to maternity, paternity and parental leave are widely used in Scandinavia, in the sense that the large majority of eligible mothers and fathers take up some of the paid leave available. However, fathers – or parents – have not opted for the opportunity of sharing the caring more equally between them. This is in marked contrast to the take-up of earmarked leave. In particular, the daddy days for fathers at the birth of their child rapidly gained popularity. In Norway, the daddy quota was an instant success, taken up by 70% to 80% of eligible fathers. In Sweden, it made little change in fathers' use of leave from the beginning (Lammi-Taskula, this volume). Large numbers of fathers taking some leave does not, however, imply that fathers generally are long-leave consumers (see Box 1.1).

In 2002, Danish, Finnish and Norwegian fathers utilised less than 10% of the paid leave days available, and Swedish fathers 17%. Apparently, a small or modest dose of fathercare is all right and is what the majority of fathers take. What remains of the leave is almost by definition for the use of the mothers. Mothers, on average, take long leave, fathers do not (Leira, 1998).

Childcare refamilised 2: cash benefits for childcare

The countries differ further in the offers of parental choice for either state-sponsored childcare or cash grants. In the 1990s, Finland, Norway and Sweden instituted cash grants for childcare as an entitlement of families that did not make use of state-sponsored childcare services for their young children. Introduced in all the countries by governments of the centre/right, the Swedish scheme was withdrawn after a short period when the social democrats returned to power (see Haataja and Nyberg, this volume). Denmark legislated a childcare leave ('børnepasningsorlov') similar in some respects to the cash grant schemes. (This entitlement was later abolished.)

Finland was the first to legislate cash grants for childcare. In Finland, in the mid-1980s, the agrarian Centre party, and the Social Democrats agreed on a national political compromise to advance a dual-track for parenthood policies. Parents were to have a choice between cash or care services: publicly funded childcare services, legislated in 1973, were to be supplemented by the legislation of cash benefits for childcare (home care allowance) (Mikkola, 1991; Anttonen, 2001). From 1990, parents of the under-threes were given a choice of cash grants (home care allowance) as an alternative to accommodation in state-sponsored childcare services. If Finnish parents prefer a place in state-sponsored day care for their children, the local authorities are obliged to provide this. In 1996 the right of choice was extended to cover all pre-schoolers.

The Norwegian scheme (legislated in 1998) offers parents of children aged 12 to 36 months the right to a cash grant for childcare, provided that the child does not attend state-sponsored day care services (part-time day care can be matched with a partial cash grant) (see also Ellingsæter, this volume). For parents opting for the cash grants, there were further choices, namely parental or non-parental, private care, and mothercare or fathercare (for this chapter, only cash grants for parental care are considered). Unlike the Finnish cash grant, the Norwegian scheme was not coupled with a real choice for parents in respect of parental care or access to public care services.

Cash grant schemes were advocated as supporting parental choice in respect of public or private care arrangements, and as a means to give parents more time with children. They have also been argued as valuing the unpaid work of mothers, and as a means of equalising the income of one-income families and dual-providers, and as supporting equality between women in equalising the incomes of employed and non-employed mothers. In contrast to the daddy quota of the parental leave, the cash grant was not planned to help recruit the parent of the underrepresented sex into childcare. Interpreted as supporting the traditional male-breadwinner family and as a backlash to gender equality, cash grants also had their antagonists. Regarded by some as undermining the right of children to attend state-sponsored day care, cash grant schemes met with opposition on these grounds, too. Making take-up conditional upon *not* using a public good is a fairly unusual element in welfare state policy, and the wisdom of the scheme was called into question.

In 2005, the cash grant schemes of Finland and Norway differed in several important respects (see, for example, Salmi and Lammi-Taskula,

1999; Leira, 2002). In both countries, however, cash grants have gained considerable popular support in the sense that they are widely taken up. Hardly surprisingly, mothers comprise the great majority of grant recipients (Salmi and Lammi-Taskula, 1999; Salmi, this volume). Whether the success of cash grants represents a return to the housewife family is disputed in Finland (Sipilä, 1995; Salmi and Lammi-Taskula, 1999; see also Mahon, 2002). According to Anneli Anttonen (2001), the grant is an expression of long-lasting Finnish maternalism, while in Norway it has been described as the state's gift to the traditional father (Andenæs, 1997). Not taking issue with the interpretations, it should be noted, that high take-up rates are set in very different labour market contexts in the two countries. In the early 1990s, the Finnish economy was in crisis and unemployment soaring. Against this backdrop, arguably, the popularity of the cash grant for childcare was a mix of a preference for mothercare and a lack of jobs. In Norway, where the labour market was tight, the high take-up of the cash benefit is not just about choice of mothercare, but also about the failure of childcare policies to deliver high-quality, state-sponsored childcare services sufficient to meet the demand (Leira, 2002).

Parenthood change and policy reform

The early 2000s show a remarkable continuity in work/family policies. Core programmes still include paid parental leave schemes and public sponsoring of childcare services. Finland and Norway, in addition, have added cash benefits for childcare. The politicising of childcare has been taken further, with the volume of childcare-related rights, regulations and provisions greatly expanded. In retrospect, two seemingly opposite trends stand out: public investment in the defamilising of the early childhood years has increased remarkably as childcare services for pre-schoolers have developed towards meeting demand. Professional care offered within the framework of specialised institutions supplements motherly or household-based care, and is part of the standard childhood experience for the older pre-schoolers. In addition, more emphasis has been put on refamilised care for the youngest children as the period of paid parental leave has been extended, and fathers included among those entitled to paid leave to care for infants. Finland and Norway add to the refamilising trend in offering the choice of cash grants for parental childcare.

The interrelationship between parenthood change and policy reform has taken different forms (Leira, 2002):

- Childcare-related policies have been instituted in response to ongoing family change. State-sponsoring of childcare services was a delayed response to the rising employment of mothers; motherhood change preceded policy reform. Later assisted by state-sponsored childcare, large numbers of mothers have been 'liberated' from full-time caring responsibilities and have entered the labour market. Gaining access to paid work, they have been able to provide economically for themselves and their children – even when splitting up with their partner.
- Parenthood policy reform has preceded parenthood change, as witnessed in the institution of paid parental leave. Mothers and fathers are freed from work – with wage compensation – and childcare is refamilised. Legislated before any large-scale change in fatherhood, the paid parental leave schemes are particularly interesting in assuming that policy intervention may speed family change, and undo – or soften – ingrained traditions for differentiating the functions of motherhood and fatherhood.
- Parenthood policies have also been provided to delay or postpone a further change away from the male-breadwinner/female-carer family, a family form long in decline in Scandinavia. Assuming that the dual-earner family resulted from necessity as much as from choice, cash grants for parental care offer the choice of prolonged familisation of childcare by either the mother or the father. Generally, the schemes have been interpreted as state support for home-based maternal care.

National parenthood policy profiles

Differences in national policy profiles are more pronounced if we consider how policies target mothers and fathers as both providers and carers. In summary, the above discussion of policy packages shows:

- Strong support for working motherhood is a characteristic of *Denmark's* parenthood policies in the period considered. In Scandinavia, Denmark is the foremost provider of state-sponsored childcare services for the under-threes, and is meeting demand for the older pre-schoolers. Full-time childcare services support the norm of the full-time working week for mothers as well as fathers. Up until the early 2000s a relatively short period of paid parental leave encouraged early return to employment. In Nordic comparison, Denmark's policy support for fathercare is the weakest.

- In *Finland*, following a relatively long period of paid parental leave, the dual childcare track means that parents of pre-schoolers have the choice of either publicly sponsored prolonged familised care or defamilised childcare services. Parenthood policies target working and domesticated mothers. For working mothers, the norm is full-time employment and publicly funded childcare services are provided on demand. More than its Nordic neighbours Finland promotes prolonged familised care by parents via a combination of paid parental leave and cash grants for parental childcare. Generally, parental care translates as mothercare. Compared to Norway, and especially Sweden, support for familised fathercare is modest.
- In *Norway*, despite promises of universal coverage, a shortage of publicly funded day care services persists. In Nordic comparison, policy support for defamilised childcare and working motherhood has for a long time lagged behind. A period of paid parental leave of up to one year has facilitated familised parental childcare, the daddy quota promoting fathercare for the very young. Following the parental leave period, a cash grant scheme supports prolonged familised parental care, mainly taken up by mothers. Policy support for caring motherhood comes second only to Finland's, while support for caring fatherhood comes second only to Sweden's.
- *Sweden's* parenthood policies have been in the forefront with respect to familisation of childcare via parental leave. By expanding the total period of paid parental leave, and as the leading quota country of the four, Swedish policies stand out as offering the strongest support for fathers as carers. At the same time, coverage of defamilised state-sponsored, full-time childcare services is evidence of strong policy support for working motherhood. Among the Nordic countries, Sweden's policies come closest to facilitating the dual-earner, care-sharing family, in which both mothers and fathers are economic providers and carers for children.

Rianne Mahon (2002) has argued that the childcare policies of Finland on the one hand and of Denmark and Sweden on the other illustrate different approaches to gender equality. Finland has taken up a neofamilist turn, while Denmark and Sweden are pursuing a gender equality track. The examination above shows a more complex picture: in policy support of working motherhood, Denmark and Sweden are rather similar, but in support for caring fatherhood rather different. This argument is more in line with that of Bruning and Plantenga (1999), whose analysis concludes that work/family policy packages of Denmark, Sweden and Finland represent three different models. Adding Norway makes a fourth.

Practising parenthood: parental choice

Increasingly since the 1990s, the drive for gender equality, both in the labour market and in the care of children, confronts the policy emphasis on gender-neutral parental choice. In all the four countries discussed, as in Western Europe more generally, one striking result of the reception and use of the parental choice entailed in parental leave is the prolonged job breaks of mothers and the familising of maternal care for very young children. In Finland and Norway, this trend is further strengthened by the use of the cash grants for childcare (Leira, 2002).

How the reception of gender-neutral parental choice reforms should be interpreted has been the subject of much debate (for example, OECD, 2001b; Leira,1998, 2002; Salmi and Lammi-Taskula, 1999; Anttonen, 2001; Lammi-Taskula, Borchorst, this volume). Among other things, the response of parents is an illustration of the limits to choice in a context in which the labour market is strongly segregated by gender, gendered wage inequalities persist, and parental obligations have remained gendered – although less markedly compared to the grandparent generation. Often interpreted as strategic, rational adaptation, the unequal sharing of breadwinning and childcare makes economic sense, since fathers are generally in better-paid jobs and the family stands to lose more if the father takes long leave.

In a gender equality perspective, it may well be asked, as do Peter Moss and Fred Deven (1999), whether parental choice is a promise or a pitfall. In Scandinavia, the normative climate and cultural traditions surrounding the mother–child and father–child relationship are still gendered. Workplace opposition to fathers taking long leave is more pronounced than it is for mothers, hence fathers may stand to lose more if pursuing prolonged familised care. While caring is an all-important element in social and cultural norms concerning 'good motherhood', it is less emphasised in the interpretation of 'good fatherhood'. For example, for fathers, spending 10 weeks of parental leave is taking very long leave; for mothers, a 10-week period of leave is considered very short, indeed, too short. Some Scandinavian studies indicate that fathers shy away from the nursery, but also that mothers see parental leave as their private property, and keep fathers at bay. Obviously, the first choice of one parent, may block the first choice of the other. Whoever has the first choice, mother or father, or whatever is chosen first, job or childcare, the unequal response of fathers and mothers to parental leave and cash benefit schemes is a reminder that mothers and fathers pursue different combinations of work and parenthood, and invest differently in their families. So far, the use made of gender-neutral parental choice has largely served to reproduce gender inequality in the care of young children, confirming mothers as the primary carer parent (Leira, 2002).

Parenthood policies: from responsibilities to social rights

Summarising main trends in parenthood policy reform, the following aspects of the transformation of parental responsibility for childcare deserve special mention: first, the care of young children, once primarily defined as the obligation of the parents, has been reconceptualised as an interest common to – or a joint venture between – the parents and the welfare state. From being selectively orientated policy instruments, childcare-related services and benefits have been developed towards becoming universally available.

Second, and increasingly since the 1970s, childcare has been interpreted as a social right of parents and children. The care of young children has been expanded to include a platform from which mothers and fathers are entitled to make claims on the welfare state. Parental responsibilities are not relinquished, rather they attain new dimensions. Childcare-related rights of parents include a right (or an opportunity) to care and not to care. The right of fathers to give priority to paid work, and not to engage in the caring of children, has been so much taken for granted that state-sponsoring of childcare is often presented as a special arrangement for mothers.

Third, in Scandinavia, the framing of childcare policies within the vocabulary of social rights, to which is added a profound political commitment to gender equality, has served to promote new models of motherhood and fatherhood. The politicising of childcare has furthered what Jane Lewis (2002) identifies as the *universal adult worker* model of the citizen-parent. State-sponsoring of childcare services has been and still is an important instrument in equalising the economic provider opportunities of mothers and fathers. Furthermore, legislation of parental leave shows policy support for a *universalising of the carer-parent model*.

Support for a specialisation of parental tasks, generally male breadwinning and female caring, has been a strong undercurrent in parenthood policy discourse, and resurfaced in the 1990s in legislation concerning cash grants for childcare. Childcare policies, in other words, are not just about the defamilising of the care for children, but also about refamilising, and very much about the commodification or decommodification of the labour of mothers and fathers (Leira, 2002).

From the 1970s Nordic parenthood policies have set new standards for 'good' motherhood and fatherhood, facilitating caring fatherhood, working motherhood and a more equal sharing of breadwinning and caring. In the social democratic welfare state, the dual-earner/care-sharing family became the predominant family model in policy-making and among partnered parents of young children. Welfare policies have advanced and facilitated the sharing of earning and caring, forwarding a model of the 'citizen-parent' − mothers and fathers who combine employment and childcare.

Parental practices show a more complex picture. The different ways in which mothers and fathers arrange for paid work and childcare indicate the increasing differentiation and perhaps polarisation among post-industrial families in the ways in which work and family are reconciled, with mothers and fathers who opt for a dual-earner/care-sharing family at one end, and families in which a traditional division of labour predominates at the other.

Despite the gender-traditional choices, in retrospect the change in parental practices is rather striking. In the 1970s, the combination of employment and care of progeny was characteristically framed as a feminine dilemma, a matter for mothers. In 2005, fathers are much more present in political discourse, in parenthood policies and everyday childcare; the balancing of work and childcare is conceptualised as a challenge for both fathers and mothers, for the workplace and the welfare state. Parental responsibilities for children are taken up in new mixes. As mothers have changed the gender balance in employment, the universal breadwinner model has come a long way. Changing the gender balance of childcare has been slower to effect. The larger gains for gender equality now are to be found in the changing of fathers' caring practices. The potential for change entailed in parenthood policies − in fact, allowing for the universal carer model of the parent − is far from fully developed or utilised. Legislation offers parents much more scope in the sharing of childcare than is actually used. A more equal sharing of caring is far from utopian − or impossible. It might even be in the best interest of all concerned.

Notes

[1] In this chapter the terms 'Scandinavia' and 'the Nordic countries' are used interchangeably, and refer to Denmark, Finland, Norway and Sweden.

[2] The presentation is based on my earlier work, where the data used is presented in greater detail. See especially Leira (1992, 1998, 2002).

References

Andenæs, A. (1997) 'Kontantstøtte en gavepakke til mannen', in *Dagbladet*, 15 September.

Anttonen, A. (2001) 'The female working citizen', *Kvinder, køn og forskning*, vol 10, no 2, pp 33-44.

Bergqvist, C., Kuusipalo, J. and Styrkarsdottir, A. (1999) 'Debatten om barnomsorgspolitiken', in C. Bergqvist, A. Borchorst, A.-D. Christensen, V. Ramstedt-Siléu (eds) *Likestilte demokratier? Kjønn og politikk i Norden*, Oslo: Universitetsforlaget, pp 129-50.

Boje, T.P. and Leira, A. (eds) (2000) *Gender, Welfare State and the Market*, London and New York, NY: Routledge.

Borchorst, A. and Siim, B. (1987) 'Women and the advanced welfare state: a new kind of patriarchal power', in A.S. Sassoon (ed) *Women and the State*, London: Hutchinson, pp 128-57.

Bruning, G. and Plantenga, J. (1999) 'Parental leave and equal opportunities: experiences in eight European countries', *Journal of European Social Policy*, vol 9, no 3, pp 195-209.

Drew, E., Emerek, R. and Mahon, E. (eds) (1998) *Women, Work and the Family in Europe*, London and New York, NY: Routledge.

Esping-Andersen, G. (1999) *Social Foundations of Postindustrial Economies*, Oxford: Oxford University Press.

Esping-Andersen, G. (2002) 'Towards the good society, once again?', in G. Esping-Andersen, D. Gallie, A. Hemenjck and J. Myles (eds) *Why We Need a New Welfare State*, Oxford: Oxford University Press.

European Commission Childcare Network (1996) *A Review of Services For Young Children in the European Union 1990-1995*, Brussels: European Commission, Equal Opportunities Unit.

Fraser, N. (1994) 'After the family wage: gender equity and the welfare state', *Political Theory*, vol 44, no 4, pp 591-618.

Gerhardt, U., Knijn, T. and Weckwert, A. (eds) (2005) *Working Mothers in Europe: A Comparison of Policies and Practices*, Cheltenham, UK: Edward Elgar.

Hantrais, L. (2004) *Family Policy Matters: Responding to Family Change in Europe*, Bristol: The Policy Press.

Hernes, H. (1987) *Welfare State and Woman Power*, Oslo: Norwegian University Press.

Jensen, A.M. (1999) 'Partners and parents in Europe: a gender divide', in A. Leira (ed) *Family Change: Practices, Policies, and Values*, Stamford, CT: JAI Press, pp 1-29.

Karlsson, G. (1996) *Från Broderskap till systerskap: Det Socialdemokrtiska Kvinnoförbundets kamp för inflytande och makt i SAP*, Lund: Arkiv.

Kautto, M., Heikkilä, M., Hvinden, B., Marklund, S. and Ploug, N. (1999) *Nordic Social Policy, Changing Welfare States*, London: Routledge.

Korpi, W. (2000) 'Faces of inequality: gender, class and patterns of inequalities in different types of welfare states', *Social Politics*, vol 7, no 2, pp 127-91.

Leira, A. (1992) *Welfare States and Working Mothers: The Scandinavian Experience*, Cambridge: Cambridge University Press.

Leira, A. (1998) 'Caring as social right: cash for childcare and daddy leave', *Social Politics*, vol 5, no 3, pp 362-78.

Leira, A. (2002) *Working Parents and the Welfare State*, Cambridge: Cambridge University Press.

Leira, A., Tobio, C. and Trifiletti, R. (2005) 'Kinship and informal support: care resources for the first generation of working mothers', in U. Gerhardt, T. Knijn and A. Weckwert (eds) (2005) *Working Mothers in Europe: A Comparison of Policies and Practices*, Cheltenham, UK: Edward Elgar, pp 74-96.

Lewis, J. (1993) *Women and Social Policies in Europe: Work, Family and the Welfare State*, Cheltenham, UK: Edward Elgar.

Lewis, J. (2002) 'Gender and welfare state change', *European Societies*, vol 4, no 4, pp 331-57.

Liljeström, R. (1978) 'Sweden', in S.B. Kamerman and A.J. Kahn (eds) *Family Policy: Government and Families in Fourteen Countries*, New York, NY: Columbia University Press, pp 19-48.

Mahon, R. (2002) 'Childcare: toward what kind of 'Social Europe'?', *Social Politics*, vol 9, no 3, pp 343-79.

Marshall, T.H. (1965) *Class, Citizenship and Social Development*, New York, NY: Doubleday.

Mikkola, M. (1991) 'Parental choice', in S.B. Kamerman and A.J. Kahn (eds) *Childcare, Parental Leave, and the Under 3s: Policy Innovation in Europe*, New York, NY: Auburn House, pp 145-70.

Moss, P. and Deven, F. (1999) (eds) *Parental Leave: Progress or Pitfall*, Brussels: NIDI/CBGS.

Nordic Council of Ministers (1994: 3) *Women and Men in the Nordic Countries: Facts and Figures 1994*, Copenhagen: Nordic Council of Ministers.

Nordic Council of Ministers (1999: 514) *Women and Men in the Nordic Countries 1999*, Copenhagen: Nordic Council of Ministers.

NOSOSCO (Nordic Social Statistical Committee) (1990: 51) *Social tryghed i de nordiske lande 1987*, (Social Security in the Nordic Countries), Copenhagen: NOSOSCO.

NOSOSCO (1999: 11) *Social tryghed i de nordiske lande 1997*, (Social Security in the Nordic Countries), Copenhagen: NOSOSCO.

NOSOSCO (2004: 23) *Social Tryghed i de Nordiske Lande 2002*, (Social Security in the Nordic Countries), Copenhagen: NOSOSCO.

OECD (Organisation for Economic Co-operation and Development) (1994) *Women and Structural Change: New Perspectives*, Paris: OECD.

OECD (1995) *Employment Outlook*, Paris: OECD.

OECD (2000) *Employment Outlook*, Paris: OECD.

OECD (2001a) *Employment Outlook*, Paris: OECD.

OECD (2001b) *Starting Strong: Early Childhood Education and Care*, Paris:OECD.

Parsons, T. (1955) 'The American family: its relations to personality and the social structure', in T. Parsons and R.F. Bales (eds) *Family Socialization and Interaction Process*, Glencoe, IL: The Free Press.

Pateman, C. (1989) *The Sexual Contract*, Cambridge: Polity Press.

Popenoe, D. (1988) *Disturbing the Nest: Family Changes and Decline in Modern Societies*, New York, NY: Aldine de Gruyter.

Rostgaard, T. (2002) 'Setting time aside for the father: father's leave in Scandinavia', *Community, Work and Family*, vol 5, no 3, pp 343-64.

Sainsbury, D. (1996) *Gender, Equality and Welfare States*, Cambridge: Cambridge University Press.

Salmi, M. and Lammi-Taskula, J. (1999) 'Parental leave in Finland', in P. Moss and F. Deven (eds) *Parental Leave: Progress or Pitfall*, Brussels: NIDI/CBGS Publications, pp 85-121.

Siim, B. (1987) 'The Scandinavian welfare states: towards sexual equality or a new kind of male domination?', *Acta Sociologica*, vol 30, no 3-4, pp 255-70.

Sipilä, J. (1997) 'Introduction', in J. Sipilä (ed) *Social Care Services: The Key to the Scandinavian Model*, Aldershot: Ashgate, pp 1-8.

Sipilä, J. (1995) 'The right to choose: day care for children or money for parents', in R. Page and J. Baldock (eds) *Social Policy Review 6*, pp 159-69.

Wolfe, A. (1989) *Whose Keeper? Social Science and Moral Obligation*, Berkeley, CA: University of California Press.

THREE

Nordic fertility patterns: compatible with gender equality?[1]

Marit Rønsen and Kari Skrede

Policies of parenthood and fertility

Is there a possible connection between policies of parenthood and fertility? This has been subject to increasing interest over the past decades, both in demographic research and on the political agenda on ageing societies in the western industrialised world. The fertility development of the Nordic countries and the possible effects of the 'Nordic model of family welfare' have received considerable attention (UN, 2000a; Demeny, 2003). The Nordic combination of high levels of female labour force participation with relatively high levels of fertility, may suggest that a sustainable level of fertility is compatible with gender equality, and that family policies play an important role in generating this fortunate situation. However, there are reasons to take a critical look at these assumptions. We shall argue that the role of family policies in maintaining high fertility levels is often overstated, and that the present Nordic fertility patterns indicate that a sustainable level of fertility in the long run is dependent on parenthood policies with stronger incentives for gender equality.

Our methodological line of argument is that in order to understand fertility dynamics, one needs to go beyond crude fertility rates. The public debate on fertility is usually based on aggregate fertility indicators – total fertility rates. However, from a demographic perspective, the total fertility rate is a superficial measure of the underlying structural elements of fertility patterns, as they develop over time with subsequent cohorts of women passing through their reproductive period. It is also vital to understand trends among different socioeconomic groups of women, not only different levels of education but also the interplay with different sectors of the labour market.

The focus of our analysis is the relationship between Nordic fertility trends and the corresponding development of parenthood policies in the Nordic countries since 1970. We start with an outline of the analytical framework and the contextual dynamics of the politicising of parenthood processes of the Nordic countries and the development of the total fertility rates of the Nordic countries in a broader comparative perspective. We continue with a presentation of earlier research findings of policy effects on fertility and return to a broader discussion of recent research findings on the fertility dynamics of the Nordic countries. The structural aspects of the development and to what extent these findings point towards a common Nordic fertility model with converging characteristics are addressed, and the role of policies of parenthood in explaining country-level patterns are discussed. We deconstruct fertility trends among different groups of women, and discuss to what extent these trends are compatible with gender equality. Finally, we return to the challenge of how a sustainable fertility level can be combined with increasing levels of gender equality.

The Nordic model(s) of family welfare – pluralism with common denominators

More comprehensive, comparative analyses of welfare states often place the Nordic countries in a common category based on criteria from present structures of welfare systems. Esping-Andersen's (1990) distinction between three different types of welfare state regimes, with the Nordic social democratic welfare regime as a common denominator for the Nordic countries, was an important contribution in this respect. However, as argued by other researchers, for instance Lewis (1992, 1993) and Sainsbury (1994), Esping-Andersen's analysis did not include the gender relations aspects. By focusing mainly on work as paid work and on welfare policies that relate to paid work (as incentives and disincentives for the decommodification of labour), his analysis missed the importance of unpaid work and welfare produced within the families, as well as considerable differences between countries within each of the three types of welfare regimes in the model.

Such differences also apply to the Nordic countries with regard to their roads to the integration of gender equality as an area of concern for public policy. Several studies have documented that there are considerable differences between the Nordic countries with regard to the historical development of their family policy regimes, and the extent to which present family policies also integrate gender equality as an explicit political goal (Leira, 1992, 1993; Borchorst, 1994; Sainsbury, 1999, 2001; Skrede, 1999; Kjeldstad, 2001). In their introductory chapter to this book, Ellingsæter and

Leira analyse differences in the present family models of the Nordic countries in relation to underlying normative aspects of the politicising parenthood debate. With regard to integration of gender equality, the most important difference between the current models lies in the normative aspects, to what extent gender-equal parenthood practices are presented as a goal or as an option.

Nordic differences in the development of opportunity structures for parenthood and parenthood practices provide an analytic framework of contextual dynamics for exploring policy effects on fertility. These differences in family policy regimes should not, however, lead us to overlook the many similarities that the Nordic countries share in political, economic and social development in the post-Second World War period in terms of educational expansion, labour market structures and participation, as well as general content of welfare policies. The Nordic countries share a common platform in the ambitious policies that were formed during the first decades of the post-Second World War period with regard to equalisation of educational opportunities. Policy measures to secure extended access to education after compulsory schooling, combined with formal admission rights for girls as well as for boys, were important foundations for the later more explicit formulation of gender equality as an area and aim for political concern (Jonung, 1983; Skrede, 1986, 1999; Leira, 1993).

The Nordic countries further share a common platform in high levels of female participation in the labour market, including the participation of mothers of small children. However, this common platform does include strongly gender-segregated labour markets and relatively high levels of part-time work, especially in Norway and Sweden[2] (see also Haataja and Nyberg, this volume, for a closer analysis of the labour market structures of the Nordic countries). It is fair to say that seemingly high levels of gender equality, judged by rates of female participation in the labour market, could be described more appropriately as 'gender equality light' in terms of differences between mothers' and fathers' working time in the labour market (Skrede, 2004a).

We should also take into account that the Nordic countries were among the first countries to grant women access to the new female-administered contraceptives (the Pill and the IUD). Finland was the first country of the region to approve the Pill (1961) and Norway the last (1967) (TemaNord, 1999). After its introduction, the new contraceptive technology was rapidly in fairly widespread use in all the Nordic countries (Østby, 1983). During the 1960s and 1970s the Nordic countries also gradually changed their legislation on procured abortions from very restrictive to more liberal regulations.

In relation to the development of fertility trends, it should be noted that the abortion rates of Denmark, Finland, Norway and Sweden have declined substantially since the late 1980s. For Denmark and Finland this decline started as early as the early 1970s (Knudsen et al, 2003).

Consequently, when we turn to the discussion of the possible relationship between family policy regimes and fertility trends at the Nordic level, we should bear in mind that part of the possible influence between policy regimes and fertility trends is likely to be indirect effects. It is difficult to measure indirect effects related to the broader context of the economic, social and political development. However, given that the Nordic countries share a common denominator in the development towards increased female autonomy, both with regard to women's economic role and with regard to reproductive rights, it is reasonable to assume that such indirect effects are also part of the relationship.

Contrasting fertility trends

Like many other countries, the Nordic region experienced a baby boom after the Second World War. However, the boom lasted longer in Norway than in the neighbouring countries, and at the beginning of the 1970s the total fertility rate in Norway was still as high as 2.5 children per woman. In comparison, the fertility level of the other Nordic countries (except Iceland) was already below 2 children per woman (Figure 3.1).

Figure 3.1: Total fertility rate, Nordic countries (1970-2002)

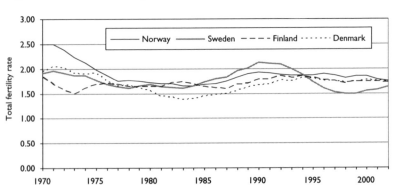

Source: Council of Europe (2003)

Throughout most of the 1970s, fertility was declining in the region, except in Finland where there was a temporary rise during the mid-1970s. In the early 1980s, fertility in Norway and Sweden had stabilised at around 1.6 to 1.7 children per woman, with a so far all-time low in 1983 for both countries. In Denmark, fertility continued to decline into the early 1980s, but hit a historic low in exactly the same year as in Norway and Sweden, with a rate just below 1.4. In contrast to the other Nordic countries, Finland had a short period of rising fertility in the early 1980s, succeeded by a temporary fall to a level of about 1.6 in 1986-87.

The development of rising fertility in all Nordic countries from about the mid-1980s caught the attention of researchers and politicians far beyond the region. The reason, of course, is that this pattern was in sharp contrast to the experience of most other European countries, where fertility continued to fall to unprecedented low levels. The decline has been particularly strong for countries in the south and in the east. To illustrate the different country trends we will use Norway and Spain as examples (Figure 3.2). As in Norway, fertility fell in Spain during the 1970s, but less rapidly at first. However, contrary to Norway, the decline did not stop in the early 1980s, but continued on into the 1990s, levelling off at about 1.2 children per woman in 1995. A similar low fertility level is also found in several other European countries, such as Italy, Bulgaria, the Czech Republic, Slovenia, and countries of the former Soviet Republic.

Figure 3.2: Total fertility rate, Norway, Spain and Japan (1970-2000)

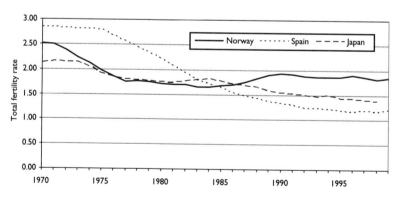

Sources: Council of Europe (2003); Japanese Ministry of Health and Welfare Statistics Department (1998); Takahashi (2001); Kojima (2001)

Kohler et al (2002) have labelled a total fertility rate at or below 1.3 *lowest-low fertility*, and have estimated that such levels could imply a halving of a country's population size in less than 45 years if they persist over a long time in a contemporary low-mortality context. The potential of immigration to substitute for the lack of domestic births has further been shown to be rather limited (UN, 2000b). In Italy, for example, the immigration needed to offset the projected decline in population would be about 250,000 per year during 2000–50, while the number assumed in the medium variant of the United Nations projections is substantially lower, just 6,000 per year. A growing number of countries in Europe thus view their low birth rates with resulting population decline and ageing as a serious problem, jeopardising the basic foundations of the nation and threatening its survival (Chamie, 2004; Stark and Kohler, 2002). Furthermore, the public debate over low fertility is not limited to Europe. In several Asian countries there is now considerable concern about a prevailing low fertility level. In Japan, for example, fertility has fallen more or less gradually since the early 1970s, from a reproduction level of more than two children per woman to today's level of just below 1.4 children (Figure 3.2). Thus, the present level in Japan is not very different from the lowest-low fertility countries of today's Europe.

Policy impacts on fertility – hypotheses and findings

Not surprisingly, the rising fertility pattern in the Nordic countries during the 1980s and early 1990s stirred a renewed interest in the possible pro-natalistic effect of the Nordic model of welfare policy and stimulated research in this area. An interesting question is why the Nordic pattern is so different from most other European countries and what can be learned from these differences. Unfortunately, there is no simple answer to this question, but one feature frequently pointed out is the relative generosity of Nordic family policies, including long, wage-compensated parental leave and a well-established, albeit still not quite sufficient, supply of publicly subsidised childcare.[3] These measures certainly reduce the costs of fertility and may thus encourage women to have more children.

A crucial question is how to assess the impact of public policies. Certainly, a very crude approach is to draw conclusions based on comparisons of levels and trends across countries, using aggregate statistics. Even if this may give a first indication of a possible effect, there are obviously many pitfalls, as there may also be other time trends that correlate with the trends being analysed. For example, both fertility and policy expansion may be correlated with upturns and downturns in the economy. To control for the bias of other influences, one may analyse the time series using multivariate analysis techniques. This is, for example, the approach of Gauthier and Hatzius (1997), who analyse the total fertility rate from 1970–90 based on aggregate data from 22 industrialised countries, using a model that includes indicators of maternity leave (duration and benefits-to-earnings ratio) and child benefits in addition to other fertility determinants. Their results suggest that fertility may be positively related to child benefits, while there were no significant effects of maternity leave.

Although useful as a period indicator of a country's fertility level, the total fertility rate is a poor measure when it comes to uncovering differences in the underlying trends. Hence, countries that appear quite similar when comparing their total fertility rates may turn out to be quite different when the fertility pattern is examined in more detail. The UK or the US may, for example, look quite similar to the Nordic countries as both have relatively high total fertility rates (1.6 and 2.1, respectively, in 2000: UN, 2003), but compared to the Nordic countries, they have much higher levels of teenage fertility and larger differences in the composition of birth rates by ethnic groups. To get to grips with such variation, it is necessary to deconstruct the fertility trends by parity (birth order) and to analyse the timing of childbearing and final number of children by socioeconomic characteristics. In this connection it is important to distinguish between the *postponement of fertility* related to the timing of entrance into parenthood and the *recuperation of fertility* ('catching up' on fertility) related to the timing and spacing of later births and the final number of children.

A remaining problem with aggregate data is that the sum of individual behaviour may not necessarily reflect average individual behaviour. Hence, individual-level data is a better source for impact analyses. To analyse the timing and spacing of fertility, a further requirement is that the data are longitudinal, that is they contain information about individuals over their life course. Before the 1990s, such data were in short supply, but later data from similar Family and Fertility Surveys conducted in about 20 industrialised countries have been available for analyses. Based on the Swedish and Norwegian surveys, several authors have addressed the role of public policies, and so far the results seem to indicate that there is a certain impact. Most evident is probably the effect of the so-called 'speed premium' in Sweden (Hoem, 1993). This is a unique feature of the Swedish parental leave system whereby a mother maintains the same benefit level as with the previous child if she has another child within 30 months (before 1986: 24 months), even if she does not return to work between the births. As might be expected, this has encouraged mothers to have their second and third chilsen sooner (Oláh, 2003; Berinde, 1999).[4] An interesting additional finding from Sweden by Oláh is that women are more likely to have a second child if the father takes parental leave with the first child, suggesting that features that encourage an active participation from the father in childcare may stimulate fertility.

Evidence based on Norwegian data at the individual level indicate that there may be a slight positive effect of increasing day care supply on third births, but the effect is most pronounced at low levels of day care coverage, and among highly educated women (Kravdal, 1996). The latter is an interesting finding, but may partly reflect that highly educated mothers have been a driving force behind the vast expansion of day care centres. Such interdependence between family policies and childbearing is difficult to disentangle, and deserves closer attention in future research. From Finland and Norway there is also some support for the hypothesis that the extension of parental leave may have stimulated fertility (Rønsen, 2004a). The effect is most significant for Finland, which had more extensions during the analysis period (about 1960-90), and is mainly limited to the probability of having a second or third child.

Is there a Nordic pattern of fertility?

Existing evidence thus indicates that the positive development of fertility trends in the Nordic countries may have been a demographic bonus of the Nordic welfare model. Yet, the evidence is mainly from the period prior to 1990, and there have been a series of changes in the family policy programmes of several Nordic countries since. The effects of the latest expansions are thus not included in the assessment.[5] Further, it has not been possible to distinguish between short-term and long-term effects on fertility. In particular, the question of possible policy effects on completed fertility for cohorts who started their reproductive period after the fertility decline of the 1960s and 1970s is of interest. During the 1990s these cohorts were approaching the end of their fertile period. Consequently, there is a great need for follow-up studies that also include more recent years. These and other issues are presently being addressed by a network of researchers collaborating within the framework of an ongoing Nordic project. In the following we shall present some preliminary findings from this network.[6]

A comparative overview of recent trends and patterns of childbearing in three Nordic countries – Denmark, Norway and Sweden – can be found in Andersson (2004a). Combining data from three countries into a single dataset, this study provides a very accurate picture of the relative differences in fertility rates between the three countries. To some extent, the trends have been fairly similar, but each country also has its own specific pattern. Swedish fertility, for instance, has fluctuated much more strongly than in the two neighbouring countries, while Danish and Norwegian fertility have evolved more gradually. A shift to shorter birth intervals in Sweden during the 1980s is specific to that country. Trends in Denmark seem to have lagged somewhat behind the childbearing development in Norway and Sweden, as a turnaround from decreasing to increasing levels of childbearing is evident in 1977 in both Norway and Sweden, while for Denmark, a similar turnaround does not occur until 1983. For Norway a pattern of higher first-birth rates among young women (aged 15-29) appears. The country-specific shift to shorter birth intervals in Sweden corroborates previous conclusions that the 'speed premium' has had an effect. Besides, greater fluctuations in fertility in Sweden are likely to be related to the sudden and large rise in unemployment in that country in the early 1990s (Andersson, 2000). The elevated first-birth rates at young ages among Norwegian women is also an interesting result, as it may partly be linked to the special support scheme for lone mothers that is unique to that country (Skrede, 2003; see also Skevik, this volume). Our ambition is to address these and other dissimilarities more fully at a later stage.

Recent single-country analyses shed more light on the determinants of the latest development in each country. In a study of birth rates up to 2002, Andersson (2004b) documents a uniform trend reversal towards the end of the 1990s in Sweden, as falling rates have been replaced by increasing birth propensities at all parities. That is, both first and second and higher order birth rates have been increasing, but the rise in first-birth rates has mainly been limited to women in their thirties. In another study Duvander and Andersson (2004) follow up on the question of a possible relationship between the use of parental leave and continued childbearing. In line with previous analyses based on survey data from the 1970s and 1980s (Oláh, 2003), they find a positive effect of the fathers' use of parental leave, but only for leave of moderate lengths. A positive effect is also evident for mothers who take extended leave, but only on the likelihood of a third birth. Interestingly, Vikat (2004) has made a parallel finding for Finland. Analysing the fertility trend from the late 1980s to 2000, he shows that women who make use of extended leave related to the Finnish home care allowance (HCA) have higher third-birth rates. But, as

Vikat duly remarks, this may primarily be because more family-oriented women opt for the HCA as part of their plan to have another child. Times of recession and poor labour market prospects may be an added incentive to realise such plans, which we shall discuss further below.

In line with previous results for Sweden (Andersson, 2000), Vikat also finds that a woman's economic activity and income have positive effects on childbearing in Finland, but the effect is most pronounced for first births. Since a positive effect is the opposite of what is predicted by standard economic theory (for example Becker, 1981, 1991), one may argue that the Nordic welfare model has loosened the traditional negative link between a woman's effort and remuneration in the labour market and fertility, by making employment and childbearing more compatible and reducing the opportunity cost of having a child. In a comparative Nordic perspective we would then expect that the effect of women's economic activity and income would be least negative (or most positive) in countries with the most generous family policies. This is a hypothesis that will be pursued further in work in progress within our Nordic network.

The accumulated evidence from past and present analyses thus supports the notion that there are positive effects of welfare policies on fertility, but as demonstrated by the Swedish trend in the 1990s, a generous family policy programme is no guarantee of a high fertility level. In the early 1990s, Sweden experienced a period of slack in the economy that soon led to a sharp rise in unemployment, and young people and people with low education were hit particularly hard. For the first time ever, there were also cutbacks in the financial support to families. Soon afterwards, fertility declined, from 2.1 children per woman in 1992 to about 1.5 in 1997. Thus, economic cycles and economic prospects also clearly have important effects on fertility, and the observed negative effect of rising unemployment is probably both a result of poorer income prospects for the present and, possibly even more important, a greater feeling of insecurity about the future.

However, as suggested in comparisons of Sweden and Finland, adverse macroeconomic conditions may not have the same adverse effects on fertility in all countries. In Finland, unemployment also rose very quickly and to higher levels than in Sweden in the early 1990s, but fertility remained at a relatively high level. Evidently, the recession did not have a noticeable influence on the childbearing behaviour of Finnish women, as is also documented by Vikat (2004). Vikat suggests that one explanation for the divergent fertility response in Finland and Sweden may be that the Finnish welfare state was able to retain most of its important functions during the recession. Besides, the HCA had been fully implemented just before the downturn of the economy, and this may have encouraged some women to have a child and take extended childcare leave with the support of the HCA while the labour market conditions were unfavourable. A couple of Swedish studies likewise suggest that fertility in Sweden may exhibit stronger pro-cyclic patterns because its family policy is more closely linked to prior employment activity (Jonsson and Dlab, 2003; Björklund, 2006). Compared with Finland, the income replacement in the parental leave scheme is higher in Sweden, while the minimum amount received by those with little or no previous income is much lower. Along the same lines one might speculate that the transitional allowance to lone parents in Norway may have been a buffer during the spell of the relatively high youth unemployment rate in the early 1990s, as the first-birth rates in Norway did not seem to be much affected. Hence, fairly generous cash benefits or minimum allowances may serve as a counter-cyclical measure and have a stabilising effect on fertility during times of recession.

Converging patterns at cohort level

So far we have seen that the Nordic countries share similarities in being forerunners with regard to the fertility decline that started in the 1960s – now commonly recognised as the second demographic transition (van de Kaa, 1987; Lesthaeghe, 1995). The future will show whether the common pattern of rising fertility rates from the mid-1980s also implies that the region will be forerunners with regard to the recuperation of fertility ('catching up' of delayed births – for a closer discussion see Lesthaeghe, 2001). What we can study already, however, is the outcome of the period pattern for completed fertility (cohort fertility) among Nordic women. Here we shall look at selected cohorts of women born in the 1930s and later who have completed most of their reproductive period (Figure 3.3).

The trend in cohort fertility has been fairly similar throughout the Nordic region, but more stable in Sweden than in the other three countries. In the 1930 cohort, completed fertility in Sweden was relatively low, at about 2.1 children per woman, while contemporary Nordic cohorts had about 2.5 children per woman. In the whole region, completed fertility fell across cohorts born before the Second World War, but less so in Sweden than in the other countries. The decline was especially rapid in Finland, where the 1945 cohort completed their

Figure 3.3: Completed fertility of female birth cohorts, Nordic countries (1930-63)

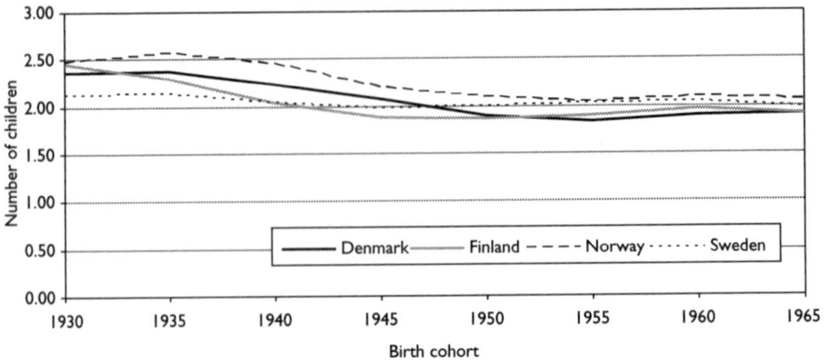

Source: Council of Europe (2003)

childbearing with fewer children than the corresponding Swedish cohort, at 1.88 and 1.98, respectively. In Denmark and Norway, cohort fertility continued to fall in the cohorts born after the Second World War, to 1.84 and 2.05 in the 1955 cohort. Among younger cohorts there has been a slight increase in cohort fertility in all countries, resulting in levels varying from 1.90 in Denmark to 2.09 in Norway for the 1960 cohort. The actual number of children born to Nordic women who have completed most of their reproductive period thus fluctuates around 2 children per woman, which is close to reproduction level. So far these cohorts have thus given birth to almost enough children to replace themselves and their spouse.

The apparent stability of the total picture in Figure 3.3 may obviously conceal some divergent trends among different groups of women. For Norway, previous analyses by education have revealed increasing dissimilarities in birth patterns across cohorts, and work in progress within our Nordic network will reveal whether similar patterns may also be observed in other countries. Here we use Norway as an example, as the comparative Nordic results are still preliminary. We would argue, however, that Norway is also a very interesting case, as it still has the highest cohort fertility of the four Nordic countries, and as its family policy historically stands out as the most ambivalent, with incentives directed both at the promotion of the dual breadwinner model, and at support schemes that put more emphasis on parents' freedom to choose[7] (see Ellingsæter, this volume).

The Norwegian analyses show that there is an increasing postponement of motherhood among highly educated women compared to women with low education, but when it comes to the final number of children, the difference between educational groups is becoming smaller. Women with higher education thus 'catch up' on some of the fertility gap later in their fertile period. The declining dissimilarity is further found to be mainly a result of a larger reduction in the number of children in the lowest educational group. In fact there has been a slight increase in the average number of children among women with a long tertiary education[8] born after the Second World War (Lappegård, 2000; Rønsen, 2004b).

Childlessness is still highest among the highly educated, however. The contrasting development across cohorts is, however, interesting (Figure 3.4). The only group with a falling trend in childlessness is women with university education born before 1944-48, while the trend among their contemporaries with lower education is relatively stable or moving slightly upward. There is thus a slight convergence

Figure 3.4: Childlessness by educational level at age 40, Norwegian women born 1935-61

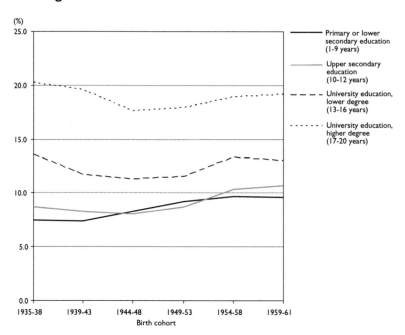

Note:

Change of cohort definition from 1944:

1935-43: Resident population by 31/12/1998.

From 1944: Women born in Norway, controlled for outmigration and deaths prior to age 40.

Sources: Population Statistics System and Educational Statistical System, Statistics Norway

in childlessness between educational groups across these cohorts. There may be several reasons for this, but one explanation often encountered is that the expansion of family policies made it increasingly easier for labour market-oriented women to combine children and paid work. Besides, women with a long tertiary education constituted a very small and select group in the older cohorts, but as the proportion of women with higher education has grown, they have become less select over the years. Hence, their choice to have or not to have a child may have become more similar to that of other women. However, among women born in the 1950s, childlessness is increasing in all educational groups, and in the 1959-61 cohort the proportion with no children was 19% among women with a long tertiary education and 10% among those with primary or lower secondary education.

In recent Nordic fertility research, attention has not only been given to *level* of education, but also to *field* of education. An interesting finding is that field of education may be an even stronger determinant of fertility than level of education. For example, for Norway Lappegård (2001) finds that childlessness is almost as low among nurses and teachers with a university degree as among women with no education beyond secondary school, and having become mothers, the former groups have a higher expected number of children at age 40 than the latter. A similar pattern has also been observed in Sweden (see, for example, Hoem, 1994; Stanfors and Svensson, 1999). One reason for the relatively high fertility among nurses and teachers is probably that this is a group that is both family oriented and work oriented and thus has strong preferences in both directions. A large public sector with ample job opportunities and flexible part-time arrangements may have been conducive for the realisation of the dual strategies implied by such preferences (Ellingsæter and Rønsen, 1996). Another and related reason is that workers within these sectors may have little to lose from employment breaks in terms of future career opportunities and earnings potential, mainly due to the high proportion of female workers and a relatively flat income profile over the working life.

Sustainable fertility – a challenge for Nordic gender equality

Figure 3.3 shows that all the Nordic countries did reasonably well with regard to the recuperation of fertility during the 1990s. Cohort fertility rates at reproduction level or very close to it indicate that the increase of mothers with three or more children by age 40 among younger cohorts to a large extent have compensated for the increase of childless women and one-child mothers. From this perspective, it is reasonable to conclude that the Nordic countries need to worry to a lesser degree than most other European countries about the present level of fertility with regard to the challenges of an ageing population. Moreover, in addition to the assumed 'general' effects of the Nordic models of family welfare, the analyses referred to above indicate that improvement in family policy support schemes also have contributed marginally to raising second- and third-birth rates during the 1990s. This is at least the case with regard to Norway, which also is the country with the most pronounced improvement in family support schemes during this period. As shown in Figure 3.3, Norway is also the Nordic country with the best recuperation record, with a relatively stable cohort fertility around reproduction level for the 'post-transition' cohorts born in the 1950s and early 1960s.

This does not mean, however, that the present Nordic fertility trends in all respects represent a robust and sustainable road in relation to the present challenges from social and demographic development within these societies. Given that gender equality both in the labour market and in the parental share of childcare has been stated as the main goal for the Nordic models of family welfare, some elements of the present fertility trends give reason to question the sustainability of development in relation to these goals. As mentioned above, earlier analyses of the fertility patterns of Norway and Sweden indicate that women with an education for the female-dominated professions in the public sector contribute higher levels of fertility than women with an education for the less gender-segregated or male-dominated sectors (Lappegård, 2001, 2005). Norway and Sweden have slightly higher rates of cohort fertility, but also higher levels of gender segregation by industry and higher levels of part-time work than Finland and Denmark (TemaNord, 1999). The differential fertility by educational type indicates that the good catch-up of fertility at cohort level may be explained to a considerable extent by a 'family-friendly', gender-segregated labour market and an underlying selection of women with strong preferences for children and for work in a 'family-friendly' context into occupations in these sectors. Recent analyses by Kravdal (2001) support the hypothesis that such selection effects can partly explain the earlier finding of a positive effect of education on the probability of having a third child.

The postponement of first birth and increased rates of childlessness in the younger cohorts are additional indications of preference heterogeneity both in educational choice and in entrance into motherhood. A recent analysis of the effects of education on young Norwegian women's transition to motherhood over the period 1971 to 2001 indicated that there is a career-adjustment effect in women's entry into motherhood related to field of education (Lappegård and Rønsen, 2005). This career-adjustment effect may be related both to differences in the opportunity costs of a career break by sectors and to preference heterogeneity. Finally, increasing educational differences in the timing of motherhood among younger cohorts suggest that long parental leaves and generous family benefits may fit better with a career track in the public sector and within female-dominated professions than among highly educated young women in the private sector and within jobs and professions with more male competition.

In this perspective, the rising trends of childlessness for highly educated women also indicate that family formation and the transition to parenthood represents a greater challenge for today's and tomorrow's young generations than for the first post-transition cohorts born in the mid and late 1950s. Here we should also take into account the changes that have taken place in men's family formation and entrance into fatherhood. Recent analyses of register data for male Norwegian birth cohorts born between 1940 and 1980 show both a strong increase in childlessness for men at ages 40 and 45 and a stronger socioeconomic selection into fatherhood for men in the younger cohorts. A more pronounced 'recirculation' of eligible men is also part of the picture (Skrede, 2004b).[9]

It is also worth noting that among highly educated[10] women and men in cohorts born between 1961 and 1970, the rate of childlessness in 2001 (at age 31–40) was even higher for men than for women, with respectively 35.4% and 30.3% childless by Census date.[11] Unless the catch-up of first births after age 30 among the highly educated considerably exceeds the corresponding rates of preceding cohorts, we must expect a considerably higher level of permanent childlessness for highly educated women in the younger cohort than in the older (17.8% for women born between 1951 and 1960). Moreover, the high level of childlessness for highly educated men is a new phenomenon, compared to the older cohorts. This indicates that part of the increase in childlessness for highly educated women may also be ascribed to difficulties in finding a man who is willing to share parental duties at a more equal level. An alternative explanation for the increased postponement of fatherhood among younger highly educated men is the possibility of negative attitudes from their employers towards active fatherhood roles. From this perspective, the postponement can be seen as a strategy for establishing a solid foothold in the labour market prior to fatherhood (Skrede, 2005). Earlier research indicates that men employed in career jobs in the private sector often experience negative attitudes from employers towards taking longer parental leave than the daddy quota (Brandth and Kvande, 2005).

Consequently, the current cohort fertility rates close to reproduction level should not be taken as a litmus test, neither of the sustainability of the fertility development nor the compatibility with gender equality in the long run. Both the increasing intra-cohort differences in younger female cohorts with regard to completed fertility (childlessness and number of children born) and the present variation in parenthood practices indicate that current birth patterns are based on a *gender equality deficit* in parents' time use in employment and care. This is evident in the more differential fertility patterns of younger cohorts. First, the higher third-birth propensities are most pronounced among women who we would expect (from their choice of education and occupation) to have relatively strong preferences for family and children, including a willingness to reduce their engagement in paid work during childrearing phases. Second, as mentioned earlier, 'gender equality light' is an appropriate description of the gendered pattern of paid and unpaid work for the majority of couples with small children, in Norway as well as in the other Nordic countries.

The indications of a positive fertility response to current family policies from parents practising 'gender equality light', confirm that family policies facilitating the combination of childrearing and labour market participation may be necessary prerequisites for a sustainable level of fertility. From the perspective of gender equality, a 'gender equality light' division of paid and unpaid work has positive aspects compared to a traditional single breadwinner model in terms of increased economic autonomy and a foothold in the labour market for the part-time worker. However, with regard to further advancement towards gender equality it also contains pitfalls in terms of perpetuating the present gender-segmented labour market and the lower incomes of women compared to men. In this respect, the current fertility pattern also gives reason to doubt the compatibility with gender equality in the long run.

Questions related to the unequal gender division of paid and unpaid work over the life course cannot be neglected in the search for future sustainability of demographic development. In a long-run perspective, it will not be easy to reach more balanced shares of paid and unpaid work between women and men, unless the incentives of family policies more strongly motivate such changes. Consequently, in addition to the need for generous family policies motivating a sustainable level of fertility with regard to social reproduction, the policies should also contain more normative elements towards gender equality.

Notes

[1] The perspectives and research results presented in the chapter are based on earlier work by the authors, in particular Rønsen (2004b) and Skrede (1999, 2004a, 2004b, 2005), as well as ongoing work within a network project financed by the Welfare Research Programme of the Nordic Council of Ministers, entitled 'Family policies, fertility trends and family changes in the Nordic countries'.

[2] The division between part-time and full-time employment now varies considerably between Norway and Sweden on the one hand, and Finland and Denmark on the other. In the case of Finland, however, a high overall female employment rate and a very high share of full-time work put Finland in another division from the start of the post-Second World War period. In the later part of the 1990s, full-time rates decreased in Finland and increased in Denmark. By 1998 the employment structures for Finnish and Danish women appear very similar with regard to the shares of full-time and part-time work respectively, while the full-time employment rates of the two other countries are substantially lower and the part-time rates correspondingly higher (TemaNord, 1999).

[3] More details on the family policy programmes of Finland, Norway and Sweden can be found in Rønsen and Sundström (2002), among others.

[4] The same result is obtained when using individual-level register data; see, for example, Hoem (1993) and Andersson (1999).

[5] For example, the expansions comprise the introduction of a 'daddy quota' in Norway and Sweden (1994 and 1995 respectively), a cash benefit for childcare in Finland ('home care allowance', fully implemented in 1990) and Norway ('cash-for-care benefit',

implemented 1998/99), and an extension of the paid parental leave period from 22 weeks (1988) to 52 weeks (1993) in Norway.

[6] See note 1 for more information on the network. A common platform for the network analyses is longitudinal data from administrative registers. A disadvantage of administrative data is that there is less information on each person in registers than in specially designed surveys, implying that there are fewer variables available for analysis. However, a great advantage of register data is that they cover the whole population and allow for analyses of very small groups. Another advantage is that the administrative data systems of the Nordic countries are very similar, and as such they constitute an excellent foundation for comparative analyses. This facilitates an intra-Nordic comparative perspective, which may throw more light on possible differences in fertility patterns *between* Nordic countries.

[7] Since the late 1980s, Finnish family policy has also put more emphasis on freedom of choice with arrangements such as the home care allowance (HCA).

[8] More than four years of tertiary education.

[9] The proportion of childless men (without registered children) at age 40 increased from 16.7% in the 1945 cohort to 25.6% in the 1960 cohort, while the proportion of childless women at age 40 increased from 9.3% in the 1945 cohort to 12.6% in the 1960 cohort.

[10] In this case defined as a university degree at Masters level or higher.

[11] Census date: 3 November 2001. Source of information on childlessness by Census date: Norwegian Population Systems.

References

Andersson, G. (1999) 'Childbearing trends in Sweden 1961-1997', *European Journal of Population*, vol 15, pp 1-24.

Andersson, G. (2000) 'The impact of labour-force participation on childbearing behaviour: pro-cyclical fertility in Sweden during the 1980s and the 1990s', *European Journal of Population*, vol 16, pp 293-333.

Andersson, G. (2004a) 'Childbearing developments in Denmark, Norway, and Sweden from the 1970s to the 1990s: a comparison', *Demographic Research*, Special Collection 3, article 7, pp 153-76 (available at: www.demographic-research.org).

Andersson, G. (2004b) 'Demographic trends in Sweden: an update of childbearing and nuptiality up to 2002', *Demographic Research*, vol 11, article 4, pp 93-109 (www.demographic-research.org).

Becker, G.S. (1981, 1991) *A Treatise on the Family*, London/ Cambridge: Harvard University Press.

Berinde, D. (1999) 'Pathways to a third child in Sweden', *European Journal of Population*, vol 15, pp 349-78.

Björklund, A. (2006) 'Does family policy affect fertility? Lessons from Sweden', *Journal of Population Economics,* vol 19, pp 3-24.

Borchorst, A. (1994) 'Welfare state regimes, women's interests and the EC', in D. Sainsbury (ed) *Gendering Welfare States*, London: Sage Publications, pp 26-44.

Brandth,B. and Kvande, E. (2005) 'Fedres valgfrihet og arbeidslivets tidskulturer', *Tidsskrift for Samfunnsforskning*, vol 46, pp 35-54.

Chamie, J. (2004) 'Low fertility: can governments make a difference?', Paper presented at the annual meeting of the Population Association of America, Boston, MA, 1-3 April (available at: http://paa2004.princeton.edu).

Council of Europe (2003) *Recent Demographic Developments in Europe*, Strasbourg: Council of Europe Publishing, December.

Demeny, P. (2003) 'Population policy dilemmas in Europe at the dawn of the twenty first century', *Population and Development Review*, vol 29, pp 1-28.

Duvander,A.-Z. and Andersson, G. (2004) 'Leder delad föräldrapenning till fler barn?', *Riksförsäkringsverket Analyserar*, p 15.

Ellingsæter,A.L. and Rønsen,M. (1996) 'The dual strategy: motherhood and the work contract in Scandinavia', *European Journal of Population*, vol 12, pp 239-60.

Esping-Andersen, G. (1990) *Three Worlds of Welfare Capitalism*, Princeton, NJ: Princeton University Press.

Gauthier, A.H. and Hatzius, J. (1997) 'Family benefits and fertility: an econometric analysis', *Population Studies*, vol 51, pp 295-306.

Hoem, B. (1994) 'Lärare föder flere barn', *Välfärdsbulletinen*, no 3, pp 17-19.

Hoem, J.M. (1993) 'Public policy as the fuel of fertility', *Acta Sociologica*, vol 36, pp 19-31.

Japanese Ministry of Health and Welfare, Statistics and Information Department (1998) *Vital statistics of Japan, 1998*, Tokyo: Ministry of Health and Welfare, Statistics and Information Department.

Jonsson, A. and Dlab, B. (2003) 'Sysselsätting och fruktsamhet i Sverige och Finland', Uppsats, Nationalekonomiske institutionen, Stockholms Universitet.

Jonung, C. (1983) 'Kvinnor och mäns yrken', in M. Lundahl and I. Persson-Tanimura (eds) *Kvinnan i Ekonomien*, Malmö: LiberFörlag, pp 53-69.

Kjeldstad, R. (2001) 'Gender policies and gender equality', in M. Kautto, J. Fritzell, B. Hvinden, J. Kvist and H. Uusitalo (eds) *Nordic Welfare States in the European Context*, London: Routledge, pp 66-97.

Knudsen, L., Gissler, M., Bender, S.S., Hedberg, C., Ollendorff, U., Sundström, K., Totlandsdal, K. and Vilhjalmsdottir, S. (2003) 'Induced abortion in the Nordic countries: special emphasis on young women', *Acta Obstreticia et Gynecologia Scandinavica*, vol 82, pp 257-68.

Kohler, H.-P., Billari, F.C. and Ortega, J.A. (2002) 'The emergence of lowest-low fertility in Europe during the 1990s', *Population and Development Review*, vol 28, pp 641-81.

Kojima, H. (2001) 'Determinants of Japanese attitudes towards fertility and policy interventions: A comparative analysis of the 1990/1995 IPP Surveys and JGSS-2000', Paper presented at the Second Annual Meeting of the Population Association of Korea, 1 December 2001, Seoul, Korea.

Kravdal, Ø. (1996) 'How the local supply of day-care centers influences fertility in Norway: a parity-specific approach', *Population Research and Policy Review*, vol 15, pp 201-18.

Kravdal, Ø. (2001) 'The high fertility of college educated women in Norway: an artefact of the separate modeling of each parity transition', *Demographic Research*, vol 5, no 6, pp 187-215 (available at www.demographic-research.org).

Lappegård, T. (2000) 'New fertility trends in Norway', *Demographic Research*, vol 2, article 3 (available at www.demographic-research.org).

Lappegård, T. (2001) 'Valg av utdanning – valg av livsløp?', *Tidsskrift for Samfunnsforskning*, no 3, pp 409-35.

Lappegård, T. (2005) 'Impact of labour market attachment and employment structure on mothers' second- and third-birth rates in contemporary Norway', Essay submitted as part of PhD dissertation in Sociology, University of Oslo, Norway.

Lappegård, T. and Rønsen, M. (2005) 'The multifaceted impact of education on entry in motherhood', *European Journal of Population*, vol 21, pp 31–49.

Leira, A. (1992) *Welfare States and Working Mothers: The Scandinavian Experience*, Cambridge: Cambridge University Press.

Leira, A. (1993) 'The 'woman-friendly' welfare state? The case of Norway and Sweden', in J. Lewis (ed) *Women and Social Policy in Europe*, Aldershot: Edward Elgar Publishing Ltd, pp 49-71.

Lesthaeghe, R. (1995) 'The second demographic transition in western countries: an interpretation', in K.O. Mason and A.-M. Jensen (eds) *Gender and Family Change in Industrialized Countries*, Oxford: Clarendon Press.

Lesthaeghe, R. (2001) 'Postponement and recuperation: recent fertility trends and forecasts in six western European countries', IPD-WP 2001-1, Interuniversity papers in demography, Vrije Universiteit Brussels, Belgium.

Lewis, J. (1992) 'Gender and the development of welfare regimes', *Journal of European Social Policy*, vol 2, no 3, pp 159-73.

Lewis, J. (ed) (1993) *Women and Social Policy in Europe*, Aldershot: Edward Elgar Publishing Ltd.

Oláh, L. Sz. (2003) 'Gendering fertility: second births in Sweden and Hungary', *Population Research and Policy Review*, vol 22, pp 171-200.

Østby, L. (1983) '20 års utvikling i samliv, prevensjon og abort', in K. Skrede and K. Tornes (eds) *Studier i kvinners livsløp*, Oslo: Universitetsforlaget, pp 105-38.

Rønsen, M. (2004a) 'Fertility and public policies – evidence from Norway and Finland', *Demographic Research*, vol 10, article 10, pp 141-70 (available at www.demographic-research.org).

Rønsen, M. (2004b) 'Fertility and family policy in Norway – a reflection on trends and possible connections', *Demographic Research*, vol 10, article 10, pp 263-86 (available at: www.demographic-research.org).

Rønsen, M. and Sundström, M. (2002) 'Family policy and after-birth employment among new mothers – a comparison of Finland, Norway and Sweden', *European Journal of Population*, vol 18, pp 121-52.

Sainsbury, D. (ed) (1994) *Gendering Welfare States*, London: Sage Publications.

Sainsbury, D. (1999) 'Gender and the making of the Norwegian and Swedish welfare states', in B. Palier and D. Bouget (eds) *Comparing Social Welfare Systems in Nordic Countries and France*, Nantes: MIRE, vol 4, Maison des Sciences de l'Homme, Ange-Guépin, pp 153-68.

Sainsbury, D. (2001) 'Gender and the making of the Norwegian and Swedish welfare states', *Social Politics*, vol 8, pp 113-43.

Skrede, K. (1986) 'Gifte kvinner i arbeidslivet', in L. Alldén, N.R. Ramsøy and M.Vaa (eds) *Det norske samfunn III*, Oslo: Gyldendal, pp 145-68.

Skrede, K. (1999) 'Shaping gender equality – the role of the state: Norwegian experiences, present policies and future challenges', in B. Palier and D. Bouget (eds) *Comparing Social Welfare Systems in Nordic Countries and France*, Nantes: MIRE, vol 4, Maison des Sciences de l'Homme, Ange-Guépin, pp 169-99.

Skrede, K. (2003) 'Opening the black box: some preliminary findings on early transition to parenthood and the role of cohabiting unions in early family formation in Norway', Paper presented at the workshop: Das vernachlässigte Geschlecht in der Familieforschung: Analysen zum Heirats und Geburtenverhalten von Männern in Deutchland, 27-28 February, Max Planck Institute for Demographic Research, Rostock.

Skrede, K. (2004a) 'Familiepolitikkens grense – ved 'likestilling light'?', in A.L. Ellingsæter and A. Leira (eds) *Velferdsstaten og familien – Utfordringer og dilemmaer*, Oslo: Gyldendal Akademisk, pp 160-96.

Skrede, K. (2004b) 'Færre menn blir fedre', *Økonomiske Analyser*, vol 23, no 6, pp 57-68.

Skrede, K. (2005) 'Foreldreskap i forandring – færre menn blir fedre', *Tidsskrift for Kjønnsforskning* (formerly *Tidsskrift for kvinneforskning*), vol 29, no 2, pp 4-22.

Stanfors, M. and Svensson, L. (1999) 'Education, career opportunities and the changing patterns of fertility: a study on 20th century Sweden', Paper presented at the Seminar on Women in the Labour Market in Changing Economies, Rome, 22-24 September.

Stark, L. and Kohler, H.-P. (2002) 'The debate over low fertility in the popular press: a cross-national comparison, 1998-1999', *Population Research and Policy Review*, vol 21, pp 535-74.

Takahashi, S. (2001) 'Demographic investigation of the process of declining fertility in Japan', Paper presented at the IUSSP Seminar on International Perspectives on Low Fertility, Tokyo, Japan, 21-23 March.

TemaNord (1999: 514) *Women and Men in the Nordic Countries: Facts and Figures 1999*, Copenhagen: Nordic Council of Ministers.

UN (United Nations) (2000a) 'Below replacement fertility', *Population Bulletin of the United Nations*, Special Issue Nos 40/41 1999, New York, NY: UN.

UN (2000b) *Replacement Migration: Is It a Solution to Declining and Ageing Populations?*, New York, NY: UN.

UN (2003) *World Fertility Report 2003*, Economic & Social Affairs, Population Division, New York, NY: UN.

van de Kaa, D.J. (1987) 'Europe's second demographic transition', *Population Bulletin*, vol 42, pp 1-57.

Vikat, A. (2004) 'Women's labor force attachment and childbearing in Finland', *Demographic Research*, Special Collection 3, article 8, pp 175-212 (available at: www.demographic-research.org).

Part Two
Gender equality and parental choice in welfare state redesign

FOUR

Nordic men on parental leave: can the welfare state change gender relations?

Johanna Lammi-Taskula

Promoting fatherhood at the policy and institutional level can produce more symmetrical definitions of women and men as parents than will exist without such promotion. But does the politicising of fatherhood really 'make men into fathers' (Hobson, 2002)? Men are facing a challenge to increasingly share the responsibilities of family life at the same time as women have become an important part of the labour market. From the early 1990s, fatherhood has been a focus area in the development of parenthood policies. In order to encourage more men to take parental leave, individual and non-transferable rights for fathers have been legislated.

Changes in gender relations at the institutional level are expected to change the gendered practices of work–family reconciliation. The way men and women think, act and feel is, however, also influenced by the workplace culture (Haas et al, 2002) as well as by family negotiations (Olsen, 2000). Thus the politicising of parenthood to promote fathercare does not necessarily produce radical changes in the division of paid and unpaid work in everyday life.

In the Nordic countries, parental leave schemes have been available for men since the 1970s, but men have not taken up the opportunities nearly as much as had been expected (Leira; Borchhorst, this volume). The daddy quota of parental leave has been the main instrument in promoting fathers' take-up of the leave. The introduction of a quota has increased the number of men who take parental leave (Brandth and Överli, 1998; Haas et al, 2002; Rostgaard, 2002). The quota is a challenge to the traditional division of care work. Decisions about sharing or not sharing parental leave are no longer totally up to the parents. The idea of the quota is the same in all countries – this leave period is reserved for the father – but there is variation in the actualisation in different Nordic countries

(Rostgaard, 2002). The timing and the policy arguments have been different. The length of the quota varies, as well as the level of individual care responsibility, in other words, whether the father is the primary carer during his leave. Variation at the institutional level is related to differences in the gendered division of labour and power in everyday life, that is, to the take-up patterns of parental leave and the effects these patterns have for women's and men's positions in the labour market as well as at home.

Focusing on the politicising of fatherhood, this chapter compares the current entitlements of fathers for taking parental leave in five Nordic countries: Sweden, Norway, Denmark, Iceland and Finland. Next, reviewing both qualitative and quantitative research, the chapter goes on to examine the socioeconomic and cultural conditions of actualising leave possibilities, and considers especially negotiations of gender relations in the everyday life of families and workplaces. The conclusion returns to a main question raised: does the politicising of fatherhood change gender relations in infant care?

Fathers' rights to leave

The time that may be taken free from employment by a father to care for his child is not determined by one form of leave but several different policy elements. Some entitlements are individual and non-transferable, such as paternity leave and the daddy quota; some are transferable parental leave. First, the father can take a short paternity leave soon after childbirth when the mother is also at home with the baby. Paternity leave is meant to promote the father–child relationship and to provide help for the mother. The length of paternity leave is three weeks in Finland and two weeks in all other Nordic countries. Iceland has no special paternity leave.

Second, the father can share parental leave with the child's mother, according to their mutual decision. This time period varies from three months in Iceland to one year in Sweden. In principle, only one parent at a time stays at home on parental leave, taking full responsibility for childcare, while the other parent is at work or studying. In practice, however, it is possible and quite usual for the other parent – in this case the mother – to take annual holiday or sabbatical leave in order to stay at home together with the father and child (Rostgaard, 2002; Haataja, 2004).

Third, the father can take the daddy quota of parental leave, which is a non-transferable leave period, meaning that it cannot be taken by the mother if the father decides not to use it. The length of the daddy quota varies from two weeks in Finland to three months in Iceland. Denmark is the only Nordic country with no daddy quota at the moment as a two-week quota has been abolished (see Borchorst, this volume). Also the two-week 'bonus leave' in Finland has a somewhat different character than the daddy quotas in Sweden, Norway and Iceland because it is conditional. The father only gets his two extra leave weeks if he first takes two weeks of the transferable parental leave.

There are some differences between the Nordic countries in the eligibility criteria for a father's parental leave. Only in Norway does a father's option to take parental leave depend on both his and the mother's employment; in order for the father to take parental leave, both parents must have been employed for six of the previous 10 months (Brandth and Kvande, 2003). Danish fathers are eligible for parental benefit if they have been in the labour market for at least 13 weeks before the leave and have during this time worked at least 120 hours; but also unemployed fathers can take parental leave (www.bm.dk). In Sweden and in Iceland, a father can take parental leave if he has been employed for at least six months; in Sweden also if he has worked altogether at least 12 months during the past two years (www.fk.se; Drew, 2005).

In Iceland and in Finland, a father living together with the mother of their child is entitled to parental benefit and parental leave regardless of the mother's position in the labour market (Gislason, 2004; www.kela.fi). In Finland, in order for the father to receive parental benefit he must have lived in Finland for at least 180 days before the due date, and the mother of his child must have taken a postnatal medical examination five to 12 weeks after childbirth (www.kela.fi). In Sweden, fathers who do not live with the mother are also entitled to parental benefit and parental leave if their child lives in Sweden and the parents have shared custody (Nyman and Petterson, 2002).

The above-mentioned forms of leave are part of the social insurance system, which usually means that an earnings-related compensation is paid during the leave period. There are, however, some exceptions: during paternity leave, quite a large flat-rate benefit is paid in Denmark (Rostgaard, 2002) and in Norway wage compensation during paternity leave is not statutory but negotiated in collective agreements (Leira, 1998). Unpaid periods are also included in the parental leave scheme in Norway, where both parents have the right to a one-year period of unpaid parental leave in addition to the period with compensation. In Sweden, a low flat-rate benefit is paid during the last three months of the parental leave period (Haataja, 2004).

The level of the earnings-related parental benefit is highest in

Norway (80% to 100% of previous income) and lowest in Finland (about 70% of average income). The level of the Danish flat-rate benefit is 56% of the average male production worker's income (Rostgaard, 2002). Benefits are important for the family economy, but they also symbolise the importance of care work as it is evaluated by the state. As men's wages are in general higher than women's, a low compensation level may result in a lower take-up of leave by fathers (Haataja and Nyberg, this volume).

Flexibility in the parental leave schemes has been seen as facilitating men's take-up of leave (Rostgaard, 2002). In all the Nordic countries, parental leave can be taken on a part-time basis. The alternatives for full-time parental leave in Sweden are 70%, 50%, 25% or 18% of leave combined with part-time employment. In Norway, the time-account scheme allows parents to work part time 50%, 60%, 75%, 80% or 90% of the time and to receive a partial parental benefit that is paid for a longer period than the full-time leave benefit (Haataja, 2004). The daddy quota can, however, only be taken full time (Rostgaard, 2002). In Denmark and in Iceland, parents can take part-time leave if they are able to negotiate it with their employers (Rostgaard, 2002; Gislason, 2004).

Compared to the other Nordic countries, Finland is a latecomer in creating part-time possibilities for parental leave. Part-time parental leave was first legislated for in 2003 and, unlike in the other Nordic countries, it is conditional: part-time parental leave can be taken only if both parents shorten their working hours at the same time and take turns in childcare for at least two months (Haataja, 2004). The Finnish system is more rigid also in regard to the timing of leave periods and taking leave over a longer time span. Whereas parents in Denmark, Sweden and Iceland can take periods of parental leave until the child is eight to nine years old, in Finland this is possible only until the child is about 10 months old. If the father has not taken up his leave entitlements during this period, he can no longer receive the income-related parental benefit.

However, in Finland and Norway there is still the possibility of full-time or part-time leave with a flat-rate benefit after the paternity and parental leave periods, until the child is three years old. During this period, a cash-for-care benefit is paid to a parent who stays at home with the child instead of using public child day care services (see Ellingsaeter, Leira, this volume).

High popularity of short leave periods

The possibilities for sharing the care of young children between the parents are quite extensive in the Nordic countries at the institutional level, but in practice the gendered division of labour in families is still far from symmetrical. Although large numbers of Nordic fathers are taking some form of parental leave, sharing the transferable period of parental leave between mothers and fathers so that the father bears the primary care responsibility is still a marginal phenomenon. The introduction of the daddy quota has resulted in take-up by fathers in greater numbers as this part of parental leave cannot be transferred to the mother. The daddy quota has also increased the sharing of parental leave outside the quota between fathers and mothers in Norway and in Iceland (Brandth and Kvande, 2003; Gislason, 2004). On the other hand, the quota has shortened the average length of leave periods taken by fathers in Finland and in Sweden (Haataja and Nyberg, this volume).

The popularity and the high take-up of the father's individual leave rights – paternity leave and the daddy quota – have been referred to as 'everyman's mass movement' (Lammi-Taskula, 1998) or 'a father revolution' (Holter, 2003) as these leave periods are taken by a majority of fathers with different socioeconomic backgrounds. In Norway, the two-week paternity leave is taken by more than two thirds of fathers and the one-month quota of parental leave is even more popular – when the quota was introduced in 1993, the share of fathers taking parental leave rose from 4% to more than half of entitled fathers, and has since then grown to close to 90% (Brandth and Kvande, 2003).

Similarly, rapid development has taken place in Iceland along with the daddy quota of parental leave. During the first year (2001) of the new parental leave system with a one-month daddy quota, the take-up of leave by fathers grew from less than 1% to more than 80%. The take-up has remained as high with the extension of the quota to two months in 2002 and three months in 2003 (Gislason, 2004; see Chapter One, Table 1.1, p 23). The success of the daddy quota in Norway and Iceland may at least partly be due to the fact that the quota was added to the existing parental leave period, whereas in the other countries it was partly or totally taken from the existing transferable parental leave that had mainly been taken by mothers.

In Sweden, another aspect explaining why the daddy quota has not increased the take-up of parental leave by fathers as rapidly as in Norway and in Iceland is that leave can be taken during a much longer period, until the child is eight years old. Before the quota in

1993, about one in four parents taking parental leave were fathers, but in 2001 the share of fathers was almost 40%. Half of the entitled fathers take some parental leave on a yearly basis, and during a five-year period only one in four fathers has not taken any leave (Nyman and Petterson, 2002).

In Finland and in Denmark, more than half of fathers take one or two weeks of paternity leave, but longer parental leave – which requires taking full responsibility for childcare and which needs to be negotiated with the mother – has been taken by only a few men (Rostgaard, 2002; Lammi-Taskula, 2003). The daddy quota has been more popular than the common parental leave among fathers, but not nearly as much as in the other countries. Before the two-week daddy quota was abolished in Denmark, it was taken by one in five fathers (Rostgaard, 2002). A similar popularity to that in Denmark was predicted in Finland as the new father's bonus leave ('quota') was introduced (Haataja, 2004). However, during the first year the quota was taken up by only about 5% of fathers in Finland (Kela, 2004).

The length of parental leave taken yearly by fathers is longest in Iceland, where the average number of fathers' parental leave days has grown from 39 days in 2001 to 87 days in 2003. The one-month quota was taken by most fathers, and the two-month quota was also possible for a large majority. In 2002, about nine in 10 fathers took the whole two-month quota period. In 2003, three in four Icelandic fathers took all three months of their parental leave quota (Gislason, 2004.)

Contrary to Iceland, the fathers' parental leave periods have become shorter in Sweden and in Finland after the introduction of the daddy quota. In Sweden, the average length of leave taken by fathers was 40 days in 1993 but only 27 days in 2001 (Nyman and Petterson, 2002). In Finland, parental leave periods taken by fathers averaged 64 days in 2002 but only 37 days in 2003 (Kela, 2004; see Box 1.1, Chapter One). As the fathers' take-up rate of parental leave is very low in Finland, the average length of all leave (paternity and parental) among fathers was only 17 days in 2003 (Kela, 2004).

In Denmark the mean length of parental leave taken by fathers in 2000 was one month. The same year the mean length of leave taken by fathers in Norway was 25 days; according to a survey those taking the daddy quota stayed at home on average for six-and-a-half weeks (including paternity leave) whereas those who did not take the quota only took on average one-and-a-half weeks of leave (Brandth and Kvande, 2003).

However, as fathers mainly take short leave periods, their share of all parental leave days is low, ranging from less than 1% in Denmark (Rostgaard 2002) to 17% in Sweden (JämO, 2005). In Norway, fathers take 8.5% of all leave days (Rikstrygdeverket 2002/ www.likestilling.no) and in Finland only 5% (Kela, 2004; see Chapter One, Table 1.1, p 23). In addition to the short total length of leave periods taken by fathers, leave is also not always taken continuously but split into several periods. For example, in Iceland, because of the lack of paternity leave, many fathers take the first two or three weeks of their quota right after the birth of their child when the mother is also at home, and the rest later (Gislason, 2004).

The high popularity of paternity leave and the daddy quota of parental leave indicates that taking some leave from work to take care of one's child has become 'normal' among Nordic fathers. However, fathers' leave periods are mainly quite short and their share of all the parental leave days taken in each country is low. Following the expansion of the parental leave period and of individual non-transferable leave rights, Iceland has during recent years been the only Nordic country where both the number of fathers taking parental leave and the length of leave taken by fathers have been growing at the same time. Iceland is thus in the forefront of revising the hegemonic pattern of 'a small dose of fathercare' (Leira, 2002) and moving towards more symmetric gender relations.

Marginal but not marginalised: socioeconomic patterns of take-up

Compared to paternity leave and the daddy quota, the transferable parental leave has been taken only by a minority of fathers. One could say that this minority is marginal – only a small proportion of all fathers – but the socioeconomic composition of this group shows that the leave-sharing families are not by any means marginalised. Quite the contrary: according to statistics and surveys, the fathers who share the common parental leave come from relatively well-off families in all the Nordic countries. These fathers have a high education level, their earnings are reasonably high, and they have a spouse with a good position in the labour market (Olsen, 2000; Nyman and Petterson, 2002; Brandth and Kvande, 2003; Lammi-Taskula, 2003). Reports of the socioeconomic patterns of fathers' take-up of parental leave are not available from Iceland.

According to a Norwegian survey of 1,377 men whose child was born in 1994-95, the take-up of parental leave was higher among fathers whose spouse worked full time and did a lot of overtime work, whereas the spouse's part-time work was related to a low take-up of parental leave by fathers. On the other hand, fathers with part-time employment or with a temporary work contract took more parental leave than full-time employees with a permanent position (Brandth and Kvande, 2003). Another survey of 1,661 men in Norway – who became fathers in 1995 – showed that parental leave beyond the four-week quota was taken especially by men with an academic degree and by those employed in white-collar positions (Brandth and Överli, 1998).

Among a sample of about 4,000 Danish families with children born in 1995, the mother's high education and income level increased the chance of the father taking parental leave (Christoffersen, 1997). In Finland, a survey of 1,400 fathers and 3,300 mothers of children born in 1999 showed that men taking parental leave had a higher education level and were more often in a white-collar expert position than those who took only paternity leave. However, the father's academic degree increased the possibility of his taking parental leave only when the mother also had an academic degree, as these mothers took shorter leave periods than mothers in general (Lammi-Taskula, 2003).

The Swedish Social Insurance Institute (Riksförsäkringsverket) analysed the take-up of parental leave by fathers of children born in 1996 during a four-year period (1996-99). Leave was more often taken by men with longer education and higher income, as well as by men whose spouse had a higher education level. The fathers who did not take any parental leave had more often been unemployed and received other social benefits, and they were more often born outside of Sweden (Nyman and Petterson, 2002).

As the families sharing parental leave are by no means economically or socially marginalised, the arguments concerning the importance of the negative economic consequences of fathers' parental leave for the family can be questioned. Of course, the economic argument is real as men in general have better wages than women – partly because of gender segregation in the labour market but also because of discrimination (Vartiainen, 2001) – and as the compensation level during parental leave is in most cases less than 100%. Thus, a family usually loses more money if the father takes parental leave than when the mother does so (Leira, 1998). The higher the family income level, the bigger the losses are in absolute terms, but their relative importance for the family economy can still be smaller.

Despite gendered wage differences and actual losses experienced by families, economic constraints are experienced as a relevant argument for parental leave only in a minority of Nordic families. In a Swedish survey of 317 fathers working in the private sector in 1997-98, a majority (61%) reported no economic obstacles to taking leave (Haas et al, 2002). In a Danish sample of over 700 parents, even though 60% of the families would have lost income if the father took parental leave, only one in five said the father's leave would have been an economic burden for the family (Rostgaard et al, 1999). A third of the Norwegian fathers with children born in 1995 who had taken the four-week quota said the economic compensation had been important for them (Brandth and Överli, 1998).

Even when economy is seen as an obstacle for sharing leave in one's own family, the assumed economic losses related to the father's parental leave are not necessarily verified by making calculations. Of Finnish parents with children born in 1999, more than half of those fathers and mothers who did not share parental leave referred to negative economic consequences as an argument against the father's leave, but less than one third had done any calculations (Lammi-Taskula, 2003). Obviously, the economic justification can only partly make sense of the gendered division of labour in childcare; this justification is often founded on assumptions based on statistical facts, that is, the general pay gap between women and men, rather than facts that are significant in one's own family life.

Negotiations in families

Qualitative studies on parental leave have pointed out that in addition to the socioeconomic factors, negotiations in families between mothers and fathers are an important part of the reproduction of the gendered division of labour. Relationships between economic rationality, family time and emotional aspects are outlined in everyday life practices in the context of prevailing norms and ideologies of motherhood, fatherhood and gender equality (Olsen, 2000; Plantin, 2001; Brandth and Kvande, 2003).

The importance of family negotiations has also been addressed in several surveys. The results from Swedish workplaces showed that the partner's willingness to share parental leave was a significant predictor of a father's decision to take leave (Haas et al, 2002). Nearly half of the Norwegian fathers who did not take parental leave said an important reason was the mother's intention to stay at home, and another half reported that the parents were united in their willingness to prioritise the father's career (Brandth and Kvande, 2003). In Finland, a survey among parents of young children showed that discussions about parental leave were more common among highly educated parents who had also shared leave more often than others: 72% of fathers with an academic degree, compared to 44% of fathers with no occupational education said they had discussed the take-up of parental leave with their spouse. Lack of discussion was partly due to lack of information, despite the fact that the fathers' possibilities have existed for almost two decades. Young first-time fathers as well as the less educated ones knew less about the parental leave system than fathers in general (Lammi-Taskula, 2003.)

Often the family negotiations about parenting and parental leave are subtle and implicit rather than exhaustive and explicit. When there is little discussion, the status quo of gender relations is often taken for granted. Swedish couples interviewed at the end of the 1990s expressed a strong consensus about the division of parental responsibilities; in the context of gender inequality in working life they saw the mother's parental leave as a gain for the family (Plantin, 2001). On the other hand, equal parenting practices can also be based on implicit shared understandings. A Norwegian father who took six months of parental leave said that sharing leave was an easy decision based on mutual desire: 'It was completely natural for me to stay at home and I really wanted to stay at home, I was very happy that she agreed and there was not much discussion really, or any arguments' (Brandth and Kvande, 2003, p 84).

The father's own needs, such as hoping for a break from work (Brandth and Kvande, 2003) or the child being a long-awaited fulfilment of hopes and dreams (Olsen, 2000), also motivate him to take parental leave. In family negotiations, these needs are not necessarily the first to be mentioned. When Finnish parents' justifications for the take-up of parental leave were compared, both mothers and fathers reported their own needs, for example getting out of the rat race and being together with their child, as more relevant than their spouse's needs (Lammi-Taskula, 2004). In other words, parents were not always aware of their spouse's needs. The mother's willingness to return to work may be combined with the father's tiredness with his own work, but what is often emphasised as a main argument is the child's best interests. For example, 90% of the Norwegian fathers taking their parental leave quota at the end of the 1990s said they took leave so that their child could be in home care as long as possible and enjoy a good father–child relationship (Brandth and Kvande, 2003).

What do they say at the workplace?

A conception of the father's indispensable occupational expertise can be behind the lack of negotiation about parental leave in families. When the work situation is constructed as a considerable obstacle to the father's parental leave, he is simply not seen as able to leave his work, and discussion of alternatives is useless. According to Jouko Huttunen, who has studied fatherhood in Finland, having a family and being a father is usually seen as a positive achievement for a man in worklife, but fatherhood can be practised only within certain limits (Huttunen, 1999). Taking parental leave can be perceived as going beyond this limit and disturbing paid work too much. The responses at the workplace are significant for the take-up of leave: a survey among Swedish fathers at the end of the 1990s showed that fathers who considered their companies to be supportive towards caring fatherhood, as well as gender equality, were more likely to take parental leave (Haas et al, 2002).

In the survey among parents of young children in Finland, half of the fathers who did not take parental leave said there would have been problems at the workplace if they had taken leave. However, only one in 10 of these fathers reported the employer's actual negative attitudes towards parental leave, so a majority had based their conception of the work-related barriers on assumptions (Lammi-Taskula, 2003). Job-related reasons were also reported as the major obstacle to parental leave by Norwegian fathers: 64% of those who did not take their parental leave quota said it would have been difficult to combine leave with work tasks (Brandth and Kvande, 2003).

Despite widespread assumptions and experiences of the work situation or work culture as obstacles to the father's parental leave, certain branches of worklife can be characterised as more 'father-friendly' than others. Take-up rates of parental leave by fathers employed in different sectors show that men employed in the public sector have taken parental leave more often than those employed in the private sector in all the Nordic countries (Riksförsäkringsverket, 1993; Christoffersen, 1997; Brandth and Överli, 1998; Lammi-Taskula, 2003). According to the survey of parents from Finland, take-up rates are especially high in the public health and social care sector, whereas fathers employed in private industry or commerce have taken leave least often (Lammi-Taskula, 2003).

Several explanations have been given for the higher take-up of parental leave by fathers employed in the public sector. In Denmark, public sector employees received a supplement to the parental benefit and thus the probability of sharing parental leave between parents was higher in the 1990s when the father was employed in the public sector and the mother in the private sector (Christoffersen, 1997). Public sector – especially health and social care – organisations are female-dominated in all the Nordic countries (Nordic Council of Ministers,1999). In these organisations, absences of employees due to parental leave are usual. As routines in arranging substitutes and reorganising tasks during parental leave have been created, it is also easier for men working in female-dominated occupations to take leave (Olsen, 2000).

The attitudes of managers can also be different in public and private sector organisations. In the mid-1990s, Danish managers in the public sector were more positive towards parental leave than those in the private sector, and female superiors – who are more typical in the female-dominated public sector – were more supportive than male superiors (Andersen et al, 1996). Compared with Danish private sector companies, leave periods in public sector organisations were less often perceived as a sign of lower commitment and weaker performance (Carlsen, 1994).

The attitudes of colleagues in the workplace may also be significant to a father's decision to take up parental leave. Norwegian studies carried out in the mid-1990s showed that men taking parental leave received a lot of positive attention from their female colleagues (Brandth and Överli, 1998). In a study involving 15 workplaces in Finland, it was found that middle-aged, white-collar female employees were particularly positive towards fathers' parental leave (Salmi and Lammi-Taskula, 1999).

The work culture, including attitudes and reactions in the workplace towards parental leave, is interrelated with the organising of work. Lisbeth Bekkengen (1999) distinguishes between individual and team work as relevant to the possibilities of men (and women) taking parental leave in Sweden. If work is based on individual specialisation, the absence of an expert has more relevance for the totality of the work process rather than for other expert colleagues concerned with their own, specialised tasks and projects. The attitudes towards parental leave in specialised workplaces can thus be negative among the management whereas the reactions of colleagues can be neutral or positive when someone takes leave. The absence of one employee from a more collectively organised work process, on the other hand, is not as relevant for the management as it can be for the colleagues. The re-division of tasks can add to the workload of colleagues and they may need to spend time in tutoring a substitute employee.

In the early 2000s, tasks are more and more tied to individuals with special expertise, and employees are expected to bear responsibility for the company's success, and so leave can be interpreted as a sign of weaker commitment. The long-hours culture at dynamic workplaces and the mixed messages from management may prevent fathers from taking leave (Haas et al, 2002). Critical comments have been made by corporate management in the Finnish media about men even taking paternity leave, which is seen as incompatible with a work culture based on maximum efficiency and complete devotion to work (Laaksonen, 2003).

There may be both individually and collectively organised tasks – carried out by specialists and experts as well as those whose work can more easily be replaced – within the same workplace. This means that the attitudes and practices in regard to parental leave vary according to position and situation. The reactions of management are also related to predicting and controlling work/ family situations: at what stage are they informed about the pregnancy and plans about parental leave, how is it possible to plan ahead and reorganise tasks and how easy is it to hire a substitute? According to Bekkengen (1999), many Swedish fathers have combined a short parental leave period with a summer holiday. Prolonging holiday with parental leave may cause less negative reactions in the workplace than taking a long parental leave as such. In the early 1990s, Swedish fathers who took parental leave often had a different relationship to work than men in general: they did shorter hours and valued family life rather than paid work as the most important sphere in their life (Haas and Hwang, 1999). Perhaps this family orientation is even more threatening for employers than the temporary absence from work due to parental leave.

Outdoor daddies and household work

Sharing the responsibility of childcare also has implications for sharing the unpaid household work between parents. In general, housework is still predominantly done by women. The basic needs of the child create an inevitable frame for daily practices during parental leave. Still, there is also room for variations in practising parenting according to the mother's as well as the father's orientation and previous experience.

While there is variation among mothers as well as fathers, qualitative research on parental leave suggests that fathers tend to spend their day with the child in a somewhat different manner than mothers (Holter and Aarseth, 1994; Olsen, 2000; Brandth and

Kvande, 2003). Nordic fathers – especially Norwegian ones – seem to prefer an active outdoor and social life rather than being indoors with the child. Men creating their own practices with their babies, such as going on picnics and forest adventures, seem to be more satisfied with their parental leave than those fathers who mainly stay at home and take care of daily household duties along with childcare (Brandth and Kvande, 2003).

Going out of the home with the child is easier for those fathers who are more familiar with the childcare routines. A lack of experience means it is more difficult to recognise the child's needs and adjust sleeping and eating patterns so that longer outdoor trips are possible. Those Danish fathers who – often because of work – had not practised the basic care of their child before they started their parental leave needed to spend much more time and energy in learning the daily routine. They said in the interview study that it came as a surprise to them how time-consuming childcare could be, and frustration resulted when things did not work out as planned (Olsen, 2000).

In addition to basic childcare, a lot of housework is included in the everyday life of parents of young children. Even if unpaid housework may be quite equally shared by a childless couple, a redivision happens when a child is born (Ahrne and Roman, 1997). This work of cleaning the home, washing clothes, buying food, preparing meals, washing dishes, and so on, is usually done predominantly by mothers, who take most parental leave and thus spend more time at home. A more equal sharing of household work between the parents can be expected when the father also takes parental leave (Brandth and Överli, 1998; Haas and Hwang, 1999).

Being a primary carer for the child can also mean paying less attention to household chores and concentrating on the child (Einarsdottir, 1998). Surveys in the mid-1990s among parents of young children in Sweden and Norway showed that the longer the father's parental leave period, the more equal was the sharing of daily housework. Tasks related directly to childcare such as changing nappies, feeding the child and getting up at night, as well as staying at home from work if the child was ill, were more equally shared in families where the father took a longer parental leave (Ahrne and Roman, 1997; Brandth and Överli, 1998). The division of labour may become more symmetrical due to the father's leave experience, but it is also possible that leave is taken more by those fathers who are more care oriented in the first place.

Mother's choice?

Although the statutory leave possibilities and the attitudes and practices found in working life are quite central to the division of paid and unpaid work between mothers and fathers, other social and cultural conditions are relevant as well. The availability and quality of day care places for the child as well as cultural conceptions and ideals of mothering and fathering can determine the length of each parent's leave period.

Especially in areas populated by a lot of families with young children, the supply does not always meet the demand and many parents have difficulties in finding a suitable day care place for their young children (Haas and Hwang, 1999; Rostgaard et al, 1999; Leira, this volume). For parents with a precarious position in the labour market – often mothers with a low education level – a long leave seems like a good alternative to unemployment and at the same time a solution to the day care problem as well as high day care fees (Olsen, 2000; Lammi-Taskula, 2004; Ellingsaeter, this volume).

Negative attitudes against mothers returning to work when their children are 'too young' do not make it easier to decide about the father's parental leave. The parental leave system creates a norm for the length of the period that a 'good mother' should stay at home with her child. The traditional model where the mother takes a long leave and the father takes no more than a short paternal leave is still 'the correct choice' for many Danish women (Olsen, 2000). If a mother returns to work before the right to leave is over, she faces a lot of questioning and criticism, especially from other mothers. As one Swedish mother put it: 'It would have been seen as quite weird, had I not stayed at home when the child was young' (Plantin, 2001, p 127).

When the obstacles to fathers' parental leave are listed, breastfeeding is often mentioned as 'naturally' prohibiting the sharing of parental leave between mothers and fathers (Salmi and Lammi-Taskula, 1999; Ellingsaeter, this volume). The capacity to breastfeed is indeed one of the relevant physiological differences between mothers and fathers, and rather long periods of breastfeeding are recommended by medical authorities. In Finland, full breastfeeding is recommended for six months, partial breastfeeding at least until the child is one year old (STM, 2004). However, a majority of Finnish mothers will supplement breastfeeding: in 2000, a survey among mothers showed that no more than 14% of four-month-old babies were given only their mother's milk (Hasunen, 2002).

Being unable or unwilling to fulfil the expectations created by the breastfeeding recommendations may create more pressure to be a 'good mother' by taking a longer parental and childcare leave. Instead of referring to breastfeeding as an argument for not sharing parental leave, the mother's 'choice' to stay at home is emphasised. A Norwegian mother who left her job when the second child was born said: 'In all the families with young children that I know, it is the mother who is at home. That's how it is with us, too. I am at home because I want to be at home!' (Brandth and Kvande, 2003, pp 97–8).

The 'mother's choice' argument has been criticised by pointing out that it is actually the cultural, social and practical everyday facts that 'order' the mother to stay at home (Olsen, 2000; Kivimäki, 2001). It is fathers rather than mothers who can choose whether or not to take parental leave and for how long (Bekkengen, 2002). And even when the father may be willing and able to take parental leave, prevailing conceptions of good motherhood do not encourage mothers to leave a baby in the father's care.

Do parenthood policies change gender relations?

The Nordic policies of parenthood, with independent and non-transferable leave rights for fathers, aim at a more equal division of the work and responsibility related to childcare between women and men. This is expected to promote gender equality in the labour market as well as in family life. So far, change towards gender symmetry has been modest as the development of fatherhood policies has not led to widespread actualisation of new practices of paid and unpaid work in families and in worklife.

The fatherhood policies include different leave possibilities for fathers, reflecting different kinds of ideas of parental gender relations. As paternity leave is relatively short and taken while the mother is also at home, this leave scheme does not construct symmetry in gender relations in the same way as parental leave does. During paternity leave, the mother is the primary parent and the father can be a 'visiting care assistant'. The take-up of the transferable part of parental leave is left to be negotiated and decided by parents, with no explicit suggestion to change the status quo of gender relations, that is, the mother's primacy in childcare. The daddy quota, on the contrary, is a non-transferable right, which explicitly places the father in the primary parent position. Thus, the quota countries – Norway, Sweden and Iceland – have a more determined orientation towards promoting fathercare and creating a more symmetrical division of labour between women and men in infant care. Finland and Denmark, on the other hand, are more vague in striving for gender equality in promoting fathercare. The conditional bonus quota in Finland and the abolished short quota in Denmark indicate that the actualisation of possible changes in gender relations is entrusted to individual parents.

In general, policies promoting fathercare are more significant on the symbolic level of gender relations than on the level of actual division of labour between mothers and fathers. Fathers take only a small proportion of the whole parental leave period in all the Nordic countries, with somewhat more in Sweden, Norway and Iceland than in Finland and Denmark. A daddy quota of parental leave makes the take-up rate as well as the average number of days taken by fathers higher compared with common parental leave which leaves the decision of take-up to the parents. In Norway and in Iceland where the quota was added to the existing parental leave period, it was an immediate success among fathers, whereas the rise of popularity has been less fierce in the other countries where the quota period was partly or totally separated from the existing transferable parental leave. It seems to be easier for fathers to take their individual quota when it is not 'taken from the mother'.

Parenthood policies promoting fathercare reach their target better among the white-collar than the blue-collar population. In the minority group of couples sharing parental leave, well-educated parents employed in the public sector are over-represented. For them, a couple of months' leave period taken by the father is not economically impossible, the mother has a good job to return to, and the father's employer is probably more supportive than employers in general. In addition to socioeconomic resources that support their choices, the higher reflectivity of leave-sharing couples is yet another resource for reaching a more equal division of labour. Instead of taking the prevailing gender order for granted, they have discussed, explored and evaluated different possibilities. For large numbers of Nordic parents, unverified assumptions – for example, about the economic consequences of equal sharing of parental leave as well as cultural conceptions of gender and parenthood, especially motherhood – hamper negotiations both in the family and in the workplace. Unreflected unequal gender relations are naturalised and remain unchallenged.

Worklife practices play an important role in the actualisation of family policy in everyday life. The demands of employees to be ever more productive, effective and committed to their work do not leave too much room for care responsibilities. With a simultaneous discourse of good parenting underlining the importance of early attachment for a child's well-being, the parents of young children end up in a cross-swell of undercurrents taking them towards a traditional gender pattern. In this pattern, the father is supposed to meet the demands of worklife, and the mother to be responsible for childcare. The segregation of responsibilities and tasks reproduces a gender order where women are at a higher risk of discrimination in the labour market and men can become emotional outsiders in family life.

Still, parents do have possibilities to choose a different pattern. They can start by having a discussion of the alternatives at home, and take up plans for parental leave also at the father's workplace, where unexpected support may be found. The father's parental leave can promote the deconstruction of gender segregation and hierarchy in the workplace and in the labour market. For an individual father, taking parental leave can be a turning point in his life, bringing him closer to his child and making him rethink personal priorities. For an individual mother, sharing parental leave with the father can reduce her double burden of paid and unpaid work and make the work–life reconciliation easier. More generally, take-up of parental leave by fathers can produce change in gender relations by bringing in new perspectives, ideas and practices of parenthood.

The means provided by family policy are important but not sufficient for producing any major change in gender relations. In the context of the present gender order, these means are often used to reproduce prevailing gender relations. For example, the possibility of both parents staying at home at the same time may promote higher take-up by fathers while undermining the policy aim of constructing more symmetrical gender relations in society. When the father can be on parental leave without the mother being 'defamilised', she can maintain the social status of a 'good mother' who has not given away her care responsibility.

Individual positions and characteristics of each parent such as the high education level of mothers or the employment of fathers in the more family-friendly public sector may not by themselves result in the sharing of parental leave; it takes several, simultaneously supporting social and economic factors to involve men in the daily tasks and responsibilities of infant care. As long as the pay gap between men and women exists, the economic justification for mothers' parental leave continues as one of the main arguments against fathercare, negative consequences for family economy being assumed without any reality check. The implementation of existing family policy and the actualisation of more equal sharing of parental care responsibilities also require new discourses of parenthood as well as new insight in working life. It needs to be recognised that both parents are able to provide good care for the child, and that employees, including men, have desires and responsibilities outside the workplace.

At the moment, Iceland leads the way in this respect with the longest daddy quota of parental leave. Following from new fatherhood policies, both the number of men taking parental leave and the number of leave days taken by fathers have increased. Fathercare is no longer a minority phenomenon in Iceland; it has become hegemonic among families with young children. The consequences of this rapid change of gender relations in infant care for gender equality on a more general level have, however, not yet been evaluated. More research is needed also in the other Nordic countries to see whether the politicising of fatherhood can in the long run change gender relations not only on a discursive or ideological level but also in the practices of the labour market and in the everyday life of families.

References

Ahrne, G. and Roman, C. (1997) *Hemmet, Barnen och makten: Förhandlingar om Arbete och Pengar i Familjen*, Stockholm: SOU.

Andersen, D., Appeldorn, A. and Weise, H. (1996) *Orlov: Evaluering af Orlovsordningerne*, København: SFI.

Bekkengen, L. (1999) 'Män som 'pappor' och kvinnor som 'föräldrar'', *Kvinnovetenskaplig Tidskrift*, vol 20, no 1, pp 33-48.

Bekkengen, L. (2002) *Man får Välja: Om Föräldraskap och Föräldraledighet i Arbetsliv och Familjeliv*, Malmö: Liber.

Brandth, B. and Kvande, E. (2003) *Fleksible Fedre*, Oslo: Universitetsforlaget.

Brandth, B. and Överli, B. (1998) *Omsorgspermisjon med 'Kjaerlig Tvang'*, Trondheim: Allforsk.

Carlsen, S. (1994) 'Men's utilization of paternity leave and parental leave schemes', in S. Carlsen and J. Elm Larsen (eds) *The Equality Dilemma*, Copenhagen: The Danish Equal Status Council, pp 79-91.

Christoffersen, M. (1997) *Spaedbarnsfamilien*, København: SFI.

Drew, E. (2005) *Parental Leave in Council of Europe Member States*, Strasbourg: Council of Europe, Directorate General of Human Rights.

Einarsdottir, B. (1998) *Through Thick and Thin: Icelandic Men on Paternity Leave*, Reykjavik: The Committee on Gender Equality, City of Reykjavik.

Gislason, I. (2004) 'Papporna på island', in U. Lorentzi (ed) *Vems Valfrihet?*, Stockholm: Agora, pp 92-106.

Haas, L. and Hwang, P. (1999) 'Parental leave in Sweden', in P. Moss and F. Deven (eds) *Parental Leave: Progress or Pitfall? Research and Policy Issues in Europe*, The Hague/Brussels: NIDI/CBGS Publications, pp 45-68.

Haas, L., Allard, K. and Hwang, P. (2002) 'The impact of organizational culture on men's use of parental leave in Sweden', *Community, Work and Family*, vol 5, no 3, pp 319-42.

Haataja, A. (2004) 'Pohjoismaiset vanhempainvapaat kahden lasta hoitavan vanhemman tukena', *JANUS*, vol 12, no 1, pp 25-48.

Hasunen, K. (2002) *Imeväisikäisten Ruokinta Suomessa 2000*, Helsinki: STM.

Hiilamo, H. (2002) *The Rise and Fall of Nordic Family Policy?*, Helsinki: STAKES.

Hobson, B. (ed) (2002) *Making Men into Fathers: Men, Masculinities and the Social Politics of Fatherhood*, Cambridge: Cambridge University Press.

Holter, Ö. (2003) 'Nordic studies on men: paths for the future', in J. Varanka (ed) *Developing Studies on Men in the Nordic Context*, Helsinki: STM (Ministry of Social Affairs and Health).

Holter, Ö. and Aarseth, H. (1994) *Mäns Livssammanhang*, Stockholm: Bonniers.

Huttunen, J. (1999) 'Muuttunut ja muuttuva isyys', in A. Jokinen (ed) *Mies ja Muutos: Kriittisen Miestutkimuksen Teemoja*, Tampere: Tampere University Press.

JämO (JämställdhetsOmbudsmannen) (2005) *Föräldraskap: Kunskaps – och Nulägesrapport*, Stockholm: JämställdhetsOmbudsmannen.

Kela (Kansaneläkelaitos/Social Insurance Institution in Finland) (2004) *Tilastollinen Vuosikirja 2003* (Statistical yearbook of the Social Insurance Institution), Helsinki: Kela.

Kivimäki, R. (2001) *Hoitovapaat Työpaikan ja Perheen Arjessa*, Tampere: Tampereen Yliopisto, Työelämän Tutkimuskeskus.

Laaksonen, T. (2003) 'Työhön on sitouduttava apinan raivolla', Interview with Tero Laaksonen, chief executive officer of Comptel (available at: www.bisnes.fi).

Lammi-Taskula, J. (1998) *Miesten Perhevapaat*, Helsinki: STAKES.

Lammi-Taskula, J. (2003) 'Isät vapaalla: ketkä pitävät isyys – ja vanhempainvapaata ja miksi?', *Yhteiskuntapolitiikka*, vol 68, no 3, pp 293-8.

Lammi-Taskula, J. (2004) 'Sukupuolijärjestelmä, vanhempainvapaat ja isät', in I. Aalto and J. Kolehmainen (eds) *Isäkirja*, Tampere: Vastapaino, pp 167-92.

Leira, A. (1998) 'Caring as social right: cash for childcare and daddy leave', *Social Politics*, vol 5, no 3, pp 362-78.

Leira, A. (2002) *Working Parents and the Welfare State: Family Change and Policy Reform in Scandinavia*, Cambridge: Cambridge University Press.

Nordic Council of Ministers (1999: 514) *Women and Men in the Nordic Countries*, Copenhagen: Nordic Council of Ministers.

Nyman, H. and Petterson, J. (2002) *Spelade Pappamånaden Någon Roll?: Pappornas Uttag av Föräldrapenning*, Stockholm: Riksförsäkringsverket.

Olsen, B. (2000) *Nye Fedre på Orlov*, Köbenhavn: Köbenhavns Universitet, Sociologisk Institut.

Plantin, L. (2001) *Mäns Föräldraskap: Om Mäns Upplevelser och Erfarenheter av Faderskapet*, Göteborg: Göteborgs Universitet, Institutionen för socialt arbete.

Riksförsäkringsverket (1993) *Vilka Pappor kom Hem?*, Stockholm: Riksförsäkringsverket.

Rostgaard, T. (2002) 'Setting time aside for the father: father's leave in Scandinavia', *Community, Work and Family*, vol 5, no 3, pp 343-64.

Rostgaard, T., Christoffersen, M. and Weise, H. (1999) 'Parental leave in Denmark', in P. Moss and F. Deven (eds) *Parental Leave: Progress or Pitfall? Research and Policy Issues in Europe*, The Hague/Brussels: NIDI/CBGS, pp 23–44.

Salmi, M. and Lammi-Taskula, J. (1999) 'Parental leave in Finland', in P. Moss and F. Deven (eds) *Parental Leave: Progress or Pitfall? Research and Policy Issues in Europe*, The Hague/Brussels: NIDI/CBGS, pp 85–121.

STM (Finnish Ministry of Social Affairs and Health) (2004) *Lastenneuvola Lapsiperheiden Tukena: Opas Työntekijöille*, Helsinki: STM.

Vartiainen, J. (2001) *Sukupuolten Palkkaeron Tilastointi ja Mittaaminen*, Helsinki: STM.

FIVE

The public–private split rearticulated: abolishment of the Danish daddy leave

Anette Borchorst

Introduction

In 2002, the two weeks' daddy leave in the Danish parental leave was abolished after an intensive debate in the media from March to July 2001, and at the same time the parental leave was extended from 26 to 52 weeks. The decision was passed by parties from the right-wing government, which had just taken office. Parental leave had not been placed high on the political agenda for many years, and the politicisation was triggered by the fact that the debate constituted a prelude to the electoral campaign preceding the parliamentary election in November 2001. Earmarking part of the leave for fathers turned out to be a very controversial issue during the debate.

The daddy leave, which was not transferable to the mother, had been adopted four years previously by a Social Democratic–Social Liberal government together with the left, and it had the intended outcome. From 1998 to 2001, the take-up rate of fathers increased from 7% to 24%, contrary to the very modest take-up rate of fathers during the 10-week period that could be shared by the father and the mother in parental leave from 1984 to 2000. During this period, only 5% of the fathers opted for leave. Compared to this, the earmarking was a veritable success, and yet, it was not portrayed as such in the media. This has to do with the success of the right-wing parties, and above all the Agrarian Liberals, who triggered the debate, in framing earmarking negatively as government interference in the private affairs of the family.

In this way, a public–private dichotomy that had played a modest role in Danish politics for many decades was rearticulated. The centre and left did not frame the daddy leave positively as entitlements of fathers, and they did not manage to activate a debate on the impact of the gendered construction of the leave. In this way, the gendered practices were reduced to being a matter of individual choices of fathers and mothers. The debate was not moved beyond arguments about the choices of the individual mothers and fathers, such that the significance of the structural aspects of the parental leave, such as its gendered constructions and impact on, for instance, employers' attitudes to men opting for parental leave, was not brought into the focus.

The failure of the centre-left to challenge the rhetoric of the right may be explained by the fact that several of the parties, including the Social Democrats, were internally divided on the issue. On a more general level, the case reflects that the political game among other things is played out as a contest over meaning. In this particular case, it was reinforced by the fact that a call for an election was expected. A surprisingly large number of politicians participated and much of the debate, which would normally take place in Parliament, was played out in the media. The debate on parental leave also exposed a particular Danish policy paradox regarding gender equality as a policy logic. Gender equality is a strong informal norm, but a weak explicit policy norm. Denmark has for many decades been in the forefront in terms of expanding public childcare facilities, and it has had record high coverage with childcare facilities for pre-school children, which has been very significant for facilitating women's paid work. On the other hand, policies of gender equality have been relatively weak and confined to a policy niche. They relate primarily to formal anti-discrimination in the labour market and have been kept separated from welfare and childcare policies, which by and large have had a gender-neutral underpinning.

Strategies for achieving gender equality have above all been aimed at facilitating women's breadwinning, and this has been accomplished by expanding welfare policies. The role of Danish men as carers and fathers within marriage has not been politicised to the same extent as in Sweden and Norway, where the integration of fathers in caring responsibilities was placed high on the governmental agenda in the late 1980s and the 1990s. Danish fathers' entitlement to parental leave was granted in 1984, which was 10 years later than in Sweden and seven years later than in Norway. The daddy leave was also introduced later in Denmark, and at the time earmarking leave for fathers was abolished in Denmark, it was extended in Sweden.

In this chapter, I focus on the background for the decision to abolish the Danish daddy leave in 2001. First, I approach problem definition, agenda setting, path dependence and social constructivism as approaches to public policy-making. Next, I address the timing of different policies influencing changes in the position of women from the 1960s and onwards more generally, and subsequently I deal with childcare policies and policies of gender equality in particular. After this, I briefly provide a long historical perspective on parliamentary negotiations on maternity and paternity leave from 1901 till the late 1990s, after which I analyse the decisions to adopt a daddy leave in 1997 and abolish it in 2001. Finally, I discuss Danish gender equality paradoxes.

Agenda setting and the contest over meaning

Policy analysts have for many years engaged in discussions about what determines policy output. During the last two to three decades, new approaches have gained ground, challenging above all the idea that policy-makers react to objective conditions, and that they do it in a rational way. Problems do not exist objectively; they are portrayals of people's experiences and interpretations (Edelman, 1988; Stone, 1988). Issues may get to the political agenda for all sorts of reasons, and politicians do not consider all alternative solutions. Many scholars have directed their attention to agenda setting and problem definition as decisive for decisions. Another important point is that policies are time-bound and deeply shaped by context and varying economic, political and discursive opportunity structures. Timing is therefore important. At particular moments, policy windows may open, for instance due to political events and specific problems that surface and attract public attention (Kingdon, 1984).

Historical institutionalists ascribe specific significance to the particular historical path of policies. Actors can play a key role at a certain time, but institutionalisation of organisational structures, policy logics and discourses may imply that policies follow the path that was initially chosen. The concept 'path dependence' is an indication of this. It leads to the rather broad conclusion that 'history matters', and the intriguing question is what mechanisms create it, and what causes path-breaking elements in politics (Thelen, 1999).

Another somewhat different but compatible approach stems from the impact of social constructivism on policy analysis. It has been labelled 'the argumentative turn' in policy analysis, and it focuses on how political problems are interpreted and how they are discussed (Fischer and Forester, 1993). This tradition also challenges the idea that political issues exist as objective phenomena. Policy-making involves a constant discursive struggle over criteria and framing of issues, and the way they are framed attributes meaning to them. Some aspects are brought to public attention, others are downplayed, and competing problem interpretations often coexist. The terms of the political discourses have become a dimension of politics in itself, and political parties use arguments strategically to make some interpretations dominate and outcompete others.

Comparisons of political debates in different countries expose considerable differences in when and how political issues reach the political agenda, and the framing of political problems is also often surprisingly different. Bacchi, who focuses on the problem definition regarding women's inequality in the US, Canada and Australia (1999), demonstrates that there are considerable differences in the way pay equity, abortion, childcare and four other areas have been constructed as political problems, and this has been significant for the different policies that have been adopted.

A central issue for determining specific policies of parenting and gender equality is what is framed as a public concern, and what is defined as private, which the state should not interfere in. The outcome of discursive battles on this distinction mirrors patterns of gendered power and dominance relations (Fraser, 1989, p 166ff).

In my empirical work on what has shaped public policies that particularly influence the gendered construction of parenting, I have applied all the above-mentioned approaches, and I have kept the question of decisive mechanisms for policy outputs empirically open. The following sections are based on my findings.

Changes in family structures and women's position in the 1960s and 1970s

The golden age of the male breadwinner family model lasted only 15 years in Denmark. From the early 1960s it was undermined by a number of interrelated changes in family structures, which may be summarised as follows: the number of married women in paid work grew from a quarter to a half during the 1960s, and fertility took a sharp downturn from 1966 (see also Rønsen and Skrede, this volume). Marriages decreased drastically from the mid-1960s, and divorces accelerated in the late 1960s and during the first half of the 1970s (Borchorst and Dahlerup, 2003, p 199).

The timing of events may be explained by changes in the economic opportunity structures. The women's rights organisations had for several decades promoted education and integration in paid work as the optimal route to gender equality. They did not, however, gain much support for this strategy immediately after the Second World War due to the cold-war climate and the economic recession. Public committees recommended collectivisation of housework and public policies to support a dual-earner family model, but these ideas remained dormant throughout the 1950s. The economic opportunity structure changed with the boom in the Danish economy in the early 1960s, and the unmet demand for labour produced a shift in attitudes towards women's participation in gainful employment. Yet, it does not fully explain the *scope* of the changes, which stretched into a period of economic downturn in the first half of the 1970s.

Political and discursive opportunity structures were also subject to considerable changes. The expansion of welfare policies and the significance of the new feminist movement in the 1960s and 1970s paved the way for an historical shift in gender perceptions and hegemonic norms (Dahlerup, 1998), and this was interlinked with the increasing secularisation that characterised the country. Initially, competing discourses on the proper position of women triggered a heated debate, not least among women. A recurrent theme was who should care for pre-school children. In the 1950s and the early 1960s, women were framed as bad mothers if they engaged in paid work; 10 years later this position had lost ground, and working mothers had become the hegemonic norm (Biza et al, 1982).

The extension of the educational system generated irreversible changes from mothers to daughters, and tax policy reforms mitigated economic hindrances to gainful employment for married women. When the Danish economy was struck by the increasing oil prices in the early 1970s, and unemployment started to rise, inclusion of part-time workers in the unemployment insurance system represented another hindrance to sending women back to the family as housewives.

The integration of women into the labour force was facilitated by changes in reproductive policies. The Pill was released in 1966, and this and other types of contraceptive enhanced women's bodily autonomy. Furthermore, abortion within 12 weeks of pregnancy became legalised in 1973, and it was offered as part of the public tax-financed health system. Of particular significance for breadwinning as a lifelong perspective for women was the strengthening of maternity leave entitlements and the expansion of public childcare facilities.

Before I focus on the debates on parental leave, I will deal with the timing, content and framing of childcare policies and policies of gender equality.

Universalist childcare provision

The competing images of ideal family structures were reflected in the political debates of the early 1960s. Childcare was subject to somewhat contradictory framing. Leading Social Democrats saw the family as a solution to consequences of rapid technological and economic changes, and initiatives were taken to adopt a coherent family policy founded on traditional family patterns. Policy recommendations suggested that mothers should take care of their own children, at least for the first three years. During the same period, it was widely debated whether childcare facilities were beneficial to children or not. Several attempts to ask experts to settle the matter generated ambiguous conclusions. Traditional family policy promoting a male breadwinner family model, however, never gained ground in Denmark, which until 2004, had only had a Ministry of Family Affairs for one-and-a-half years.

It was decisive that the first steps towards preparing changes in the legislation on childcare facilities were already taken in 1961 (Borchorst, 2002). In 1964, the universalist principle was instituted in the childcare legislation. The 1964 Child Care and Youth Care Act marked a radical shift in state efforts dedicated to subsidising childcare. Residual measures targeted at needy families were replaced by universal measures aimed at children from all social groups. The change involved a whole new set of values concerning care for infants. Whereas the staff had previously been preoccupied with hygiene and regularity, and the legislation had dealt with preventive child welfare, the cornerstone was now social pedagogic childcare offers, founded on the integration of care and education. The key objective of the provisions now focused on play and social interaction. The diffusion of these ideas was nurtured by the introduction of a three-year education for childcare pedagogues in 1969.

Recommendations from progressive pedagogues, who had for many decades served as experts and advisors to public authorities, greatly influenced the content and framing of the decisions. The women's rights organisations were also active in promoting the issue on the political agenda. Among the political parties, the Social Democrats and the left in particular induced the policy change, but it is noteworthy that all political parties in Parliament supported the Act. Although satisfying the need for labour was an important incentive, especially for the right-wing parties, the overall policy logic was child centred. The problem definition of the legislation was related to the needs of small children, not to the lack of economic independence for women or the demand of labour.

The number of childcare facilities grew steadily from 1966, and coverage ratios increased and have remained among the highest in Western Europe, particularly for 0- to three-year-olds (OECD, 2001). Childcare represents one of the few areas where Denmark was at the forefront of the Scandinavian development, and it is partly explained by the path dependence of the policies.

The state's commitment to support childcare was introduced in the 1919 Budget, and this was earlier than most other governments started to subsidise childcare. It was generated by a unique coalition of progressive pedagogues and leading Social Democrats in Copenhagen. This responsiveness to forces in civil society characterised many welfare policies in Denmark. From early on, policies were founded on the integration of care and education, and private idealistic initiatives played a central role in the establishment of facilities. The public commitment, which was targeted at needy families, was gradually extended and strengthened. In 1949, an element of universalism was introduced when support for facilities accommodating children of all social backgrounds was allowed.

The 1964 Act on childcare therefore exhibits continuity and a radical shift at the same time. The considerable public commitment was influenced by the legacy of the 1919 decision, the institutionalisation of the child-centred policy logic and the cooperation between politicians and pedagogues. The timing of the new Act was also of some importance. Preparations were started before the position of women was politicised, and childcare became a hot issue.

Gender equality policy: a political niche

In the middle of the 1970s, gender equality was established as a new policy area. The development was triggered by international initiatives, such as the United Nations' call to establish women's policy machinery and United Nations' International Women's Year in 1975. The European Community also had an impact on the development in Denmark, which joined in 1973 as the only Scandinavian country at the time.

The first step towards instituting gender equality was the establishment of a women's commission in Denmark in 1965, inspired by similar Swedish and Norwegian initiatives. Whereas the other two countries established small, powerful commissions, the Danish Social Democratic Prime Minister allowed representation by numerous organisations, according to the strong corporatist spirit that prevailed in policy-making at the time. The fact that so many vested interests were involved hampered the commission's ability to agree on policy recommendations, and this in turn curtailed its opportunities to influence the political agenda. Moreover, it took nine years to complete its tasks, and by then opportunity structures had altered radically (Borchorst and Dahlerup, 2003, chapter 3).

The economic downturn and the so-called landslide election in 1973 transformed Danish politics. Denmark was hit hard by the oil crisis, and unemployment increased drastically. Furthermore, the election transformed Danish politics fundamentally. It eroded the stable party system based on the four old political parties, the Social Democrats, the Social Liberals, the Conservatives and the Agrarian Liberals, and this undermined the political consensus on which the welfare state had been founded and extended during the previous many decades. Two newly formed political parties challenged gender equality as a hegemonic political norm. The Progress Party, a tax denial party on the extreme right, obtained considerable representation, and it articulated open resistance and ridiculed almost all political decisions on gender equality. The much smaller Christian Democratic Party's pro-family rhetoric emphasised childcare within the family. The two parties did not gain major support on the actual policy-making, but their presence prompted a shift in the discursive opportunity structure.

Hence, the timing and sequencing of events implied that Denmark was much more reluctant to establish gender equality policy machinery than Sweden and Norway. The support for political measures to enhance gender equality was modest, especially among the right-wing parties. An exception was the Social Liberals, a small but very significant party in Danish politics, which has a long tradition of promoting gender equality. Outside Parliament, the feminist movement, which had adopted a rather hostile attitude towards the state, had a considerable influence on the changing discourses. It put pressure on the political parties to address the subordination of women. The right turn in Danish politics did, however, undermine the extra-parliamentarian pressure to include gender issues on the political agenda (Christensen and Siim, 2001).

The political majority in Parliament including the Liberal government was against establishing a policy machinery for gender equality, but Denmark got one anyhow, when a Social Democratic Prime Minister acted upon an administrative order in 1975 and founded the Equal Status Council. As a consequence, its room for manoeuvre was curtailed. Until its legal confirmation in 1978 it primarily dealt with inquiries and complaints from individuals, and it only engaged in a few considerations on strategies for achieving gender equality. The family was excluded from its general field of operation, due to the resistance of the Christian Democrats, and childcare and other welfare policies were kept separated from these policies, too. Hence, the dominant policy logic related to labour market issues and education only, even though the reconciliation of family and work constituted a significant problem for many women. Gender equality was very vaguely defined in the legislation, and the instruments were selected from a restricted repertoire. Affirmative action and special treatment were allowed, but the actual options were very restricted, since it required an exemption from the Act on Equal Treatment in each case. In the 1980s, gender equality was strengthened as policy logic, but less than in Sweden and Norway which strengthened their policies of gender equality policies and the implementation of them (Borchorst, 1999a, 1999b).

There was, however, one attempt to merge welfare and family policy with gender equality. The Council of Equal Status and the Child Commission, which was appointed in 1979, cooperated to strengthen a child-centred perspective, incorporating gender equality as a policy logic. Together, they managed to influence political discourses for a while, but the cooperation did not materialise as significant policy changes.

During the 1990s, gender as a political category lost further momentum in public policies. Internal turbulence in the Equal Status Council and conflicts between feminist organisations and men's groups about the focus on men undermined gender equality as a political project. Policies with extremely gendered outcomes, such as the Childcare Leave Scheme which granted parents a right to leave for one year to take care of their children, were framed as gender-neutral family policies, and they were negotiated with very limited focus on gender (Borchorst, 1999c). Another factor that may explain this development is the disappearance of the feminist movement as a strong extra-parliamentarian pressure that influenced discursive frames. It was also apparent that open resistance to gender equality measures in the majority population had stretched from the extreme right to the Agrarian Liberals and the Conservatives, which had previously supported many decisions on gender equality. To this it should be added that gender equality plays a very restricted role in the political parties in Denmark (Borchorst, 2004).

In sum, the gender-neutral welfare policies adopted during the 1960s generated major reforms for women, but gender equality policies from the 1970s were weak, and the process towards establishing gender equality as a key policy area was punctuated by the fact that the economic crisis coincided with the landslide election and the turn to the right. Attempts to coordinate the objectives of family policies and policies of gender equality capsized in the 1980s. Towards the end of the 1990s, they were still strictly separated, and policies concerning the adaptation to a dual-earner family model were still predominantly directed towards women. Hence the weak and narrow policies of gender equality may be explained by path dependence and unfavourable opportunity structures.

Maternity and paternity leave on the political agenda, 1901-97[1]

Legislation on maternity leave was first subject to regulation in Denmark in the factory law of 1901, which introduced two weeks' mandatory maternity leave for female factory workers after an intensive debate on special protection of female workers. A unique alliance between bourgeois women's organisations and female unions outside Parliament succeeded in preventing a ban on women's night work, and they also managed to persuade the male politicians to allow social assistance to women during maternity leave. In the interwar period, the assistance, which was means tested, was gradually improved, and it was granted to more groups of women.

The following decades saw only modest changes in the legislation, but in the early 1960s, path-breaking changes were made. More groups of women employees gained access to benefits during maternity leave, and in 1966, statutory rights to maternity leave were extended to almost all groups of women in the labour market, and the leave was extended to 14 weeks. The changes were adopted during a period when many welfare benefits were improved; universalist principles were strengthened and insurance-based criteria were downplayed. The integration of women into the labour force was a central political objective, but the improvements of the maternity leave were not highly politicised.

Throughout the 1970s, leftist parties and the Social Liberals in particular made attempts to include fathers in parental leave entitlements. Outside Parliament there was strong and persistent pressure from social movements and unions and above all the new feminist movement to prolong the leave and entitle fathers to leave. The issue was presented as a solution to women's double workload, but also as a benefit for fathers and children. The extra-parliamentarian pressure was not successful, however, above all because the economy was in bad shape.

The economic downturn implied that the politicians engaged in fierce conflicts on which issues should be given priority. Within the Social Democratic Party there was a conflict between leading politicians in favour of a restoration of Kastrup Airport and female politicians, who pushed for the extension of the parental leave. The political strength of the female politicians was weakened by the fact that female trade unionists opposed statutory rights for fathers because they found that the leave for mothers was too short. They criticised the fact that four weeks' pregnancy leave was deducted from the leave after the birth, because this was disadvantageous to women employed in hard physical work. They also questioned whether the fathers would actually participate or just go fishing if they were granted leave.

Finally, in 1984, after numerous unsuccessful proposals, the leave was extended from 14 to 24 weeks, and fathers became entitled to 14 days after the birth together with the mother. Furthermore, father and mother could share the last 10 weeks. The entitlements of fathers were dependent on the status of the mother, and men who had children with students or housewives were not entitled to leave. This was changed in 1991, when fathers gained statutory rights independently of their wives and partners.

The debates during the 1990s were characterised by a reluctance to deal with gender equality objectives. The stipulation of parental leave entitlements had since 1989 been laid down in the Equal Treatment Act. This was motivated by technical arguments, since European Union directives required the reversal of the burden of proof in connection with the dismissal of pregnant women and people opting for parental leave. It did, however, not revoke further reflections on the gendered construction of the parental leave neither in 1989 nor in 2001.

By and large, the decisions from 1901-97 had been characterised by consensus between the political parties, with the centre and left as the most proactive agents for promoting and improving the parental leave.

Daddy leave 1997-2001 – from low to high politics[2]

In 1997, the parental leave was prolonged from 24 to 26 weeks, and the decision marked a radical shift in the construction of the leave, since the additional two weeks (25 and 26) were earmarked for fathers. The adoption of a daddy quota was inspired by the Norwegian *fedrekvote* from 1993 and the Swedish *pappamånad* from

1995, both for four weeks (Lammi-Taskula, this volume; Leira, 2002 and this volume).

The decision was passed as part of a centre-left agreement on the budget, which did not include the right-wing parties. The left–right fight marked the shift from gender equality as a consensual political norm among the major political parties, except for the Progress Party at the extreme right, which had systematically opposed all decisions on gender equality. Given this left–right cleavage, it is remarkable that the right did not politicise the decision and profile their opposition to it in Parliament or in the media. The decision went largely unnoticed by the public. It was subject to a very short parliamentary debate and a very restricted debate in the media. It is not uncommon that issues that are included in budget agreements are not subject to longer debates in Parliament, but it is noteworthy that several of the issues that triggered a heated debate four years later did not surface when the leave was introduced.

The Social Democratic government coalition framed daddy leave as a benefit to the father, the child and the mother and as a means to increase gender equality. This win–win interpretation was not challenged by the right, which, however, questioned whether fathers would take up the leave. They suggested that the question should be settled by the social partners in collective agreements, in which case extending the leave would be financed by the partners themselves through collective agreements. They did not frame the daddy leave as an interference with the free choice of families, nor did they label it as a coercive measure. Indeed, both right and left argued that the proposal did not imply coercion.

The leave did not get a special name to distinguish it from the two weeks' leave to which fathers were entitled immediately after the birth together with the mother. Furthermore, the government did not launch comprehensive campaigns to encourage fathers to use this option as the Swedish and Norwegian governments had done.

In 2001, parental leave and the daddy quota reappeared on the public agenda on 8 March, International Women's Day. It happened by coincidence, and it became highly politicised, because it triggered a pre-election debate, during which the Agrarian Liberal Party together with the Conservatives challenged the Social Democratic coalition, which had been in office since 1993. Hence, the upcoming election constituted the policy window that opened for politicising a new decision. It was a new phenomenon that gender equality occupied a central position in an election debate, since it had for decades been almost non-existent as an electoral issue.[3] The leading oppositional party, the Agrarian Liberals, saw the issue as a means to profile itself as an alternative to the Social Democrats, who headed the government. By supporting a central welfare policy, the Agrarian Liberal party sought to reinforce a pro-welfare profile. They also used the daddy leave as a tool to orchestrate a campaign framing the Social Democrats as old-fashioned and tutelary, and finally, the issue was chosen as a means to attract female voters, who tended to prefer other parties.

The notion of coercion became a dominant discourse of the right. The arguments also drew on the strong resentment which is evoked in the Danish public when something is labelled as a quota. Quotas and affirmative action are by far the most controversial gender equality instruments in Denmark. Initially, the coalition parties were caught on their heels, because extending the parental leave violated central objectives to increase the labour supply and prevent a rise in public expenditure. The Social Democrats, who have been characterised as the primary architects of the Danish welfare state, were squeezed, since they opposed a welfare reform proposed by the right.

They and their coalition partner yielded some months later after an intensive media debate, when the remaining seven parties all supported the proposal. At this point, they engaged in a discussion about earmarking part of the leave for fathers as a way of distinguishing their proposal, but they were constrained by internal divisions.[4] The parliamentary group was deeply divided over the issue. The Party's spokespersons for labour market and social policy affairs and several ordinary members opposed the daddy leave in the media and framed it as coercion. They labelled the Social Democratic Minister of Equal Opportunities a fundamentalist because she was in favour of the so-called 3-3-3 model that had been adopted in Iceland, reserving three months for mothers, three for fathers and three to be shared. The Prime Minister initially supported this model, but he retreated due to the opposition in the Party. The conflict that was generated within the Party was by and large of a gendered nature. The proponents were mainly women, and the opponents mainly men. Gender conflicts within political parties are rarely exposed in Denmark, because unlike the sister parties in Sweden, the Danish Party does not organise women's caucuses within the party. In this particular situation it became visible, since their disagreements were played out in the media.

The media controlled the timing, when the issue was put on the agenda, but during the ensuing phases, the politicians and the political parties kept the process going due to the impending election. An extraordinary number of politicians became engaged in debate on the issue as it overlapped three policy areas – social, labour market and equal opportunities policies – and because the high politics status of the proposal brought out all the party leaders. The process was not visibly marked by other actors. The civil servants played a minor role, which is usual practice in the agenda-setting phase, but in this case it was also due to the high political nature of the issue and the upcoming election. The media were critical opponents of the parties' proposal to extend the parental leave, because it contradicted central political goals to reduce public expenditure and increase the supply of labour, but some newspapers systematically took over the coercive metaphoric as the dominant frame for the daddy leave. Feminist organisations warned against the combined effect of prolonging the leave and abandoning the daddy quota, but it is noteworthy that men's organisations did not voice support for the entitlements of fathers. These organisations have, however, mainly organised men on the issue of the rights of men at marital dissolution.

The Agrarian Liberal and Conservative Parties had outlined a strategy profiling themselves as parties that supported central welfare issues. They presented themselves as a renewal, as a contrast to the old-fashioned policies of the government of the day. Freedom of choice and welfare constituted the key framework in the Agrarian Liberals' profiling, and they used the daddy quota to label the Social Democratic policy as coercion, guardianship and a limitation of the individual's freedom of choice. The Social Democrats did not profile themselves in earnest with an alternative interpretation of the coercive metaphoric, which should be viewed in light of the internal disagreement in the Party.

It was noteworthy that neither during the media debate in 2001 nor in the parliamentary debate in 2002 was the daddy leave presented as a success. The increase in the take-up rate of fathers stated in the introduction to this chapter was never used as an argument for earmarking. The figures were available at the national statistical office, but they were not included to inform the decision-makers. The newly elected Conservative Minister of Gender Equality even defended the abolishment of the daddy leave by arguing that the fathers did not use it.

The focus on gender during the debate in 2001 points to a change since the 1990s when gender, as noted above, occupied a modest role in political debates. This shift may also be traced in the rearticulation of a public–private split in relation to work and family issues.

The public–private split

The mobilisation of women and their increased parliamentary presence in politics from the 1960s and 1970s has all over the Western world challenged the public–private divide, and it has been demonstrated that this divide is neither fixed nor unchangeable. The new feminist movement, which claimed that 'the personal is political', attempted to politicise the private sphere with a radical emancipatory project, and it managed to put issues such as domestic violence on the political agenda in many countries.

There was, and to some extent still is, however, a considerable difference between countries. A public–private dichotomy has permeated liberal societies and ideologies, and feminist scholars have analysed its liberal patriarchal legacy (Pateman, 1980). They have demonstrated how this divide has constituted a barrier to women's full citizenship (Lister, 1997).

In Scandinavian countries it lost some of its significance; a public–private mix emerged when the welfare states expanded their responsibility for reproductive tasks and thereby strengthened their woman-friendly potential (Hernes, 1987; Siim, 2000).

The process is, however, by no means a gradual or automatic process that works one way, and discursively political parties especially from the right have from time to time rearticulated gendered divisions of care and breadwinning. In 1974, the Danish Prime Minister Poul Hartling, who was also the leader of the Agrarian Liberal Party, argued that strengthening girls' interests in vocational training, changing the distribution of household tasks between spouses, and strengthening women's interest and motivation for participating in the labour market were not a governmental concern, nor were they aspects that could not be enhanced through legislative action (*Folketingstidende*, 25 October 1974). During the following years, the integration of women in vocational training and into the labour force was indeed considered central to governmental policies, and as noted earlier, public childcare facilities have been expanded drastically. On the other hand, the historical analysis has revealed that the caring role of fathers within marriage has been subject to a relatively weak politicisation in Denmark, compared to the other Scandinavian and Nordic countries. During the 1980s and 1990s, the political disagreements about statutory rights of fathers were largely framed as disagreements on economic priorities, and it did not revoke major ideological battles about the public–private split.

In 2001, the abolishment of the daddy leave did, however, trigger a discursive battle on limits to public interference, and a public–private split was rearticulated as a means of profiling the right from the centre-left in Danish politics. Politicians from the centre-right parties voiced concurrently that it was not a task for the public sector to influence the division of labour by gender, and the daddy leave was interpreted as politicians invading people's privacy. The Social Democratic Party was inhibited due to internal disputes over gender equality as a parameter in the legislation and did not challenge the predominant opposition on this issue. The trades union movement was also divided with regard to the subject.

Yet, discourse and practice are not necessarily in accordance. The family has been subject to numerous regulations since this time, and the current government has gone considerably further by setting an age limit at 24 for marriage between Danish citizens and non-citizens. Furthermore, it has not been problematised that parental leave is premised on female responsibility for small children, since a relatively long period of the parental leave is earmarked for the mother. Leave for the first two weeks after the birth is mandatory for women, and after this, 12 weeks are reserved for the mother. Historically, the arguments for this have been considerations for the recovery of the mother and the focus on promoting breastfeeding, but it is noteworthy that the Danish leave today has the most gendered construction in the Nordic countries, since it has the relatively longest period earmarked for the mother.

The rearticulation of the public–private split in relation to the daddy leave was chosen strategically to profile the right-wing parties in relation to the Social Democratic Party, and the upcoming election was the factor that opened the policy window and triggered the discursive battle. Another explanation for this development is the character of Danish policies of gender equality.

Gender equality policy paradoxes

The narrow Danish gender equality project may be explained by the disadvantageous opportunity structures that shaped policies of equal opportunities in the initial phase. These policies do not enjoy strong support, neither in the political parties, nor in the population at large. It is also not likely that this development will be reversed, because the feminist movement has disappeared, more or less.

Danish welfare policies still secure women's economic autonomy, and traditional family policies never gained a strong foothold in Denmark. The government appointed a new Minister of Family Affairs in 2004, but it remains unclear whether this signals new policy measures or mainly governmental concern about the problems with reconciling work and family that especially women are concerned about. Female breadwinning and dual-income earner family structures have become a hegemonic and most likely also an irreversible norm. The care of small children will remain on the political agenda for the years to come, but it remains to be seen whether fathers will organise in relation to the right to care not only at marital dissolution, but also within marriage.

During later years, new challenges and cleavages have surfaced, and this has generated new gender equality paradoxes. For the first time in several decades, the right profiles itself on gender equality. This is related to the fact that the situation of refugees and immigrants has been placed high on the political agenda. The parties in government argue together with the extreme right that especially Muslim groups do not comply with the Danish norms of gender equality. In this way these parties seek to profile themselves on a gender-political agenda that does not require significant policy initiatives. The centre-left has adopted a defensive strategy because it is internally divided on the question, and furthermore these parties do not know how to tackle the recognition of difference between ethnic groups and equality between the genders at the same time.

It is very likely that this paradox, that the right-wing parties, which have not profiled themselves on gender equality for many years, during the past five years have articulated a strong concern for gender equality among the minority ethnic groups, will persist during the coming years. It remains to be seen whether the centre-left manages to promote a vision for gender equality, or whether the right has taken the lead in terms of framing gender equality discourses. It is, however, also clear that women have become a strategic electoral group, and this implies that all the political parties have to tackle issues such as female representation and the gendered division of care and breadwinning.

The abolishment of the daddy quota reveals that the fight over meaning has become an integral part of the political game and the competition for electoral support. If it is true that politics also is played out as a contest over meaning, it implies that things will not change merely if a new election brings a turn towards the left. A re-adoption of daddy leave hinges on the ability of the centre-left to produce an alternative frame to the free choice rhetoric that became hegemonic during the debate in 2001. Furthermore, unless the leave is extended further, which is not unlikely, it will be difficult to argue convincingly for earmarking a period for fathers, because it will be presented as curtailing women's access to leave.

The question remains whether the relatively weak institutionalisation of gender equality will lag behind as a social practice in Denmark. This may be the case in terms of political representation and female management and gendered practices in the care of the newborn, but there are also indications that point in the direction of less pessimism. First of all, comparisons of welfare and family policy models rank Denmark relatively high in terms of achievements in gender equality (Korpi, 2002). Furthermore, comparative data on the attitudes of parents from the mid-1990s suggest that the support for egalitarian gender norms are stronger among Danish parents than among Swedish and Norwegian parents, and they are also more optimistic in their evaluation of prevailing gender equality patterns (Ellingsæter, 1998). This may, of course, relate to the hegemonic discourses of gender equality as an accomplishment, but seen together these findings may be interpreted as a sign of gender equality as a strong informal norm, especially among women. Furthermore, it is interesting to note that the gender gap in party choice has been persistent. Since the early 1980s, women vote more to the left than men, and the gender differences in political attitudes are even more pronounced. During the 1990s, the gap between women's support for economic redistribution and welfare benefits and men's preference for tax reduction has become considerable, and it is today higher than ever. The gender gaps are larger in Denmark than in Sweden and Norway (Andersen and Goul Andersen, 2003; *Mandag Morgen*, 2004).

Notes

[1] This section sums up my own empirical work in Borchorst (2003). This work is based on many different sources, which are indicated in the references.

[2] This section sums up my own empirical work in Borchorst (2003). This work is based on many different sources, which are indicated in the references.

[3] When the election was called in October, the issue disappeared, and refugees and immigrants became the leading theme of the campaign.

[4] It was abandoned the same year, when a Social Democratic government took office.

References

Andersen, J. and Goul Andersen, J. (2003) 'Køn, alder og uddannelse: fe unge mænds sejr', in J. Goul Andersen and O. Borre (eds) *Politisk Forandring: Værdiforandring og Nye Skillelinjer ved Folketingsvalget 2001*, Åarhus: Systime.

Bacchi, C. (1999) *Women, Policy and Politics: The Construction of Policy Problems*, London: Sage Publications.

Biza, L.C., Krebs Lange, B. and Lous, E.K. (1982) *Ude og Hjemme*, Speciale, Aarhus: Historisk Institut, Aarhus Universitet.

Borchorst, A. (1999a) 'Equal status institutions', in C. Bergqvist, A. Borchorst, A.-D. Christensen, V. Ramsteat-Siléu, N.C. Raaum, and A. Styrkasdoffir (eds) *Equal Democracies? Gender and Politics in the Nordic Countries*, Oslo: Scandinavian University Press and Nordic Council of Ministers, pp 167-89.

Borchorst, A. (1999b) 'Gender equality law', in C. Bergqvist, A. Borchorst, A.-D. Christensen, V. Ramsteat-Siléu, N.C. Raaum, A. Styrkasdoffir (eds) *Equal Democracies? Gender and Politics in the Nordic Countries*, Oslo: Scandinavian University Press and Nordic Council of Ministers, pp 190-207.

Borchorst, A. (1999c) 'Den kønnede virkelighed – den kønsløse debat', in J. Goul Andersen, P. Munk Christiansen, T. Beck Joergensen, L. Togeby, and S. Vallgaarda (eds) *Den Demokratiske Udfordring*, København: Hans Reitzels Forlag, pp 113-32.

Borchorst, A. (2002) 'Danish child care policy: continuity rather than radical change', in S. Michel and R. Mahon (eds) *Childcare Policy at the Crossroads: Gender and Welfare State Restructuring*, New York, NY: Routledge, pp 267-85.

Borchorst, A. (2003) *Køn, Magt og Beslutninger: Politiske Forhandlinger om Barselsorlov 1901-2002*, Aarhus: Magtudredningen.

Borchorst, A. (2004) 'Skandinavisk ligestillingspolitik tur-retur, på dansk billet', *Nytt Norsk Tidsskrift*, no 3-4, pp 264-74.

Borchorst, A. and Dahlerup, D. (2003) *Ligestillingspolitik som Diskurs og Praksis*, København: Samfundslitteratur.

Christensen, A.-D. and Siim, B. (2001) *Køn, Demokrati og Modernitet: Mod nye Politiske Identiteter*, København: Hans Reitzels Forlag.

Dahlerup, D. (1998) *Rødstrømperne: Den Danske Rødstrømpebevægelses Udvikling, Nytænkning og Gennemslag, 1970-1985*, København: Gyldendal.

Edelman, M. (1988) *Constructing the Political Spectacle*, Chicago, IL: University of Chicago Press.

Ellingsæter, A.L. (1998) 'Dual breadwinner societies: provider models in the Scandinavian welfare states', *Acta Sociologica*, vol 41, no 1, pp 59-73.

Fischer, F. and Forester, J. (1993) *The Argumentative Turn in Policy Analysis and Planning*, Durham and London: Duke University Press.

Fraser, N. (1989) *Unruly Practices: Power, Discourse and Gender in Contemporary Social Theory*, Cambridge: Polity Press.

Hernes, H.M. (1987) *Welfare State and Women Power: Essays in State Feminism*, Oslo: Norwegian University Press.

Kingdon, J.D. (1984) *Agendas, Alternatives and Public Policies*, New York, NY: Harper Collins College Publishers.

Korpi, W. (2002) *Velfærdsstat og Socialt Medborgerskab*, Aarhus: Magtudredningen.

Leira, A. (2002) *Working Parents and the Welfare State: Family Change and Policy Reform in Scandinavia*, Cambridge: Cambridge University Press.

Lister, R. (1997) *Citizenship: Feminist Perspectives*, Suffolk: Macmillan Press Ltd.

Mandag Morgen (2004) 'Regeringen har tabt kvinderne og 1968-generationens børn', 24 August.

OECD (Organisation for Economic Co-operation and Development) (2001) *Employment Outlook*, Paris: OECD.

Pateman, C. (1980) *The Disorder of Women*, London: Polity Press.

Siim, B. (2000) *Gender and Citizenship: Politics and Agency in France, Britain and Denmark*, Cambridge: Cambridge University Press.

Stone, D. (1988) *Policy Paradox and Political Reason*, New York, NY: Harper Collins.

Thelen, K. (1999) 'Historical institutionalism in comparative politics', *Annual Review of Political Science*, no 2, pp 369-404.

SIX

The Norwegian childcare regime and its paradoxes

Anne Lise Ellingsæter

Childcare matters are increasingly central to contemporary welfare state debate and policy reform. The organisation of childcare affects the gender relations of parenthood, and boundaries between work and parental care are one of the most contested issues. Three family policy models with assumedly different implications for childcare and gender equality are commonly distinguished: states supporting the dual-earner family, states supporting a traditional male breadwinner family, and states leaving it to individuals to find private or market-based solutions (Korpi, 2000). Scandinavian policies are usually associated with the dual-earner family model, or at least as moving in that direction. National policy models are often more complex than this typology suggests, however, as they combine different policy elements. Besides, policy models change over time, and recent policy developments display increasing complexity and diversity that may blur conventional typologies (for example, Daly, 2000; Daly and Lewis, 2000; Mahon, 2002a; Michel and Mahon, 2002).

Historically, Norway has actually been acknowledged as a family policy 'hybrid', combining dual-earner support with traditional breadwinner elements, including generous cash transfers to families (Ellingsæter, 2003). This *family policy dualism* (Ellingsæter, 2003, p 421) has been noted as the Norwegian 'ambivalence' or 'double-track' (Leira, 1992; Skrede, 1999). Some scholars perceive it as part of a more general divergence from the Scandinavian model of gender and welfare – the Norwegian 'puzzle' (Sainsbury, 2001). Gender traditionalism and ambivalence towards employed mothers have been characteristic. It is possible to argue that the policy 'hybrid' is reproduced in recent policy reforms. Yet, the very meaning of policy dualism may change over time, as the contexts of policies do change. Hence, the analysis of the politics of childcare needs to be 'placed in time' (Pierson, 2004).

Placing the Norwegian childcare regime in the present time, the mid-2000s, examining the regime's boundaries between work and parental care and the implications for the gender relations of parenthood, is the ambition of this chapter. Regulations on parents' right to work versus childcare in the early stages of parenthood – the central contemporary battlefield for these issues – are the focus of attention. A multi-causal, contextual approach is needed in the study of parenthood policies (Ellingsæter, 2003). National case studies are particularly valuable, as they attend to complexity, context and chronology within the national setting (Daly and Lewis, 1998). In exposing the dynamics of actors, ideas and practices shaping policy content and outcomes, case studies are indispensable. Furthermore, the present study's approach to childcare policies as a 'regime' – examining the main care policy elements *jointly* – is advantageous. In any case, analyses that emphasise the simultaneous operation of different policy principles add further insights about policy dynamics (see Daly, 2000), and help uncover contradictions inherent in particular policy configurations. A 'childcare regime' is more than the sum of single policies; however, it accentuates policies as a system, in which the policies interact in generating a structure of opportunities that shape parents' practices.

The right to work versus the right to care

There are three main types of care policy elements that appear in most national welfare regimes, changing over time: paid parental leave, cash benefits for care and subsidised day care services. The three policy elements have different implications for the organisation of childcare, and different assumptions about childhood and parenthood are inscribed in them. The policy elements to a different degree support women's/parents' right to work, on the one hand, and their right to care, on the other. The right to work is supported by the provision of childcare services, defamilising childcare, and by paid parental leave, familising childcare as part of the employment contract. Thus parental leave secures the right to care among the employed. Cash benefits for care grant the right to care independent of employment status, but usually involve payment in the 'lower league of benefits' (Daly and Lewis, 1998).

Paid parental leave arrangements are usually classified as policies enhancing gender equality. However, parental leave can be ambiguous with regard to the gender equality objective, both regarding policy rationales and policy impact. A study of eight European countries concluded that: 'Taken as a whole, it would seem appropriate to question the use of parental leave as an effective instrument in the achievement of a fairer division of work and care ... the equal opportunities content of parental leave must not be overestimated' (Bruning and Plantenga, 1999, pp 207-8). Parental leave policies are influenced by social assumptions of childhood, motherhood and fatherhood, which have a bearing on our understanding both of leave policies themselves, and how and why leave policies are used (Deven and Moss, 2002).

National variations in parental leave arrangements actually reflect different purposes, from encouraging women to stay at home to promoting gender equality by supporting mothers' employment (Deven and Moss, 2002). For example, Swedish parental leave is considered more a welfare policy for children than a policy promoting gender equality, indeed constituting a risk factor for women's employment (Björnberg, 2002). Moreover, there is growing concern about the potential disadvantageous effect of long leaves for women's labour market opportunities (Pylkkänen and Smith, 2003).

High-quality and affordable childcare services are one of the most important components in supporting parents'/mothers' right to work. According to Korpi (2000), access to public childcare services for children under three is the litmus test of a modern family policy directed at the dual-earner family. Many countries provide educational programmes for children aged three and above, but these are generally not intended as gender equality measures. Childcare services for children under three are considered a main dimension in distinguishing between different *service regimes* among welfare states (Anttonen and Sipilä, 1996).

Cash-for-care benefits are usually classified as traditional male breadwinner family policies, presuming or being neutral to a traditional gendered division of labour in society as well as within the family (Korpi, 2000). A common denominator for the European countries that have introduced cash-for-care benefits is that centre-right governments stand behind them (Morgan and Zippel, 2003). Parental choice, valorisation of care and a more equal distribution of state support between employed and non-employed mothers motivate the reforms.

All the three policy elements – paid parental leave, cash benefits for childcare and publicly subsidised day care services – constitute prominent parts of the prevailing Norwegian childcare regime, resulting in a dualistic system in terms of family models supported. The parental leave is long – one year – with high economic compensation.[1] The leave taker has the right to return to her/his job.[2] Six weeks of the leave are reserved for fathers only, the so-called 'daddy quota'. A time account scheme allows a flexible uptake of leave up to two years. 'Full coverage' is the consensual political goal for childcare services.[3] Full coverage means the provision of places to all parents who want a place for their children. Access to childcare services is not institutionalised as a social right, however. There is a cash-for-care benefit for parents with children one to two years old who do not attend publicly subsidised childcare.[4] Thus not only parents staying at home with their children are entitled to the benefit; it also includes parents buying childcare outside the state-subsidised services. In the following discussion I examine these three policy elements, emphasising the policy processes shaping them and their influence on the gender relations of parenthood. Some of the paradoxes arising from this particular childcare regime are highlighted in the concluding section.

Institutionalising 'separate spheres': parental leave

The Norwegian parental leave package reflects several different policy objectives and concerns. The long leave valorises parental care in the child's first year of life. Children's particular need for fatherly care and the redistribution of care between mothers and fathers are recognised by the daddy quota. The time account system recognises families' needs for time flexibility and time sovereignty. The present leave package was a social democratic innovation, formulated in the late 1980s.[5] It was presented as part of an ambitious 'chain of care', including day care places and after-school care, emphasising society's responsibility for public childcare after the child's first year of life.

Already in the mid-1980s the goal of one year of leave gained political consensus (except for the far-right Progress Party), resting on the common objective to give parents more time with their children. Yet the political priority and the motivation for support varied across political parties. The gradual leave extensions since 1986 were effectuated in periods when the Social Democrats were in (minority) government. Moreover, while work–family reconciliation and gender equality have been central rationales for the leftist parties, the centre-right parties have persistently based their argument on the needs of the family, on children's needs for parental care. The centre-right did not support the 1993 leave extension; they proposed a cash benefit as an alternative. Neither did the parties on the right support the daddy quota, as it was considered detrimental to parental choice. The Christian People's Party, however, emphasised that the quota would give fathers an insight into women's care work and a better understanding of its importance. All parties supported the time account arrangement, including the right–wing parties, because it assumedly enhances parental choice.

Separate spheres and gender difference

The main outcomes of the parental leave package are usually summarised as follows: improved leave rights have contributed to more continuous work patterns among Norwegian mothers (Ellingsæter and Rønsen, 1996). Mothers on parental leave return earlier to work after giving birth than mothers not entitled to leave. The daddy quota has been very efficient in increasing men's take-up rate, from less than 5% prior to its introduction, to the current high level of about 85%. The time account system has had minor impact, however; less than 5% use this option.

This picture has a complementary side, however. In contrast to the policy ambition of work–family reconciliation and gender equality, parents' practices institutionalise work and family as 'separate spheres' and reproduce gender difference to a considerable degree, in both childcare and worklife. Work–family reconciliation in practice thus reinforces work–family *separation*. Full-time parenting, in reality full-time mothering, is established as a principal practice in the child's first year of life. Accordingly, alternative arrangements meet great difficulty, both in terms of organisation and social norms. The practices establish long absences for women as a main norm, based on the right to return to the job. Parents' practices conform to the ideal of full-time parental care for infants that underpinned the parental leave extension. The aim was 'to improve the family's opportunity to give the youngest [children] intimacy and care.... The best is if parents themselves can take the care responsibility in the home the first year' (St. meld. [White Paper] no 4 (1988-89), p 32).[6]

The new norm of full-time parental care acts together with a trend towards stronger emphasis on children's rights and needs. A strengthened child-oriented ideology is reflected in legislation and in the range of professional groups monitoring how parents fulfil their parental responsibilities (Ericsson, 2001). Expansion of the officially recommended breastfeeding period points in this direction. From 2002 mothers are recommended full breastfeeding (the baby is nourished by the mother's milk only) until the baby is six months old (compared with four months previously), and to prolong breastfeeding until the child is one year old, because it is beneficial to the baby's health. Mothers' practices are far removed from the recommendation; less than half practised full breastfeeding when the child was four months old, and only one in three still breastfed when the child was one year old. Personnel in maternal wards and child health centres are expected to be active in effectuating these recommendations. Full breastfeeding is a full-time activity for the mother and hence incompatible with returning to work and a necessary succeeding period of gradual reduction of nursing implies that full-time work is not possible. The breastfeeding policy is a main argument against reserving more of the leave period for fathers.[7] A mother of four with children in the 1-12 age range experiences the normative shift during her own reproductive career this way:

> Now everything is organised according to the baby. That is the signal we get already from the birth. The baby is to decide everything. There is little talk about structure and that you can manage the day a little bit yourself. No, everything is to be led by the baby's needs. Thereby many are sitting and breastfeeding all the time. When you are at home with the baby a year and everything has been led by the child's needs, it easily continues that way. (*Aftenposten*, 12 January 2005, p 16)

The proportion of mothers entitled to leave has been rather stable, about three in four, but entitled mothers take up more leave: the proportion of mothers choosing the longest leave alternative, 52 weeks at 80% compensation, increased significantly in the 1990s, from 58% in 1993 to 79% in 2000 (Danielsen and Lappegård, 2003). The causes are uncertain; there are several possible interpretations: long leaves might be considered the best for the child; parents can afford longer leaves; suitable childcare is lacking (Danielsen and Lappegård, 2003). There are reasons to believe that the transition between parental leave and return to work is particularly problematic regarding childcare. The near non-existence of day care for children under and around one year old is part of the picture.

Most of the leave has been free to share among the parents since 1978. But fathers' take-up rate was very low, and this was the background to the introduction of the daddy quota: 'to strengthen the father's place in the life of the child, it is important that in the first year of the child's life he already participates in the childcare. A part of the leave therefore should be reserved for the father' (St. meld. [White Paper] no 4, 1988-89, p 32). While the daddy quota is a success story regarding the impact on fathers' frequency of leave uptake, fathers' share of the total leave uptake is low, about 9% (Box

1.1, Chapter One, this volume). Moreover, quite a lot of fathers, almost half of them, take their quota when their partner also is at home (Brandth and Kvande, 2003). In these cases the leave is less likely to contribute to a less traditional gender division of labour in the family, and it also weakens the fathers' chance to establish an autonomous caring role.

High take-up rates indicate that the quota establishes a new norm for fathers – the normal thing for fathers to do. Although the reform was launched as a 'loving force' on fathers, fathers themselves clearly consider the quota a positive right. That the quota is a right, and that fathers thus do not have to negotiate individually with employers, is thought to be the most important reason for its success (Brandth and Kvande, 2003), although it should be added that the quota hardly 'disturbs' workplaces in the same way that women's longer leaves do, as it is no more than the length of a normal holiday.[8] But there is potential for change – about 50% of both mothers and fathers with pre-school age children want to extend the daddy quota within the existing leave (Pettersen, 2003).

The reasons for the limited success regarding fathers' share of leave take-up are probably complex (see also Lammi-Taskula, this volume). One factor is family economy. That fathers earn more than mothers do and thus families will lose money if fathers take more leave is an argument frequently mentioned in the policy debate. While there is no research in Norway to validate this argument, research on Swedish parents has shown that income loss is only a part of the problem; a progressive tax system moderates the effect, among other things (Björnberg, 2002; Haas, 2003). Moreover, women's economic loss in the longer term needs to be entered into the equation.

It has been quite common to assume that fathers' resistance to change is a main part of the problem. However, recent research suggests that mothers' reluctance to share might be as important as fathers'. Some mothers consider the leave as their entitlement and privilege, and their partners take only as much leave as mothers let them have (Magnussen et al, 2001). Some consider the one-year leave as a luxury they just want for themselves. But fathers may also consider parental leave as a welcome break from a hectic and demanding working life (Edin, 2005). Biological motherhood is also an argument for disproportional leaves for mothers; mothers have to recuperate after birth, and they need time for breastfeeding (Brandth and Kvande, 2002). A main argument against policies extending the daddy quota within the existing leave arrangement is that it takes 'rights' away from mothers. That the current parental leave except for the daddy quota is considered a 'mother's right' may not be surprising, as mothers take 92% of the leave time. But when the majority of women practise this 'privilege' as individuals, this aggregates to symbolise women as a different sort of worker at the societal level. If time off work to care for children remains the practice mostly of mothers, the conception of young women as a group with less than full labour market capacity will stick to them, and represent a risk factor in the hiring process and in career development.

This is reflected in the Gender Equality Ombud (2004) report of a growing number of complaints about illegal discrimination from pregnant women and mothers (and some fathers) on leave.[9] The complaints exhibit three main problems: (1) cases related to the hiring decision: some women experience that their pregnancy results in job offers being withdrawn or is stated as the reason why they are not hired, while others experience that their temporary work contract is not prolonged; (2) cases related to the return to work after parental leave: some are dismissed, while others experience a change in job content because of their absence; (3) cases related to wages and other benefits: persons on parental leave are excluded from local wage negotiations and performance-related benefits (bonuses and so on). The complaints from men mainly relate to wage compensation for parental leave (some employers compensate women's wages above the standard economic ceiling, but not men's). These problems are found in all areas of working life, and the Ombud maintains that discriminatory practices are supported by surprisingly many employers, including the largest employers' organisation (NHO), which defended such practices in public.

The time account was introduced with the expectation that more parents would choose part-time leave, which gives the possibility of reduced work hours in the child's first two years. One particular aim of the time account scheme was that flexible options would make fathers take more leave, and that it in general would relieve the time pressure in families with small children (NOU, 1993). The social profile of those who make use of the time account is quite skewed; users are concentrated among highly educated parents (Holter and Brandth, 1998). Several constraints concerning its use are reported. Complex rules and lack of information are reasons mentioned by parents. Problems with combining employment and family are one of the most important factors.

One reason may be lack of flexibility in the workplace. The mechanisms operating may be parallel to those affecting the use of sick leave among pregnant women. Full sick leave is often the 'easiest' solution for pregnant women. While the large majority of Norwegian women are employed during pregnancy, the proportion on sick leave has increased significantly (Strand, 2002). Between 55% and 72% of employed pregnant women are estimated to take some sick leave during their pregnancy (Nergaard et al, 2003). In understaffed workplaces, reduced work capacity/partial leave may cause irritation among colleagues, as it is often not compensated by substitutes (Nergaard et al, 2003). Pregnancy-related absence or reduced work capacity is more often considered disloyal vis-à-vis the workplace than other causes of sick leave (Strand, 2002).

'Free choice': cash for care

The overall objective of the cash-for-care benefit was to 'improve the opportunities of families with small children to provide good childcare' (St. prp [White Paper] no 53, 1997-98, p 5). Three aims were specified. One was that families should be secured more time to care for their own children. A second was that families should be given a real 'free choice' regarding the form of care they want for their children. A third aim was just distribution of state subsidies to families with children, independent of how childcare is arranged.

The reform was passed by a centre minority government with support from the two parties on the right, with the left wing, the Labour Party and the Socialist Party, in fierce opposition. The Christian People's Party particularly fought relentlessly for this reform for years, it being the Party's main reform proposal. Like no other reform, the cash benefit brought the conflicting positions of Norwegian family policy out in the open. These conflicts did not surface in the earlier debates about parental leave, but had been visible in the different policy motivations. A main dividing line is between different ideal models of early childhood: family-based care versus a parent/institutional care mix (see also Leira, 1998). The policy debate was extremely polarised. Opponents saw the reform as an attack on gender equality, and predicted serious setbacks for mothers' employment and for gender equality in general. The public childcare system was expected to face serious problems, as a decline in the demand for public day care was expected because hiring private childminders would become much more profitable.

A slow down in mothers' employment growth

The majority of parents with children aged one to two years old receive the cash benefit, of which a negligible number are fathers.

There has been a marked drop in the proportion of parents receiving the benefit ever since its introduction, declining from 74.8% of all parents with children aged one to two years old in 1999, to 57.8% in 2005. The proportion is highest among parents with one-year-olds, 63.9%, compared with 51.7% for parents with two-year-olds. Contrary to expectations, evaluation studies of the effects so far indicate that the reform has led to only modest adjustments in mothers' employment, while parents' demand for childcare services is higher than ever.

Not unexpectedly, the reform did not affect employment and working hours of fathers much. More surprisingly, however, is the modest short-term impact on mothers' time in employment, documented in a series of studies based on various data sources (see a review of the earliest studies in Baklien et al, 2001; Ellingsæter, 2003). A recent analysis based on labour force surveys shows a high level of *stability* in the employment rate of mothers with children aged one to two years old in the years after the reform (Håland and Næringsrud, 2004). In the period 1997-2003, about 70% of the mothers were employed, a stability similar to that of all women in the 25-49 age group. Thus, the previous long-term trend of *growth* in mothers' employment rates has levelled off, which might be an effect of the reform. The average number of hours worked among employed mothers shows a small but consistent increase in the period, from 27.8 to 29.7 hours, mainly caused by increasing full-time work. In comparison, average working hours among women aged 25-49 declined somewhat, due to a reduction in hours in full-time work. Qualitative studies a couple of years after the introduction of the reform also suggested that parents' decisions about work and care are to a small extent influenced by the cash benefit. Many parents believe that they would not have acted differently without the cash benefit (Bungum et al, 2001; Magnussen et al, 2001).

Some studies try to estimate what is *likely to have happened* if the cash benefit had not been introduced. One such study, based on register data up to 2001, suggests a modest effect on mothers' total labour supply. Mothers' hours in paid employment (note: not employment rate) could have been 6% higher if the cash-for-care benefit had not been introduced (Schøne, 2002). The estimated potential effect is mainly visible among mothers of one-year-olds; and significantly less so among those with two-year-olds (Schøne, 2004). A third study based on similar methods using survey data of parents in 1998, 1999 and 2002 estimates the potential effects of the benefit on mothers' employment to be larger (Rønsen, 2005). That is, if the cash benefit had not been introduced, mothers' employment rates and working hours would have grown further and been significantly higher than at present. This study also estimates a potential negative effect on fathers' time in employment. Rønsen interprets this as the long-term effect of the cash-for-care benefit.

These kinds of estimates are always associated with uncertainty. Moreover, estimates are also open to alternative interpretation. For example, if more potential negative effects are estimated, it is not necessarily an indication of the long-term effects of the cash benefit reform. It might equally reflect a temporary adjustment, as the cash benefit may well interact in new ways with other changes taking place. It is likely that parents' work/care strategies in the transition period from parental leave and return to work are changing. The shortage of public day care at the end of leave continues to represent a serious constraint on mothers' employment, but the situation is improving. The ongoing expansion of day care places among the youngest children is reducing parents' expected time on day care waiting lists, and unpaid leave for a few months may be preferred to getting a private childminder for a rather short period. Thus, extended unpaid leave with cash benefit might be the preferred alternative, and might also involve fathers.

Parents' preference for public childcare has turned out to be much stronger than anticipated. The lack of day care poses a severe constraint on mothers' employment, and choice is illusionary. The newspapers are filled with stories about distressed parents:

> 'New parents start to worry about day care as soon as the child is born.... If I had wanted to stay at home it would have been fine, but I want to work ... ' [mother]

> 'We considered whether Charlotte should quit her job and stay home [with the child]. Then she would receive unemployment benefit and cash for care. It is frustrating that in 2005 you do not have a real choice.' [father] (Mother and father of a nine-month-old child, *Dagbladet*, 23 April 2005, p 12)

The reform is in principle gender neutral, it is directed at 'parents' and 'families'. An argument for the 'free choice' rationale was that parents should be trusted to choose the best form of care for their children. In the public debate the reform was framed as a time issue, helping parents to solve the 'time squeeze' (Ellingsæter, 2006).

It was based on a negative conception of mothers' employment as conflicting and stressful, and the assumption that many mothers are employed out of economic necessity, and would prefer to stay at home with their children.

The cash benefit presumes a family with an additional full-time wage. Traditional family values underpin the freedom of choice argument, valorising the homemaker role. Family care is considered the best for children aged under three. The emphasis is on enhancing the situation of the one-income family and thus the opportunity to choose *parental care* (Ellingsæter, 2006). However, the content of the cash reform is in part inconsistent with its major aim, as mothers do not have to change their employment practices to get hold of the benefit. The benefit is paid to all those not using public care, whatever other care arrangement they have (use of nannies, and so on).

The reform's rather modest effects probably have two causes. One fundamental factor is the economic environment. The Norwegian labour market has been favourable in the reform period. Unemployment has been fairly low (4% to 5%), thus most mothers have had a real choice regarding work. Second, the reform runs contrary to profound long-term processes of change. It underestimates mothers' integration in the labour market and parents' preference for public childcare (see Ellingsæter, 2003, for a more detailed discussion). The reform is based on an outdated opposition between 'working mothers' and 'stay-at-home mothers'. Today most Norwegian mothers are linked to the labour market in some way. Only 15% of mothers with children aged one to two years old report that they are conventional 'stay-at-home-mothers' (Knudsen, 2001). For most mothers the choice is not between working or staying at home, rather between different ways of combining care and employment.

The unrecognised 'care squeeze': childcare services

Norway has a huge *childcare gap*, which is history in the rest of the Nordic countries. Particularly for the one- to two-year-old age group there is an excessive demand for services (Ellingsæter and Gulbrandsen, 2004). Among parents with two-year-old children, 46% have a place in day care for their child, but an additional 41% have applied for a place or want a place (Ellingsæter and Gulbrandsen, 2004). A similar gap is found among parents with one-year-olds: 22% have a place in day care, and an additional 48% have applied for a place or want a place. These gaps entail long waiting lists and frustrated parents:

Parents without day care become world champions in little satisfactory ad-hoc solutions. We export children to other parts of the city, reduce working hours, swap children, try out nannies, child park when the weather is good and so on. (*Aftenposten*, 20 May 2003, p 33)

The policy of 'full coverage'

How did this gap mount up? 'Full coverage' has turned out to be a moving target. Successive governments have had to adjust upwards the rate estimated to measure full coverage. In 2002 about 67% of children aged one to five were enrolled in day care institutions (Ellingsæter and Gulbrandsen, 2003, p 34). The last estimate of full coverage is 80% of children aged one to five years old (Ellingsæter and Gulbrandsen, 2003), and was to be achieved in 2005. The demand for places already exceeded 80% in 2002.

After the parental leave extension in 1993 almost all the political energy in the family policy field went into the controversy over the cash benefit reform. The centre-right pressure for the cash benefit acted as an efficient stoppage for a stronger emphasis on day care. The introduction of the cash-for-care benefit was indeed expected to *reduce* the demand for childcare services. While the parties on the left have stated childcare services as a central measure in their gender equality and family policy strategy, for the centre-right, gender equality is not a main objective in their childcare policy. However, the centre-right government (2001-05) had to recognise that sufficient childcare services were necessary as part of the 'free choice' policies regarding childcare: 'The Government wishes to secure all families with young children free choice in the care solution for children. Full coverage is a precondition of reaching this goal' (St. meld. [White Paper] no 24, 2002-03, p 6).

Childcare services were placed firmly on the political agenda in the early 2000s. With the cash-for-care benefit legislated, this controversy was out of the way at least temporarily, and a main focus on childcare services became viable. In 2003 the centre–right government was pressured into a political agreement, *The Day Care Compromise*, by the majority opposition, including the Progress Party.[10] A target for maximum payment for childcare services was set, after the Swedish model of '*max taxa*'.

In the shadow of the 'time squeeze'

Judged by increasing coverage rates, the 1990s was the 'decade of childcare services' in Norway. But a main cause of the improvement was political reforms that removed a large number of children from the long waiting lists. The expansion of parental leave to one year in 1993 and the lowering of the compulsory school age from seven to six in 1997 virtually removed two birth cohorts from the childcare market. The expansion in terms of places was modest, the increase was at a lower pace than for the two preceding decades. However, for children aged three or more the coverage rates did increase significantly, and have reached a balance between demand and supply in most municipalities. But childcare services for one- and two-year-old children remain a great problem. Most new places for this age group in the 1990s were in 'family day care', typically one employee caring for four to five children in a private home (Ellingsæter and Gulbrandsen, 2003). These units resemble private nanny arrangements, except for the state subsidy and some public control of the operation. Family day care was an inexpensive strategy to improve coverage rates among the youngest children.

The long waiting lists for children aged one to two years old were well known, but under-communicated in the family policy debate of the 1990s. Parents' lack of childcare services, their 'care squeeze', was completely overshadowed by the dominant focus on the 'time squeeze', highlighting 'more time for children'. Also, parents' high degree of satisfaction with day care has been underestimated. To many parents it is quite a mystery that the affluent Norwegian welfare state has not been able to supply the childcare services they need:

> Every time a spaceship lands on one of the planets out in space, I think of that we have not yet managed to get full childcare coverage in Norway. (Editor Kjersti Løken Stavrum, *Aftenposten*, 29 January 2005)

The current situation also mirrors a legacy of controversy and ambivalence about childcare services. The huge increase in mothers' employment has represented a continuous political pressure towards expansion in services, but the growth in mothers' employment has been running far ahead of public childcare provision (Leira, 1992). The first serious attempts to expand childcare services in the 1970s were met with strong opposition (Leira, 1992). The psychological development and pedagogical needs of children was the main policy rationale of the proponents. The needs of working parents for services were not articulated, despite the preceding strong growth in mothers' employment. The pervasive attitude was that the care and education of young children was the responsibility of the family. At best, day care centres represented only a supplement to parental full-time care.

Ambivalent attitudes still prevail for children under three. For example, health nurses, in important positions advising new parents, express ambivalent attitudes toward extra-parental care for these children. Some believe that care at home is the best solution, arguing that children under three are not in need of contact with other children, contrary to expert knowledge. Some consider a private childminder to be better than a day care centre. The ideal seems to be 'quiet and tranquil' and 'family like': in the home of a childminder there will normally be a more 'calm atmosphere and more direct contact between children and adults' (Gulbrandsen and Sundnes, 2004). Other health nurses consider parental care and day care to be equivalent as long as children have access to activities and stimulation.

Yet Norway is on the road towards universal childcare services. Parents' high demand for day care is the driving force in this development (Ellingsæter and Gulbrandsen, 2004). The cash-for-care reform did not change this at all. More children in the one- to two-year-old age group than ever are enrolled in public childcare (Ellingsæter and Gulbrandsen, 2003). Parents choose day care despite the substantial economic loss they experience when they do not take the cash benefit; the price for day care has been comparably high in a Nordic perspective. Moreover, the 2003 reform reducing parents' payment is estimated to increase mothers' labour supply and the demand for day care (Kornstad and Thoresen, 2003). The price reform has already increased the demand for services. A larger share of the increase in capacity is converted into expanding part-time to full-time places for children who already have a place, than into new places, however (Asplan Viak, 2004).

Childcare paradoxes and gender relations

Every welfare state displays notions about what type of childcare is appropriate, reflected in financial arrangements, care subsidies, policy assumptions in policy documents and so on, conveying cultural messages to parents about how children should be cared for (Kremer,

2002). The present Norwegian childcare policies for early childhood appear as a dualistic family policy regime, composed of elements supporting different family models. Parental leave has been structured so as to facilitate more equal sharing of parental childcare among mothers and fathers, but prolongation of the regime's dualist structure was secured by the introduction of the cash-for-care benefit, intended to increase parental choice. Thus, the Norwegian policy regime accentuates the tension between the gender equality ambition and 'free choice', a struggle of increasing relevance to many welfare states (Kremer, 2002; Morgan, 2002; Salmi, this volume). Furthermore, until very recently, policy emphasis has been directed more towards mothers' right to care than to their right to work, as day care services have been acutely short in supply. This is an indication of a continuation of a legacy of hesitance in promoting day care as a means of supporting working mothers.

These regime qualities suggest that current policies have unfolded along an unmistakable 'path', articulating a path dependence of policies. It is important to note, however, that the current regime is not the product of political consensus. Childcare for the youngest children is a contested policy field, in which the social democratic/left versus centre-right cleavage is significant. Thus, path continuity in this case, following Mahon (2002b), is not the autonomous result of institutions; rather it is the power relations underlying the policy configurations that shape the outcomes. Policy regimes are social products, and thus unfinished ones (Mahon, 2002b). Governments have a measure of political choice, although limited by existing power relations, public opinion, policy configurations and institutional arrangements (Huber and Stephens, 2001). For example, the introduction of the cash benefit depended on the particular government and party constellation at the time, and the more recent emphasis on day care services was made possible by highly unusual alliances among the majority opposition in Parliament. The role played by small political parties with a few leading issues should not be underestimated in political systems dominated by minority coalitions.

Paradoxes integral to the current Norwegian childcare regime emerge, in policy content and in the relationship between policy intention and parents' practices. The long parental leave has institutionalised a norm of full-time parental care of children aged under one year old. Childcare services are virtually non-existent for children under one (see Box 1.1, Chapter One). Parental leave practices establish work and family as separate spheres – work–family reconciliation thus equals work–family separation. Separating work and family apparently is the easiest thing for parents to do, and it is easiest for women. Full-time mothering is (re)-instituted, creating a potential negative risk for women's labour market position. Most fathers take their monthly leave quota, almost half of them with the mothers present; very few take more than the quota. Flexible practices, combinations of work and care, are very rare at the earliest stage of parenthood. The 'unused flexibility', the low utilisation of the time account scheme in parental leave, is puzzling. So also is the cash-for-care benefit, following after the parental leave period and aimed at the one- to two-year-olds. It is received by the large majority of mothers, but only with a modest negative effect on mothers' time use in employment. Even more surprising is the unexpected strong increase in parents' demand for public day care after the introduction of the benefit. The huge childcare gap, the gap between demand and supply of day care services, makes 'free choice' regarding childcare an illusion. But parents' increasing demand for day care for the youngest children makes parents key actors in generating normative change, mounting a significant pressure for political change.

Clearly, gender equality outcomes cannot always be read from the gender equality assumptions of policies. For several policies, the relationship between policy intentions and parents' practices is far from straightforward. Some policies have wide effects, others a surprisingly modest or negligible impact. What is important to take into account, is that the effect of single policies depends on *context*, of the existence of other policies, as well as the broader economic and social opportunity structures that policies are part of. For instance, the general expectation that many mothers will choose a cash-for-care benefit if it is introduced, is unwarranted. Whether such a benefit is chosen or not depends on the *alternative opportunities of choice*. Another example: access to public day care is considered the most important support of mothers' right to work, but with the universalisation of day care the correlation between mothers' employment and childcare is weakened. Norwegian parents increasingly consider public day care as welfare that is good for children, irrespective of the employment status of mothers, and this tends to reduce the previous middle-class bias in parents' demand (Ellingsæter and Gulbrandsen, 2003).

The mounting care gap for the under-threes is in many ways the most striking paradox in the current Norwegian childcare regime. Instead of reducing the well-known long waiting lists for day care for children under the age of three, the cash-for-care benefit was introduced in the late 1990s, supporting parents who *do not* use public childcare. Only recently the gap has become a top priority subject of public debate and political reform. Parents' acute 'care squeeze' was long overshadowed by a 'time squeeze' diagnosis. 'Making more time for children', as the main aim of care policies, is actually somewhat puzzling in the Norwegian setting of mothers' long leaves and frequent part-time working. However, the 'time deficit' perspective appears as part of a moral discourse, reflecting an underlying critique of modern parents who do not spend enough time with their children (Ellingsæter, 2004). Time deficit plays an essential role in the story of family decline and the demise of proper family values. The right to care is intertwined with an increasing emphasis on the duty to care.[11]

> We live in a time that, despite great support of the family, is also characterised by loneliness, dissolved unions and broken relations.... Therefore we need an strong family policy.... A good family policy is also a measure against a societal development characterised by excessive individualisation and self-centredness ... clear political signals about necessary attitudinal change in relation to care work are important. This must be strengthened, that is, by valuing care work more as a societal effort. (St. meld no 29 [the centre-right government's White Paper on the family], 2002-03, pp 5-7)

A fundamental work–family *conflict* perspective underpins the 'time squeeze' diagnosis. A common assumption is that the work–family combination is conflicting and stressful for the young child and the whole family. The problem is associated with mothers' employment, as fathers' problems with combining much longer working hours and time for children occupy only a marginal space in the public debate. Economic causes of women's employment are often exaggerated, while normative change is underestimated (Crompton, 2002). When mothers take time out of the labour market it is commonly interpreted as a result of a positive choice, complying with gender-traditional normative expectations. But various constraints influence practices a great deal. Implicit in this problem-oriented conception of the work–family relationship is the view that mothers should have a right to choose between employment and care, that is, the choice *not* to engage in paid work.

The Norwegian emphasis on the right to care supports the idea that problems associated with the work–care interface originate in, and have to be solved in the family. Problems originating in the organisation of time and cultures of time in the labour market tend to disappear. The invisibility of structural constraints increases with the rhetoric of free choice. The one-sided emphasis on the family allows gender equality-unfriendly structures and cultures in work life to persist.

A main focus of the Norwegian childcare regime has obviously been child welfare and children's rights. The centre-right government that resigned in 2005 stated that they would 'put children at the centre of family policies' (St. meld. [White Paper] no 29, 2002-03, p 6). During party conventions in the spring 2005, the Christian People's Party had 'children, children, children' as one of its main slogans, and the Labour Party 'hammered out a new family policy that places children and families with children first' (Karin Yrvin, Oslo Labour Party, *Dagsavisen*, 26 April 2005, p 3). Contemporary public policy debates are increasingly child oriented, and a potential contradiction between women's autonomy and children's interests/rights surfaces now and then. Increasing child orientation is noted in other countries as well, and some scholars express worries that a child-centred citizenship discourse may marginalise women's claims as citizens (Dobrowolsky and Jenson, 2004; Jenson, 2004). A main solution to this dilemma is to transform caring rights resting with the family into individual rights. Children's welfare should be a question not only of 'good enough' mothers, but also of 'good enough' fathers. Nor should we forget parents' welfare, that mothers and fathers are more than parents, and workers, they are also members of society at large.

Notes

[1] 54 weeks/80% compensation or 44 weeks/100% compensation (as of 1 July 2006). Nine weeks are reserved for the mother: three weeks prior to birth, to protect the foetus, and six weeks after to recuperate after the birth. The leave reserved for fathers was extended from four to five weeks in 2005 and to six weeks in 2006. The rest of the leave may be shared between the parents, as they prefer.

[2] There is an additional right to one year of *unpaid* leave, also with the right to return to the job.

[3] Except for the populist right-wing Progress Party, which in principle considers childcare to be a parental, and not state, responsibility.

[4] Introduced in 1998, NOK 3,303 per month, about 430 euros (2006). The left-centre coalition in power from 2005 has cut the benefit. Parents of children with part-time places in publicly supported services receive benefits proportional with the use of services, ranging from 80% benefit for eight hours weekly to 20% benefit for 25 to 32 hours.

[5] The analysis of parental leave is based on Ellingsæter (2006).

[6] All translations from Norwegian to English are mine.

[7] Mothers' breastfeeding featured prominently in a debate on parental leave in the autumn of 2004. Some (male) members of the Socialist Left Party proposed to divide the parental leave into three equal parts: one for the mother, one for the father, and one to be shared at the choice of the parents. The Icelandic model (see Lammi-Taskula, this volume) inspired this proposal. In the Norwegian debate the main counterargument was that an increase in fathers' leave would conflict with the breastfeeding recommendation.

[8] Annual holiday in Norway is five weeks.

[9] The reasons for an increase in complaints are probably complex. The Ombud suggests that more well-educated and more 'rights-conscious' women and a trend of frequent reorganisations in working life are likely to be important.

[10] The Progress Party's support was strategic, not a support on principle. The Party's family policy is liberalist, going against public childcare services and paid parental leave, advocating a pure cash transfer model, that is, all subsidies distributed equally to all families.

[11] Daly and Lewis (2000) have noted a general policy shift from rights to responsibilities, enforcing parental responsibilities, in the European context.

References

Anttonen, A. and Sipilä, J. (1996) 'European social care services: is it possible to identify models?', *Journal of European Social Policy*, vol 6, pp 87-100.

Asplan Viak (2004) *Analyse av barnehagetall per 20.09 2004*, Oslo.

Baklien, B., Ellingsæter, A.L. and Gulbrandsen, L. (2001) *Evaluering av kontantstøtteordningen*, Oslo: Norges Forskningsråd.

Björnberg, U. (2002) 'Ideology and choice between work and care: Swedish family policy for working parents', *Critical Social Policy*, vol 22, no 1, pp 33-52.

Brandth, B. and Kvande, E. (2002) 'Father presence in childcare', in A.-M. Jensen and L. McKee (eds) *Children and the Changing Family: Between Transformation and Negotiation*, London: Routledge Falmer.

Brandth, B. and Kvande, E. (2003) *Fleksible fedre*, Oslo: Universitetsforlaget.

Bruning, G. and Plantenga, J. (1999) 'Parental leave and equal opportunities: experiences in eight European countries', *Journal of European Social Policy*, vol 9, no 3, pp 195-209.

Bungum, B., Brandth, B. and Kvande, E. (2001) *Ulik Praksis, Ulike Konsekvenser*, Trondheim: IFIM.

Crompton, R. (2002) 'Employment, flexible working and the family', *British Journal of Sociology*, vol 53, no 4, pp 537-58.

Daly, M. (2000) 'A fine balance: women's labor market participation in international comparison', in F.W. Scharpf and V.A. Schmid (eds) *Welfare and Work in the Open Economy*, Volume II, Oxford: Oxford University Press, pp 467-510.

Daly, M. and Lewis, J. (1998) 'Introduction: conceptualising social care in the context of welfare state restructuring', in J. Lewis (ed) *Gender, Social Care and Welfare State Restructuring in Europe*, Aldershot: Ashgate, pp 1-24.

Daly, M. and Lewis, J. (2000) 'The concept of social care and the analysis of contemporary welfare states', *British Journal of Sociology*, vol 51, pp 281-98.

Danielsen, K. and Lappegård, T. (2003) 'Tid er viktig når barn blir født', *Samfunnsspeilet*, vol 17, no 5, pp 34-8.

Deven, F. and Moss, P. (2002) 'Leave arrangements for parents: overview and future outlook', *Community, Work and Family*, vol 5, no 3, pp 237-55.

Dobrowolsky, A. and Jenson, J. (2004) 'Shifting representations of citizenship: Canadian politics of 'women' and 'children'', *Social Politics*, vol 11, no 2, pp 154-80.

Edin, S.Y.L. (2005) *Moderne menn i IKT-virksomhet*, MA thesis, Trondheim: The Norwegian University of Science and Technology, Department of Sociology and Political Science.

Ellingsæter, A.L. (2003) 'The complexity of family policy reform: the case of Norway', *European Societies*, vol 4, no 4, pp 419-43.

Ellingsæter, A.L. (2004) 'Tidskrise i familien?', in A.L. Ellingsæter and A. Leira (eds) *Velferdsstat og familie*, Oslo: Gyldendal Akademisk, pp 128–59.

Ellingsæter, A.L. (2006) "Old' and 'new' politics of time to care: three Norwegian Reforms'. Paper presented to conference 'Welfare State Change. Conceptualisation, Measurement and Interpretation', arranged by CCWS, Aalborg University, Store Restrup Herregaard, 13-15 January.

Ellingsæter, A.L. and Gulbrandsen, L. (2003) *Barnehagen: fra selektivt til universelt velferdsgode*, Oslo: Nova.

Ellingsæter, A.L. and Gulbrandsen, L. (2004) 'Practices, policies and preferences – mothers' employment and childcare in Norway', Paper presented to the Work, Employment and Society Conference, Manchester, 1-3 September.

Ellingsæter, A.L. and Rønsen, M. (1996) 'The dual strategy: motherhood and the work contract in Scandinavia', *European Journal of Population*, vol 12, pp 239-60.

Ericsson, K. (2001) 'Forhandlingsfamiliens paradokser', *Fokus, Tidsskrift for familiebehandling*, vol 29, no 4, pp 243-57.

Gender Equality Ombud (2004) *Høringsuttalelse: Anmodningsvedtak fra Stortinget til Regjeringen*, Oslo.

Gulbrandsen, L. and Sundnes, A. (2004) 'Day care centres as child welfare measure', Paper presented at the 2nd Congress of the European Society on Family Relations (ESFR), Fribourg, 29 September to 2 October.

Haas, L. (2003) 'Parental leave and gender equality: lessons from the European Union', *Review of Policy Research*, vol 20, no 1, pp 89-114.

Håland, I. and Næringsrud, G. (2004) '7 av 10 mødre med barn i kontantstøtte alder jobber', *Magasinet*, Oslo: Statistisk sentralbyrå.

Holter, T. and Brandth, B. (1998) *Permisjon eller arbeid?*, Trondheim: Allforsk.

Huber, E. and Stephens, J.D. (2001) *Development and Crisis of the Welfare State: Parties and Policies in Global Markets*, Chicago, IL: University of Chicago Press.

Jenson, J. (2004) 'Changing the paradigm: family responsibility or investing in children', *Canadian Journal of Sociology*, vol 29, no 2, pp 169-92.

Knudsen, C. (2001) *Hvem lot seg påvirke? Kontantstøtten og mødres yrkesaktivitet*, Oslo: NOVA.

Kornstad, T. and Thoresen, T.O. (2003) 'Barnehageforliket – effekter på arbeidstilbud og inntektsfordeling', *Økonomiske Analyser*, no 5, pp 25-31.

Korpi, W. (2000) 'Faces of inequality: gender, class and patterns of inequalities in different types of welfare states', *Social Politics*, vol 7, pp 127-91.

Kremer, M. (2002) 'The illusion of free choice: ideals of care and childcare policy in the Flemish and Dutch welfare states', in S. Michel and R. Mahon (eds) *Childcare Policy at the Crossroads: Gender and Welfare State Restructuring*, New York, NY: Routledge, pp 113–42.

Leira, A. (1992) *Welfare States and Working Mothers*, Cambridge: Cambridge University Press.

Leira, A. (1998) 'Caring as a social right: cash for childcare and daddy leave', *Social Politics*, vol 5, pp 362-79.

Magnussen, M.-L., Godal, B. and Leira, A. (2001) *Hvem skal passe barna? Kontantstøtte, barnetilsyn og foreldres lønnsarbeid*, Oslo: Universitetet i Oslo, Institutt for sosiologi og samfunnsgeografi.

Mahon, R. (2002a) 'Child care: toward what kind of 'social Europe'?', *Social Politics*, vol 9, pp 343-79.

Mahon, R. (2002b) 'Integrating the 'socially excluded': Swedish child care policies' (available at www.civil-society-network.org/english/index.htm).

Michel, S. and Mahon, R. (eds) (2002) *Childcare Policy at the Crossroads: Gender and Welfare State Restructuring*, New York, NY: Routledge.

Morgan, K. (2002) 'Does anyone have a 'Libre Choix'? Subversive liberalism and the politics of French child care policy', in S. Michel and R. Mahon (eds) *Child Care Policy at the Crossroads: Gender and Welfare State Restructuring*, New York, NY: Routledge, pp 143–67.

Morgan, K.J. and Zippel, K. (2003) 'Paid to care: the origins and effects of care leave policies in Western Europe', *Social Politics*, vol 10, no 2, pp 49-85.

Nergaard, K. with Kristiansen, N.M. and Jordfald, B. (2003) *Gravid og i jobb: Bedriftenes politikk for tilrettelegging av arbeidet*, Oslo: Fafo.

NOU (1993) *Tid for barna*, NOU (Green Paper) 1993:12, Oslo.

Pettersen, S.V. (2003) 'Halvparten av fedrene vil ha lengre kvote', *Samfunnsspeilet*, vol 17, no 5.

Pierson, P. (2004) *Politics in Time: History, Institutions and Social Analysis*, Princeton, NJ: Princeton University Press.

Pylkkänen, E. and Smith, N. (2003) *Career Interruptions due to Parental Leave: A Comparative Study of Denmark and Sweden*, Paris: OECD.

Rønsen, M. (2005) *Kontantstøttens langsiktige effekter på mødres og fedres arbeidstilbud*, Oslo: Statististisk sentralbyrå.

Sainsbury, D. (2001) 'Gender and the making of welfare states: Norway and Sweden', *Social Politics*, vol 8, pp 113-43.

Schøne, P. (2002) 'Kontantstøtten og effekter på arbeidstilbudet: hva er en god sammenligningsgruppe?', *Søkelys på arbeidsmarkedet*, vol 19, no 1, pp 23-30.

Schøne, P. (2004) 'Kontantstøtten og mødres arbeidstilbud; varig effekt eller retur til arbeid?', *Norsk Økonomisk Tidsskrift*, vol 118, pp 1-21.

Skrede, K. (1999) 'Shaping gender equality – the role of the state: Norwegian experiences, present policies and future challenges', in B. Palier and D. Bouget (eds) *Comparing Social Welfare Systems in Nordic Countries and France*, Paris: Maison des sciences de l' Homme Ange-Guépin, pp 169-99.

St. meld. [White Paper] no 4 (1988-89) *Langtidsprogrammet 1990-93*, Oslo.

St. meld. no 24 (2002-03) *Barnehagetilbud til alle – økonomi, mangfold og valgfrihet*, Oslo.

St. meld. no 29 (2002-03) *Om familien – forpliktende samliv og foreldreskap*, Oslo.

St. prp [White Paper] no 53 (1997-98) *Innføring av kontantstøtte til småbarnsforeldre*, Oslo.

Strand, K. (2002) 'Gravid i arbeid – integrering eller fravær?', in A.L. Ellingsæter and J. Solheim (eds) *Den usynlige hånd?: Kjønnsmakt og moderne arbeidsliv*, Oslo: Gyldendal Akademisk, pp 217–32.

SEVEN

Parental choice and the passion for equality in Finland

Minna Salmi

Introduction

In international comparison, Finland is a country with well-developed policies providing support to parents who combine employment and family. This active parenthood policy has been seen as an indicator of a strong equality policy (for example, den Dulk et al, 1999) but the achievements of that policy have also been problematised (for example, Rantalaiho and Heiskanen, 1997) and even questioned as a turn to neofamilialism (Mahon, 2002). This chapter examines recent developments in Finnish policies of parenthood. How do the rationales behind parenthood policies change? How do the policy schemes meet the challenge of gender equality? Whose voice is heard when policy reforms are made? The reforms and the rationales behind them are also related to the changes in working life and the goals of present-day European politics. How do ambitions to create good policies for parents and children fit into the demands of working life and the challenges of a changing population structure?

A survey of Finnish families provides data on parents' response to the reforms. In the survey, mothers and fathers of children born in 1999 answered questions concerning their practices, wishes and opinions on how to take care of young children as well as on their experiences from the workplace when taking family leave and returning from the leave. The data were collected in 2001/02 from 3,295 mothers and 1,413 fathers.[1] As the female and male respondents do not come from the same families, the data give a picture of practices and opinions in almost 5,000 Finnish families with young children.

I will focus particularly on two topics: first, the parents' views on the arrangement of parental leave and how it should be shared between the parents, and second, the issue of parents' choice of day care or a cash grant for care. I will discuss the parents' views in relation to the rationales of the childcare reforms and the views expressed in the debate on these reforms by policy makers. I will also ask to what extent decisions on policy measures, on the one hand, and the 'choices' women make, on the other hand, can be explained by trends of re- or defamilisation, and to what extent they reflect the rather harsh development of the Western market economies, where the logic and ethos of the market seem to penetrate all areas of society (see Jacobs, 1992; Sauli et al, 2004).

Rationales of parenthood policies

In Finland, leave arrangements for parents, that is, maternity, paternity and parental leave plus home care leave and home care allowance (HCA), and leave to care for a sick child, have developed since the 1960s. During maternity, paternity and parental leave an earnings-related compensation is paid to the person on leave, whereas during care leave s/he is entitled to a flat-rate benefit. All these forms of leave include job security for the person on leave. Moreover, the benefits are resident-based and not dependent on labour market participation. Day care arranged by local authorities has been available as a general social service since 1973. In 1996 day care became a subjective right of every child under school age; since then, local authorities have been obliged to offer a day care place for every child if the parents so wish.[2]

The rationales behind the development of parenthood policies have ranged from ensuring the newborn baby's and mother's health to promoting gender equality. In the 1980s, the focus of social policy switched explicitly to parenthood policy, having earlier been on population and health policy. Social justice and gender equality were named as central policy aims. Gender equality refers here to a dual-earner/dual-carer model, although at first in a modest version. A government document of 1993 states that the aim of the long maternity, paternity and parental leave is 'to secure women's and children's health by giving *the mother* a chance to take a leave of absence from her work'; to secure the care of young children in their own homes by either the mother or the father; and to give men a chance *to support the woman* in her mothering and to establish a relationship with his child (Katsaus..., 1993; emphasis added). It is worth noting that the official policy took it for granted that mothers were employed – which was already the case in Finland by the 1950s (Salmi and Lammi-Taskula, 1999). Thus, in the case of leave arrangements, the rationale was not actually to enable women to take part in the labour market but to enable them to take a longer break from employment. Obviously, this policy can also be seen as encouraging women's high labour market activity on a continuous basis (Haataja, 2004). In the case of day care for children, the argument since the 1960s has been to realise women's right to employment while ensuring children a safe environment, and, later on, good early childhood education (Anttonen, 2003).

The Nordic countries have been characterised as women-friendly (Hernes, 1987; see also Anttonen, 2002; Borchorst and Siim, 2002) largely due to the well-developed parenthood policies. However, in Finland there are several contradictions in this policy from the point of view of gender equality. Parental leave can be taken by either of the parents, or divided between them. In practice, mothers almost always use the parental leave. From 1999 to 2003 there is a striking stability in the take-up rates of parents: fathers make use of 4% to 5% of the days available, mothers the remaining days (see also Box 1.1, Chapter One). The parental leave scheme was created to promote gender equality, but women's taking up the bulk of parental leave maintains the traditional gender pattern both in families and in the labour market, where women's position is more precarious than that of men.

The aim of paternity leave, as stated in the government document, is to enable fathers to take part in childcare and to create a close relationship with the child. However, the leave does not necessarily work this way. The short (six to 18 days) paternity leave, which is what the majority of fathers use, helps the mother in the first days after the birth. But it is far too short for a strong relationship to develop between father and child. Moreover, during the paternity leave, the father is not alone with the child, and thus not independently responsible for the child.

Developments of parenthood policies

If the actual gender consequences of parenthood policies cast a contradictory light on Finnish gender equality policy, the continuity of the development of the policies constitutes another problem. The development of the schemes almost stopped in the 1990s: the varying forms of leave were not extended, the allowances lost in their real value, and the quantity and quality of services for families with children declined (Sauli et al, 2004). The cuts were explained by the need to streamline public finances because of the economic recession, but the subsequent economic growth in the latter part of the 1990s did not lead to any expansion in the resources for families with children (see Hiilamo, this volume). The only major exception to downsizing the expenses was the right to day care, which in 1996 was guaranteed for all children under school age.

The changes to family leave arrangements were not numerous (see Salmi and Lammi-Taskula, 2005). In the 1990s, the father's parental rights were acknowledged by giving the six to 12 days' paternity leave independent status and by adding an extra six days to the leave. At the same time, reform of the regulations on paternity leave provided more opportunities to take the leave in segments (see Lammi-Taskula, this volume). The new rationale was flexibility: the change would make it easier for men to take paternity leave. Even though this would be the case, fragmented take-up fails to break the 'childcare expertise' of the mother, and maintains the idea of the father as an assistant to the mother.

The new millennium has brought with it more interesting reforms, even though the rationales remain the same: more flexibility and more gender equality. Since 2003, the fathers have had the option of an extra two weeks' paternity leave on condition that they also take the last two weeks of the parental leave. This was a special Finnish way to create 'daddy month': in total, fathers may now stay on paternity leave for up to five weeks. Also, in 2003 the opportunity to take parental leave on a part-time basis was introduced, provided both the mother and the father reduce their hours to 40% to 60% of full-time hours and take part-time leave. The move to work part time requires the employer's agreement and must last for at least two months. The benefit received during part-time parental leave is half that of the earnings-based parental allowance.

The aim of this new arrangement is to 'make the parental leave scheme more flexible' and 'more responsive to the needs of different kinds of families while at the same time maintaining the family's chance to make its own choices'. The aim is also 'to encourage the parents, especially the fathers, to use the family leaves in a more equal manner' (Government proposal 147/2002).

Flexibility and parental choice

In the government's proposal, the rationale of 'freedom of choice' is presented explicitly even though this has for a long time been a permanent argument in the debate over the issue of sharing parental leave. It has been said by politicians as well as promoters of women's role as mothers that individual, non-transferable entitlements for fathers are not attractive as they have an element of obligatory take-up, when the right way is to let the parents themselves decide which of them takes the parental leave and for how long.

However, the rationale of 'free choice of the families' is not used consistently when childcare arrangements are discussed, I contend. There has been much debate in the Finnish press lately about children's universal right to day care, both among professionals working in the fields of child policies and childcare services and among politicians and leading government officials. In this debate, questions have been raised as to whether it is appropriate that the right to attend publicly funded day care applies to every child, including those whose parent is at home on parental leave, unemployed or outside the labour market. The debaters have been worried about the signal given to the parents. On the one hand, there is the signal that 'Society' takes over the responsibility of bringing up children from (lazy or selfish or incapable) parents instead of demanding, or teaching, the parents to do the work themselves. On the other hand, the signal is said to be that the parents are made to feel inadequate or not so good as carers and educators as the professionals in day care centres. Coming from a high governmental level, this kind of criticism of day care provision has a neoliberal ring to it. Neoliberal views of the welfare state started to be heard in the 1980s and 1990s in the Nordic countries, where generally 'the state is not perceived as undermining the moral obligations of parents, but as supporting the parent-child relationship' (Leira, 2002, p 84). Government officials have also said that the universal right to day care is too generous a service in the present phase of the welfare state when national and local authorities face the financial pressure of the changing population structure with fewer taxpayers and a rising demand for services for older people.

What do the parents want? The case of parental leave

Who is to take family leave and how?

The arrangement of parental leave in Finland until the beginning of 2003 was that the six-month parental leave following the approximately four-month maternity leave could be shared between the parents, but, in practice, it was mostly taken up by the mothers. In the Family Leave Survey this practice (here called the current practice) was found to be good without reservations by one in four mothers and fathers of young children. Particularly men, but also women, quite strongly agreed with the statement that it would be good if fathers took a longer parental leave (Table 7.1).

How, then, should this goal be reached? Only a small minority of the respondents were willing without reservations to give the fathers an exclusive period of the current parental leave. A period exclusively for the fathers was considered a good idea by more fathers and mothers if that period were an extension to the current leave.

The home care leave, which is a chance to take leave from work after the parental leave and until the child turns three, is also an entitlement used almost exclusively by women, even though men are equally entitled. Over a quarter of the mothers and nearly a quarter of the fathers think that the current practice is good. A quarter of the mothers and as many as a third of the fathers think that it would be good if the fathers used more of the home care leave. However, very few of either the fathers or the mothers think that the home care leave should be shared by including a period exclusively for the fathers.

Does this inconsistency indicate double standards, with the fathers thinking that their taking more family leave would be good provided nobody actually makes them do it? In the case of home care leave, the explanation may lie more in the nature of that leave with its low flat-rate benefit and thus relatively high risk to the family economy. At least there seems to be more interest in the non-transferable fathers' segment of parental leave, where the benefit is higher.[3] Experience shows that periods of leave exclusively for the fathers do lead to more men taking the leave, but may also lead to shorter leave periods than previously (see Lammi-Taskula, this volume). Also in Finland the new arrangement of two 'bonus weeks' of paternity leave for fathers who take at minimum the two last weeks of parental leave has doubled the (still very modest) number of male parental leave users, while at the same time the average length of leave taken by fathers has shortened (Kansaneläkelaitoksen sairausvakuutus - ja perhe-etuustilastot, 2003).

Family leave on a part-time basis is not popular

The opportunity to take family leave on a part-time basis has been promoted in Finland in recent years. However, parents of young children do not seem enthusiastic about this. The general idea of taking current parental leave as a part-time leave is wholly supported by only 5% of mothers and 11% of fathers. Part-time leave gets a little more support if the parental leave were to be longer than it is currently (Table 7.1).

Table 7.1: Opinions on parental leave among parents with young children in Finland (2002) (%)

	Mothers (n = 3,295)					Fathers (n = 1,413)				
	Fully agree	Partly agree	Cannot say	Do not agree	Total	Fully agree	Partly agree	Cannot say	Do not agree	Total
The current practice is good	28	46	7	19	100	23	45	9	23	100
It would be good if fathers took a longer parental leave	31	44	18	7	100	43	41	11	5	100
The take-up of parental leave should be divided such that fathers have a part of the current leave exclusively for themselves	9	16	23	52	100	13	18	21	48	100
The take-up of parental leave should be divided such that fathers have a period exclusively for themselves as an extension of the current leave	30	30	21	19	100	30	28	21	21	100
The parental leave period should be extended on current terms	40	29	19	12	100	37	29	21	13	100
An opportunity to take parental leave in part-time periods while extending the leave should be introduced	15	26	40	19	100	21	31	33	15	100
An opportunity to take the current parental leave in part-time periods should be introduced	5	17	46	32	100	11	24	39	26	100
An opportunity to take parental leave in part-time periods should be introduced as long as both parents shorten their working hours	3	9	52	36	100	4	8	46	42	100

What do the parents think of the newly enacted reform on *part-time parental leave*?[4] They are not in favour. The suggestion of the parental leave on a part-time basis where both parents shorten their working hours and share the care of the child is supported by a very small minority of the respondents: only 12% of both mothers and fathers are even partly in favour of the conditional part-time parental leave. Half of the respondents chose a 'Cannot say' reply to this question, that is, they were uncertain of their opinion on this matter.

To take a *partial care leave*, that is to shorten one's working time to a maximum of 30 hours per week, has been possible since the beginning of the 1990s. However, only 1,000 to 1,500 families yearly have taken advantage of this possibility, which is only a fraction of those entitled to it. The parent of a child under three years old has been entitled to a part-time care allowance, which was 63.07 euros per month at the time of the survey rising to 70 euros in 2004. The respondents were willing to consider taking partial care leave if the allowance were 170 euros per month.

Issues of uncertainty

What is striking in the parents' answers to the questions concerning parental leave is the large number of respondents who express their hesitation by choosing the 'Cannot say' option. This is particularly interesting as the issues in question are precisely the ones that have been much debated in public, namely the issue of men's share of the take-up of family leave and the issue of family leave on a part-time basis (see Table 7.1).

The question concerning men's take-up of parental leave puzzles particularly women. Even though the statement 'It would be good if fathers took a longer parental leave' was clearly supported (see Table 7.1), as many as 18% of the mothers were not willing to take a stand on this, while only 11% of the fathers made the 'Cannot say' choice.

It is interesting that so many mothers cannot say what they think about this issue in this survey when the Equality Barometers indicate that large numbers of people, irrespective of gender or age, want men to take greater responsibility for the care and upbringing of their children (Melkas, 1998, 2001, 2004). The percentage of women with this opinion has remained constant at 90%, whereas among men the share in favour of men's greater involvement in parenthood has grown from 86% to 89% in six years. But there is an interesting aspect also in the Equality Barometer findings: the share of women who completely agree with the need for men's increased involvement fell from 65% in 1998 to 58% in 2004 (Melkas, 2004). Has the lively debate on men's role as family leave takers led to second thoughts among some women? This might be explained by women wishing to have a long break from the demands of working life when they eventually, on average at the relatively high age of 27 years, start a family. However, the fathers who had been on leave also said the leave was a welcome break from hectic work (see also Lammi-Taskula, this volume).

Accordingly, we might ask whether the women who are currently in the baby phase of their family lives are less willing than other women or men to give up part of the parental leave they themselves feel entitled to. The answer, it rather seems, is that women want to extend the parental leave, and preferably on current terms, which at the time of the survey meant that the parents decide on the sharing of the leave between themselves. The women's responses do not necessarily need to be interpreted as expressions of selfishness, meaning that women want to take the whole leave themselves. Women might also think of this issue from the perspective of the child; they want to extend the parental leave in order to give the child a chance to stay in home care for a longer period of time.

The issue generating the strongest hesitation is the option of taking parental leave on a part-time basis. Almost half of the mothers and a third of the fathers could not or did not want to take a stand on statements regarding this issue. Women are more cautious than men here. This might be because women are more likely to be in part-time employment. The difficulty or unwillingness to form an opinion on this topic can also be connected with the facts that, first, part-time work is not very common in Finland, and second, those who work part time often do so reluctantly (Nätti and Väisänen, 2000; Lehto and Sutela, 2004). Possibly it is also difficult to take a stand because the option is not relevant for the respondent and they have not given it much thought.

Hesitation might also result from the respondent having given much thought to part-time work and its advantages and disadvantages. It might be difficult to figure out how one's own job could be rearranged on a part-time basis. Moreover, employers might not be very keen on this either. Another reason for hesitation might be that part-time work may lead to the employee working more intensively but getting paid for fewer hours.

Obviously, part-time work is always an income issue; there are circumstances where it cannot even be considered as a childcare option.

All women, irrespective of income level, were equally uninterested in taking the current parental leave on a part-time basis, but fathers in high-income families were more interested in this alternative (17%) than fathers in low-income families (7%).

Whose passion for what equality?

Equality paradox for women

The official aim of parenthood policy has been to secure women's and children's well-being and to promote social justice and gender equality, especially women's employment opportunities and men's role as parents. The goals regarding the health of children and mothers have been achieved. But the aims have not been achieved as regards the role of men as parents and the more equal division of parenthood and work in the family, not to mention the contradictory consequences that the long leaves have for the position of women in the labour market.

The family leave schemes carry an inherent equality paradox. They were created to support women to combine employment and family, but the practical realisations of the schemes are contradictory from the point of view of gender equality. On the one hand, the leave schemes do support women's participation in the labour market while also becoming mothers. Women also value the chance to take care of their children for a long period, and they are not necessarily prepared to shorten 'their' share of the parental leave.

On the other hand, however, the present leave schemes create a trap for women as long as family leaves are taken predominantly by women. First, in families, the gendered division of labour in housework and in parenting changes very slowly (Niemi and Pääkkönen, 1990, 2002). Second, in the labour market, women are regarded as less reliable employees as they are the ones expected to take the family leaves. As a consequence, women's labour market position is more precarious than that of men. In the 1990s, this expressed itself in the increasingly common temporary employment contracts of women (Sutela, 1999). The proportion of temporary employment contracts has fallen during the first years of the 21st century, but they are still quite common among 25- to 44-year-old women; that is, women of child-bearing age (Lehto and Sutela, 2004).

Home care allowance and parental choice

From the equality perspective, another counterproductive feature of the Finnish family leave schemes is associated with unemployment and the take-up of the home care allowance (HCA). The Finnish HCA, a form of cash grant for the care of children, was realised gradually between 1985 and 1990. The grant is paid to any parent whose under three-year-old child does not use the right to a place in local authority day care. The HCA is a flat-rate benefit and clearly smaller than the financial support during parental leave, except in cases where the parent on parental leave receives only the minimum allowance.[5]

The HCA has become highly appreciated by the parents of young children. Only 17 mothers out of the total of 3,295 female respondents in the Family Leave Survey thought this benefit should be abolished. However, the smallness of the allowance has been much debated during the past years. This has been an element in the debate on whether or not the families have a real choice between staying at home to take care of their child themselves and going to work and relying on the day care services. Hardly any respondents considered the HCA big enough; the respondents suggested it be increased by at least 33%. The allowance remained the same from 1996 until the end of 2004; from the beginning of 2005 it was increased by 17%.[6]

The chance to stay at home with a child and receive an allowance, even if a modest one, for those who were not previously employed, has had some quite particular consequences. Women who use the HCA seem to divide in two groups: those who use the HCA for relatively short periods, and those who take advantage of it for a longer period. The severe unemployment of the 1990s meant that the proportion of previously unemployed women among HCA recipients grew steadily (Salmi, 2000.)

The mothers usually make use of the HCA; only one in four of the female respondents to the Family Leave Survey returned to employment directly after the parental leave. On average, the mothers stayed at home until the child was 18 months old (44% of the mothers did so). Slightly more than half of the mothers (53%) were still at home taking care of the child two years after the birth. A third of these women were already on maternity or parental leave with the next baby. However, a number of them were officially unemployed or they combined home care of children with studies or part-time work. The biggest group (42%) of women who were still at home with a two-year-old did so supported by the HCA but without a job to return to (Lammi–Taskula, 2004; see also Ellingsæter, this volume.)

The findings of the Family Leave Survey confirm that the leave schemes create two categories of mothers. Mothers with a high level of education and better chances of employment can choose between a shorter or a longer family leave period. Mothers with little education and fewer opportunities in the labour market have fewer alternatives. If a woman has not had a job prior to the birth of her child, it is more probable that she will stay at home for a longer period supported by the HCA. The HCA has, to some degree, turned into an income source for unemployed women. It does not function only as an alternative to day care, as it was meant to, but also as an alternative to unemployment (Lammi–Taskula, 2004; Leira, this volume).

Contradictory rationales?

In Finland, the labour market organisations play an important role in the drafting of all laws governing working life. Initiatives to develop the family leave schemes have been taken in the tripartite income policy negotiations. But the tripartite system can also act as a brake. Before the parliamentary elections of 1999, the 'daddy month' was much discussed. Many political parties endorsed the idea in their election manifestos. Furthermore, a group of prominent paediatricians recommended 'obligatory paternity leave' to strengthen the role of fathers and to improve the well-being of children. This attracted much media coverage. A committee on the status of fathers proposed adding 25 working days to parental leave exclusively for the father. However, the coalition government formed after the election set up a new tripartite working group to plan changes to the parental leave arrangements. The proposals of the working group were ratified by Parliament in 2002. The reform included the new arrangement for the 'daddy month' and the opportunity to take the parental leave on a part-time basis, described above.

To shorten both parents' working hours and combine part-time work with the parents' sharing of the parental leave seems an ideal solution from the perspective of gender equality. It gives both parents a chance to learn to be parents, and at the same time maintain their position in the labour market. From women's point of view this solution is good as it would lessen their risk of becoming second-class employees arising from their predominant use of the family leaves. But does this ideal solution work in practice, with the current conditions set by the labour market?

We saw above that women and men who themselves are in the young children phase of their family life were not interested in arranging their parental leave take-up in the manner laid out in the new Act. Accordingly, very few families have so far used the part-time parental leave: in 2004 there were 84 persons in receipt of the part-time parental allowance; less than 0.1% of families with a new-born child have used the new arrangement.[7] The experience with this reform suggests that politicians and labour market organisations are more enthusiastic about part-time family leaves plus part-time work than the parents in this life phase. For parents it does not seem easy to make 'free choice' of the 'flexible' arrangements.

The rationale of 'flexibility' has repeatedly been raised in the Finnish debate on promoting men's take-up of family leaves. However, it has also repeatedly been pointed out that gender consequences are influenced by the level of leave benefits (Rostgaard, 2003; see also Haataja and Nyberg, this volume). If the benefit level is low, women are likely to take the leave instead of men who have higher income. This helps us to understand why men do not become more interested in the leaves, however flexible the schemes are made. In the Finnish case, there is a clear contradiction as the schemes are made more flexible while the benefits remain at the same level, or show only moderate rises compared to the losses in their real value, and compared to the level of benefits which the parents think necessary if fathers are to consider taking up the leave.

The 'free choice' and 'flexibility' rationales may contradict with the gender equality rationale, as they easily lead to women 'freely choosing' the long leaves; or at least, the rationales do not get more men to take parental leave as expected. In Finland, as elsewhere, we still face the situation where women's considerable long-term participation in the labour market (both in numbers and in working hours) has not been matched by a similar rise in men's activity in the home. It seems that more than 40 to 50 years are required to bring about a major change in men's behaviour.

Even the situation in working life seems contradictory. In the tripartite negotiations, labour market organisations agree on extensions to paternal leave and on part-time parental leave, but in the workplaces there is no wider enthusiasm to arrange jobs on a part-time basis. Also, men report that their superiors are more critical of parental leave than of the shorter paternal leave (Melkas, 2004;

Lammi-Taskula and Salmi, 2005). My conclusion is that promotion of a better combination of employment and family has to happen not only by means of family policy measures but also through working life regulation and especially in the workplace (see also Lammi-Taskula, this volume). The balancing of employment and family cannot only be an issue between mothers, fathers and the state; working life practices play an increasingly important role in how the statutory entitlements are processed into lived everyday life (Salmi, 2003).

The parents appreciate the subjective right to day care

If there was a high degree of puzzlement in the parents' opinions on certain family policy issues, the parents of young children do have a clear opinion on one well-debated issue of family policy. They strongly favour the unconditional universal right to day care and do not support proposals to restrict this right (Table 7.2).

A clear majority of the mothers and fathers fully agree with the statement that every child's subjective right to a day care place is unquestionable. One in six mothers and one in four fathers says that they wish to use the right to a day care place for the older child during maternity/paternity or parental leave with a younger sibling.

To restrict the right to day care to part time for children whose parent is on parental leave or unemployed is fully supported only by a quarter of the mothers and a fifth of the fathers. Three in five mothers and fathers are not ready to abolish the subjective right to day care for children whose parent is on parental leave. Neither do these parents wish to abolish the right if a parent stays at home unemployed.

The strong support for the right to day care is particularly remarkable as half of the female respondents were at home taking care of their children at the time of the survey. It seems that a substantial majority of even those women who themselves have chosen another care solution want to keep the right to day care intact.

The central organisation of the local authorities and the highest official of the Ministry of Finance have suggested that the universal right to day care should be restricted even though day care for all pre-school children was granted in Finland as recently as 1996. The introduction in the 1990s of this subjective right was a result of a long struggle, with many delays during the process and a thorough debate of the pros and cons of this kind of entitlement. The debate had, in effect, been going on since the 1960s, and centred on three aspects: whether 'the best interest of the child' is best realised in

Table 7.2: Opinions on the subjective right to day care among parents with young children in Finland (2002) (%)

	Mothers (n = 3,295)					Fathers (n = 1,413)				
	Fully agree	Partly agree	Cannot say	Do not agree	Total	Fully agree	Partly agree	Cannot say	Do not agree	Total
The subjective right of every child to a day care place is unquestionable	70	15	1	14	100	77	11	1	11	100
I wish to use the right to a day care place for my older child during my maternity/paternity and parental leave	17	16	17	50	100	25	21	17	37	100
The right to a day care place should be limited to part time only if either parent is on parental leave with a younger sibling	26	33	16	25	100	19	32	21	28	100
The right to a day care place should be abolished for a child whose parent is on parental leave with a younger sibling	13	20	10	57	100	13	16	11	60	100
The right to a day care place should be limited to part time only for a child whose parent is unemployed	24	36	12	28	100	19	30	14	37	100
The right to a day care place should be abolished for a child whose parent is unemployed	12	19	9	60	100	13	18	9	60	100

home care or in day care, the right of women to employment, and how to prioritise local authority finances. In spite of the thoroughness of the earlier debate, the universal right to day care is continually being questioned – and the arguments remain largely the same (Anttonen, 2003; Leira, this volume).

In the current debate,[8] the old issues of 'the best interest of the child' and of women's right to employment have been raised, but the father's role in the care of the child has not been brought in. In this debate on 'the best interest of the child' the blame is usually put on the mother. The old arguments of how a young child can develop a deep relationship with one person only, namely the mother – familiar since the 1950s (Vuori, 2001) – have been raised again by some child psychiatrists and nursery teachers. National and local authorities use these arguments to make the case for cuts in public services for children. Among politicians, these arguments are used by those who want to prioritise higher benefits for home care as an alternative to day care services. It is seldom taken into account that, in spite of the universal right to day care, only very few children under one, one in four one-year-olds and two in five two-year-olds are actually taken care of outside the home in Finland; the proportion of all children under school age using day care services is 46%.[9] During the years from 1999 to 2003 attendance rates show an overall stability; the proportion of pre-schoolers attending day care ranges from 46% to 48% (see Box 1.1, Chapter One; Figure 8.1, Chapter Eight). The extent of the supposed 'problem' of 'groundless' use of day care services was surveyed only after the debate had been going on for quite a while, and it was found to be small: of all children entitled to day care services, only 2% to 5% have a parent staying at home (Väinälä, 2004).

In the case of day care arrangements, the situation seems to be precisely inverse to the situation described above with the parental leave. Some politicians and experts want to question the universal right to day care while parents with young children are almost unanimously in favour of it. When a more equal sharing of family leaves between men and women is debated, an often-heard argument is that this is a decision for the families to make themselves. Now, in the case of using or not using the right to day care, families seem not to be trustworthy enough to make that decision. In the former case, the authorities are not supposed to intervene in the form of legislation; in the latter case they are, at least, advised to give their 'recommendations' to parents as to their choice of form of childcare.

More contradictory rationales in the future?

An interesting shift in the documented rationales of Finnish family policy has taken place recently. In the latest strategy document (Perhepoliittinen strategia, 2003), the explicit goals again have a more demographic tone, as the first goal states that until the target year 2010 'Values in society have changed and the position of families with children has improved such that more families can have the number of children they wish to have' (p 11). A familistic tone can also be detected, as in the second goal: 'The importance of home and parents in the care and upbringing of children has grown'. On the other hand, none of the five goals or the strategic guidelines address gender equality; gender in a deeper sense is not present in this document. However, the government has also prepared a Gender Equality Programme where issues of family policy and work and family combination as well as gender equality in working life have a strong role.

Will the development towards more equally shared take-up of family leaves between women and men proceed with the help of current solutions? They seem to be planned according to the wishes of politicians and labour market organisations more than the wishes or practices of the parents themselves. To point out this discrepancy does not mean that policies should be decided by opinion polls, but some reference to the parents' everyday life and wishes would do no harm. The tripartite negotiations that today play a strong role when parenthood policies are shaped seem to be more actively involved with sewing up the schemes with small reforms like a quilt than getting acquainted with the jigsaw puzzle of parents' everyday life.

Maybe the contradiction between intended equality aims and the real outcomes, or the equality paradox mentioned above, is also a product of a sectorisation of different policies. Decisions made within certain policy areas are not necessarily evaluated from the point of view of their consequences for other policy areas, neither during nor after the decision process. The interaction between decisions and consequences on different policy areas often becomes visible only if they are analysed taking people's everyday life as a starting point. This, however, is seldom the case when policies are planned or laws drafted.

The present policy priorities in Finland are tightly tied to calculations of the changing population structure. The government has set as its primary goal the raising of the employment rate to 75%. This is an ambitious goal in a country where both men *and* women are already active in the labour market to a high degree, and where women mostly have full-time jobs. The goal is also interesting in the light of the rationales of Finnish family policy discussed above. If we wish to take seriously the ideas of giving the parents the chance to take care of their young children themselves until the children reach the age of three, and a free choice between childcare at home or in day care, we have to ask, is the goal of a high employment rate compatible with these ideas? Apparently not, as the Organisation for Economic Co-operation and Development (OECD) in its appraisal of work and family arrangements in Finland has maintained that the HCA scheme is too generous and leads to too many women staying outside the labour market for too long (OECD, 2005). However, in 2003 in the child-bearing age groups 25-44, women's employment rate was between 70% and 83% and men's between 81% and 87%. These figures indicate that there are not many idle people to employ among those who compose the target group of family leave schemes.

Closer scrutiny shows there is more to consider. The goal of a higher employment rate has been set to secure a more solid tax funding. More people are needed in the Finnish welfare state to pay taxes for a longer period of time in their lives to make ends meet. Thus, even the demographic aspect is important: the fertility rate should be kept at least at the present level of 1.7. Now, international comparisons suggest that the relatively generous family policy schemes have a strong explanatory role when the relationship of high labour market activity of women and high fertility rate in Finland is assessed (Skrede and Rønsen, this volume). If the HCA, which parents unanimously support, was abolished, and the parental leave schemes and benefits kept at the present level, there is a risk of lower fertility as a consequence. Therefore, the employment rate priority may be in contradiction with the fertility rate priority in the long run. And, in the last instance, the employment rate priority is in contradiction with itself, if interpreted in the way the OECD has done, as it may lead to fewer employees and fewer taxpayers in the future. It remains to be seen whether the doctrine of gender mainstreaming of all administration and policy making within the European Union, recently included in the programme of the Finnish government, will lead to a better balance of rationales and outcomes of policies.

The Finnish experience shows that family leaves take women out of the labour market only temporarily. First, of the respondents to the Family Leave Survey, only a few women plan to stay at home after the HCA period is over. Second, women with permanent employment contracts returned to the labour market sooner than those without a job previous to the birth of the child. A substantial proportion (43%) of mothers of a two-year-old child who were still at home taking care of the child did not have a job waiting for them. However, a great majority (70%) of women on a long family leave plan to return to the labour market (Lammi-Taskula, 2004). If they do not succeed in their plans, the problem is not in the family leave schemes but in the availability of jobs, particularly permanent jobs.

Hence, I tend to disagree with the characterisations of Finland as 'a homemaker country' (Anttonen, 2003) and the claims that the 'traditional Scandinavian model of wage-earner motherhood' is changing because of the generous cash benefits (Sipilä and Korpinen, 1998). The family leave schemes give women a chance to stay at home temporarily, but it depends not on the women but on the labour market as to whether, and how soon, they return to employment.

We might see the contradicting elements of Finnish family policy as examples of the two opposing trends in the Nordic childcare policies, those of 'defamilisation' and 'refamilisation' (Leira, 2002). The introduction of comprehensive day care provision in 1996 might be interpreted as an indicator of defamilisation, but, as such, also as a late response to women's active participation in the labour market, which started in the 1950s and grew rapidly in the 1960s. On the other hand, the cash-for-care arrangement in the form of the HCA, and the popularity of this arrangement among mothers of children under three, might be interpreted as an indicator of refamilisation; attempts to promote men's active role as parents via legislation have also been interpreted as 'familisation of fathers' (Leira, 2002).

It has even been stated that Finland has 'abandoned the egalitarian design [of childcare policy] conceived in the 1960s and 1970s for a neofamilial blueprint' as an emphasis on 'building up publicly funded collective childcare provisions has been eroded by a relative consensus on the necessity of developing cash benefits' (Mahon, 2002, p 350). This assessment seems to ignore the introduction of the universal right to day care services, not to mention the comprehensive pre-school provision which took place in the latter part of the 1990s. Also, the 'consensus' is certainly 'relative': whether to develop HCA or day care services has constantly been a contentious issue between Social Democrats on the one hand and the Centre Party and Conservatives on the other. A shift towards familism can be detected but not such a dramatic move that Mahon sketches. Actually, all the five features she puts in her 'egalitarian blueprint' of childcare policy are in place in

Finland (although faltering in the case of parental leave to 'foster an equitable sharing' of parenthood).

Actually, there are in Finland two trends both from the point of view of policy declarations (Anttonen, 2003) and from the point of view of women's action (Lammi–Taskula, 2004); one in which the parents' role in families and the fertility rate are emphasised, and women stay at home with their young children for rather long periods of time and also have more than one or two children; the other which stresses the high employment rate and where women with a high education level have to grasp their chances in the labour market, which also includes having fewer children later in life. These trends have been named 'familisation' and 'defamilisation'. But to what extent are the actions of those women who 'choose' long family leaves, or postpone having children, actually a familistic or defamilistic way of thinking, and how much of a role do the current demands of the labour market and the often absent support for work–family balance in the workplace play? My question is: do such policy measures as the introduction of a comprehensive day care provision and an allowance for home care indicate those trends? Or are they rather concrete expressions of the struggle over public expenditure, of the weak position of family policy issues in the political agenda (in the case of the late introduction of full day care provision), and the developments of working life leading to more precarious conditions of employment and more hectic work tempo (in the case of the popularity of the HCA)? It remains to be seen to what extent men's more active participation in parenthood is restricted by the male breadwinner model of the traditional gender-differentiated 'familised family' and/or the complex demands, attitudes and practices of working life.

Even though one would not be tempted to recommend the Nordic welfare states as models for other countries, one would hope they will survive in the waves of the globalising market economy and be able, on their own basis, to carve out the complicated route to more real gender equality. 'The universal caregiver model' (Fraser, 1997), in which both women and men are active participants in the labour market as well as caregivers, may seem utopian. It would require a new view of masculinity in particular, but also a more widely shared view of women as both working and caring beings, and, moreover, a will to reorganise working life. On the other hand, do we get further without utopian ideas?

Notes

[1] The survey was posted separately to mothers and fathers. The return rate of mothers was 59%. As to level of education and labour market participation, the sample is fairly representative of the general female population in the same age groups. The return rate for fathers was 49%. It was not possible to include in the survey a subsample of fathers who had not taken any family leave. Accordingly, the data on fathers do not represent all fathers of children born in 1999.

[2] This situation has led to some confusion in international comparisons. Every child under school age (seven years old) in Finland is entitled to local authority day care services, or state-subsidised private services, but only slightly less than half of the children between 0 and seven years of age actually make use of this right.

[3] During the parental leave the mother or father on leave receives an allowance related to her/his income before the birth of the child. The average allowance is 66% to 70% of the previous income.

[4] It should be noted that at the time of the survey, this reform was only at the planning stage. Hence the respondents could not have any experience of this arrangement but only assessed it as a suggestion.

[5] The HCA was 252.28 euros per month at the time of the survey. Roughly a quarter of all women on parental leave receive only the minimum allowance as they have not had any income before the birth of the child. At the time of the survey the minimum allowance was 10.09 euros for each working day (six days a week).

[6] Families can also receive an addition for siblings and a means-tested addition. A family with two children will get the maximum addition if their monthly income is less than 1,693.65 euros. In 2000, the HCA could amount to a maximum of 672 euros per month, the average being 353.53 euros per month. Some local authorities, including those in the capital area where most families with young children live, pay a municipal supplement to the HCA.

[7] Non-published information from register data; e-mail information 20 January 2005 by senior researcher Pentti Takala, Social Insurance Institution.

[8] I do not have systematic research material to back up the picture I give of this debate. The picture is based on discussions in several seminars where I myself or my colleagues have been talking to and with these professionals about the position of children and the need to develop family policy. The picture is also based on debate articles by these professionals and local authority representatives, plus newspaper and television interviews with politicians and government officials.

[9] After the right to day care for all children under school age was introduced in 1996, there was hardly any change in the demand for day care services at national level.

References

Anttonen, A. (2002) 'Universalism and social policy: a Nordic-feminist revaluation', *NORA*, vol 10, no 2, pp 71-80.

Anttonen, A. (2003) 'Lastenhoidon kaksi maailmaa', in H. Forsberg and R. Nätkin (eds) *Perhe Murroksessa*, Helsinki: Gaudeamus, pp 159-185.

Borchorst, A. and Siim, B. (2002) 'The women-friendly welfare state revisited', *NORA*, vol 10, no 2, pp 90-98.

den Dulk, L., van Doorne-Huiskes, A. and Schippers, J. (eds) (1999) *Work–Family Arrangements in Europe*, Amsterdam: Netherlands School for Social and Economic Policy Research, Thela Thesis.

Fraser, N. (1997) *Justice Interruptus: Critical Reflections on the 'Postsocialist' Condition*, New York, NY: Routledge.

Haataja, A. (2004) 'Pohjoismaiset vanhempainvapaat kahden lasta hoitavan vanhemman tukena', *Janus*, vol 12, no 1, pp 25-48.

Hernes, H.M. (1987) *Welfare States and Woman Power*, Oslo: Norwegian University Press.

Jacobs, J. (1992) *Systems of Survival: A Dialogue on the Moral Foundations of Commerce and Politics*, New York, NY: Random House.

Kansaneläkelaitoksen sairausvakuutus – ja perhe-etuustilastot 1994-2003.

Katsaus perhepolitiikan haasteisiin: Sosiaali – ja terveysministeriön julkaisuja, 1993:8.

Lammi-Taskula, J. (2004) 'Äidit työmarkkinoilla – kahden kerroksen väkeä?', *Yhteiskuntapolitiikka*, vol 69, no 2, pp 202-206.

Lammi-Taskula, J. and Salmi, M. (2005) 'Sopiiko vanhemmuus työelämään? Perhevapaat ja työpaikan arki', in P. Takala (ed) *Onko meillä malttia sijoittaa lapsiin?*, Helsinki: Edita.

Lehto, A.-M. and Sutela, H. (2004) *Uhkia ja Mahdollisuuksia: Työolotutkimuksen Tuloksia 1977-2003*, Helsinki: Tilastokeskus.

Leira, A. (2002) 'Updating the 'gender contract'? Childcare reforms in the Nordic countries in the 1990s', *NORA*, vol 10, no 2, pp 81-89.

Mahon, R. (2002) 'Childcare: toward what kind of 'Social Europe'?, *Social Politics: International Studies in Gender, State and Society*, vol 9, no 3, pp 343-79.

Melkas, T. (1998) *Tasa-arvobarometri 1998*, Helsinki: Tilastokeskus, SVT Elinolot, 1998:1.

Melkas, T. (2001) *Tasa-arvobarometri 2001*, Helsinki: Tilastokeskus, SVT Elinolot, 2001:1.

Melkas, T. (2004) *Tasa-arvobarometri 2004*, Helsinki: Sosiaali – ja terveysministeriö, Julkaisuja, 2004:20.

Nätti, J. and Väisänen, M. (2000) 'Työajat ja työsuhteet kotitaloudessa', in A.-M. Lehto and N. Järnefelt (eds) *Jaksaen ja Joustaen: Artikkeleita Työolotutkimuksesta*, Helsinki: Tilastokeskus, Tutkimuksia 230, pp 45-65.

Niemi, I. and Pääkkönen, H. (1990) *Time Use Changes in Finland in the 1980s*, Helsinki: Tilastokeskus, Tutkimuksia, 1990: 174.

Niemi, I. and Pääkkönen, H. (2002) *Time Use Changes in Finland through the 1990s*, Helsinki: Statistics Finland, Culture and the Media, 2002:2.

OECD (Organisation for Economic Co-operation and Development) (2005) *Babies and Bosses: Reconciling Work and Family Life. Volume 4: Canada, Finland, Sweden and the United Kingdom*, Paris: OECD Publishing.

Perhepoliittinen strategia (2003), Helsinki: Sosiaali – ja terveysministeriö.

Rantalaiho, L. and Heiskanen, T. (eds) (1997) *Gendered Practices in Working Life*, London: Macmillan.

Rostgaard, T. (2003) 'Social care regimes – the configuration of care for children and older people in Europe', Paper presented to the ESPAnet Conference 'Changing European Societies – The Role for Social Policy', Copenhagen, 13-15 November.

Salmi, M. (2000) 'Analysing the Finnish home care allowance system: challenges to research and problems of interpretation', in L. Kalliomaa-Puha (ed) *Perspectives of Equality: Work, Women and Family in the Nordic Countries and EU*, Copenhagen: Nordic Council of Ministers, Nord 2000:5, pp 187-207.

Salmi, M. (2003) 'Forums of supporting work – family combination: social policy or workplaces?', Paper presented to the ESPAnet Conference 'Changing European Societies: The Role of Social Policy', Copenhagen, 13-15 November.

Salmi, M. and Lammi-Taskula, J. (1999) 'Parental leave in Finland', in P. Moss and F. Deven (eds) *Parental Leave: Progress or Pitfall? Research and Policy Issues in Europe*, Brussels: NIDI/CBGS Publications, pp 85-121.

Salmi, M. and Lammi-Taskula, J. (2005) 'Leave policies and research in Finland', in F. Deven and P. Moss (eds) *Leave Policies and Research: Reviews and Country Notes*, CBGS-Werkdocument 2005/3, Brussel: Centrum voor Bevolkings - en Gezinsstudie, pp 87-96.

Sauli, H., Bardy, M. and Salmi, M. (2004) 'Families with small children face deteriorating circumstances', in M. Heikkilä and M. Kautto (eds) *Welfare in Finland*, Helsinki: Stakes, pp 20-37.

Sipilä, J. and Korpinen, J. (1998) 'Cash versus childcare services in Finland', *Social Policy and Administration*, vol 32, no 3, pp 263-77.

Sutela, H. (1999) 'Fixed-term employment relationships and gender equality', in A.-M. Lehto and H. Sutela (eds) *Gender Equality in Working Life*, Helsinki: Statistics Finland, pp 137-152.

Väinälä, A. (2004) *Selvitys kotona olevien vanhempien lasten päivähoitotilanteesta, syyskuu 2004*, Helsinki: Sosiaali – ja terveysministeriö työryhmämuistioita, 2004:16.

Vuori, J. (2001) *Äidit, isät ja ammattilaiset. toisto ja muunelmat asiantuntijoiden kirjoituksissa*, Tampere: Tampere University Press.

Part Three
Work, family and the welfare state: redefining family models

EIGHT

Woman-friendliness and economic depression: Finland and Sweden in the 1990s

Heikki Hiilamo

Since the 1970s, a distinct feature of Nordic policies has been the primacy of gender equality as a policy objective (Nyberg, 2002; Björnberg, 2002). Family and parenthood policies have promoted opportunities for both parents to combine paid employment with joint responsibility for the care of their children. In the 1970s the proportion of women working outside the home increased steadily, and most children grew up with parents who shared responsibility for supporting the family. This marked a turning point also in the policy approaches to parenthood. Politicians justified the extensive investment in public day care with the fact that mothers had already entered the labour market.

Sweden and Finland were hard hit by economic recession in the early 1990s. In Finland the economy collapsed, budget deficits soared and unemployment spiralled out of control. Gross Domestic Product (GDP) fell by more than 10%, and the unemployment rate quadrupled to almost 17% (Kalela et al, 2001, p 3). Between 1990 and 1993, the number of Swedish people in employment fell by more than half a million, GDP fell for three years running and state finances showed a sizeable deficit (SOU, 2000: 3, p 38). The unemployment rate increased from 1.6% to 8.1% (see also Haataja and Nyberg, this volume).

In this chapter I will analyse family and parenthood policy developments in Sweden and Finland during the 1990s in respect to economic equality between parents. What happened to economic equality when the mature welfare states of Sweden and Finland were hit by a deep recession? In terms of economic growth the recession was soon over in both countries. However, the government had to deal with huge budget deficits for many years. I will take economic recession and recovery as a strategic case for examining the sustainability of the gender equality ambition.

Woman-friendliness in Sweden and Finland

From an historical perspective, the Nordic countries were among the first to introduce work/family reconciliation policies as part of a deliberate attempt to increase the number of women in paid employment (Gauthier, 1996; Alestalo and Kuhnle, 2000; Pfenning and Bahle, 2000; Nyberg, 2004). This reflects the fact that there was a political will to bring about economic equality between parents by means of policies that facilitate labour force participation by mothers. Earlier family policy instruments employed in the Nordic countries and elsewhere, especially in the 1930s and the 1960s, namely pro-natalism (increasing fertility) and facilitating female employment as a solution to labour shortages, were designed to serve the interests of the markets. In the 1990s, Nordic parenthood policy included extensive maternity and paternity benefits that had a long duration and high levels of compensation for lost earnings. Parental benefits were supplemented by extensive provision of public day care. The Nordic model earned a reputation for achieving low levels of child poverty and high levels of female labour force participation (see also Skevik, this volume).

Gender equality as an objective of family policy stresses the role of the state in family welfare. The concept of gender equality is based on the different rights and duties assigned by society to women and men. With regard to family policy this fact points to inequalities in the distribution of paid and unpaid work between fathers and mothers. To follow the argument, gender equality would entail female access to paid employment and male entry into unpaid work. This definition, however, does not cover all the social and economic disadvantages women suffer as a result of prevailing gender roles, and it does not pay attention to individual preferences of both women and men. The concept of 'woman-friendliness' introduced by Helga Hernes (1987) is based on the claim that the state should not force harder choices on women than on men. This implies that the institutions of family policy should be developed so that women do not have to choose futures that demand greater sacrifices from them than are expected of men. In a woman-friendly state women could continue to have children, yet there would also be other roads to self-realisation open to them (Hernes, 1987, p 15).

The Nordic countries have received international acclaim for the outputs and outcomes of their parenthood policies (for example, Hernes, 1987; Siaroff, 1994; Kamerman and Kahn, 2001). Scandinavian scholars have pictured the Nordic welfare states as the most woman-friendly welfare states (for example, Hernes, 1987; Korpi, 2000). However, criticism and warnings have also been expressed. Nordic parenthood policies have been subject to the same criticisms as welfare policies in general: high taxation, rigid legislation, clumsy institutions, excessive state intervention, disincentives to work, and benefit dependency, among other things. All of these features have been considered obstacles to competitiveness, which in this era of globalisation is argued to call for dynamic social structures that facilitate the free flow of goods, capital and labour.

Some critics have argued that state intervention has negative effects on the family as a social institution (Popenoe, 1988; Wolfe, 1989; Kaufmann, 1993). It is clear that the outcomes of Nordic parenthood policy with regard to, for instance, child poverty and female labour force participation are excellent in international comparison. This does not mean, however, that all of the objectives of parenthood policy have been fully achieved. There is so far very little information on the relationship between policies and the realisation of gender equality (Gauthier, 1995). For example, in Sweden, parents are allowed to share the greater part of the period of parental leave (Lammi–Taskula, this volume). However, only a minor share of parental benefits is paid to fathers (see Sainsbury, 2000). The critics have also construed the high proportion of women employed in the public sector as a new form of subordination, where women are stuck in low-paid jobs (for example, Gähler, 2001, pp 20-21). Moreover, as compared to, for example, the conservative model, the Nordic welfare state has been surprisingly unsuccessful in eradicating the gender differences in paid and unpaid work. In Swedish and Finnish two-parent families with a child of under five years of age, mothers who are employed on a full-time basis outside the home spend, on average, twice as much time on childcare duties as do fathers (OECD, 2001, pp 137-41).

The Nordic model had its heyday in the late 1980s, after which it went through a rough period (Kalela et al, 2001), especially in Sweden and Finland. The early 1990s meant more than a psychological break with the past: the very existence of a model based on full employment was endangered as unemployment rose to extremely high levels and the attendant income transfers dramatically increased social protection expenditure (see also Haataja and Nyberg, this volume). All areas of social policy underwent cuts and adjustments due to huge budget deficits and problems in raising loans to cover the increased expenditure. Family policy did not remain untouched, either: the universal child benefits were cut, the compensation level of parental benefits was reduced and parental fees for child day care were raised.

Both Sweden and Finland, although with some differences in institutions, stood out as among countries with the most developed family and parenthood policies in the late 1980s (see, for example, Siaroff, 1994; Kamerman and Kahn, 2001). How did family and parenthood policies in the two countries respond to recession and recovery? How did the aim of economic gender equality fare? In short: despite harsh economic conditions may Sweden and Finland still be labelled as women-friendly welfare states?

The analysis in this chapter focuses on the implications of family and parenthood policy reform in terms of economic gender equality, or more specifically the implication for women's economic autonomy. As far as is practicable, I examine the changes in the allocation of income transfers within families, the position of women (who usually have lower incomes than men) as recipients of benefits and services, the rights of women to benefits and the tax treatment of spouses (Sainsbury, 1994). We have to keep in mind that the policy measures are not additive; in effect, they might counteract each other, for example by increasing disincentives for women to enter the labour market (such as cash benefit for childcare programmes or home care allowance). Given the disadvantaged economic position of women, economic gender equality, in this case, goes together with woman-friendliness.

In the following a minimal definition of family policy is applied; expenditure on family policy is defined solely in terms of public costs, meaning costs recorded in the annual accounts of national and local government, and as applying only to income transfers and day care services for families with children. First of all I wish to investigate how the legislative amendments to family policy have affected economic gender equality. As I am studying retrenchment rather than reform (Pierson, 1994), I will not assess if the changes take countries towards a particular family policy or welfare state model. I will only evaluate whether or not a change signifies a departure from the Nordic gender equality ambition.

My approach to family policy change takes the following form: I will analyse the most important legislative amendments to family policy in the form of tax support for families with children, universal child benefits and parental benefits. The emphasis lies on parental benefits, as they were subject to several reforms. I also briefly discuss public provisions for day care, which is a central element of parental policies. Both Sweden and Finland offer day care at low cost on a universal basis. However, due to administrative differences in the systems it is difficult to make a comparison between the countries (in this volume, see Skevik for a separate analysis of benefits for single parents, and see Lammi-Taskula for an examination of fathers' entitlements as carers; see also Haataja and Nyberg). The chosen methods mean that single policy areas are compared one by one. The summary section will provide an attempt to compare the overall 'package of changes'.

The analysis is based on a simple, crude method where the content of the selected reforms is assessed in relation to economic gender equality as a family policy goal according to three outputs (compare Haataja and Nyberg in this volume). The effect may be:

(1) positive (marked +): that is, the reform promotes economic gender equality in the family policy system;
(2) negative (marked −): that is, the reform hampers economic gender equality in the family policy system;
(3) neutral (marked 0): that is, the reform does not affect economic gender equality.

'Positive' and 'negative' concern only the effect of changes on the characteristics of the ideal model. The starting point of the analysis is not to take a stand on whether the development has been 'positive' or 'negative' as such.

The analysis shows about the level of individual reform both the direction of change and its intensity using three grade scales (−/+,− −/++,− − −/+++). It is important to note that I only consider changes in family policy outputs (or policy content), that is, at the level of the tax/benefit system, and will not relate these changes to family policy outcomes. With regard to the realisation of economic gender equality, at this point I discuss only the first-round effects. This means that I will only look into the detailed rules and regulations concerning family benefits and will not assess how the affected population reacts to changes (see, for example, Lammi-Taskula; Salmi; Haataja and Nyberg, this volume). Moreover this analysis does not permit any far-reaching conclusions about the general development throughout the whole decade. The analysis shows only how the family policy system on output level has been changed in respect to economic gender equality.

Taxation of families with children

As recently as in the late 1980s, there were major differences in two aspects of the family and parenthood policies of Sweden and Finland:

home care allowance (see Salmi; Haataja and Nyberg, this volume) and family tax deductions. Sweden abolished the child tax deduction as far back as 1948, the same year that the universal cash child benefits system was introduced there. In Finland, in contrast, tax deductions were an important element of family policy until the early 1990s. Thereafter the situation changed quickly. In the so-called family support reform of 1994, except for a small deduction for maintenance liability, tax deductions for families with children were abolished and replaced by direct support, that is, an increase in the universal child benefits. Keeping the deduction for maintenance liability was justified on the grounds that it motivates the payment of alimony (Kaurala, 1993, p 26). Liable parents were able to deduct a small amount of the paid alimony.

Finland

Until 1993, a childcare deduction from state taxation was granted to parents of children aged three to seven. In spite of the separate tax assessment of spouses in Finland, this tax deduction in practice supported the traditional male breadwinner family model: parents could choose from which spouse's income the deduction was made, and it was more profitable to make such deductions from the income of the spouse with the better income, that is, usually the man's. The man was thus offered better chances – due to lighter taxes – to support the family. Further, the possibility of choice favoured families with two breadwinners at the expense of one-parent families. In 1993 the childcare deduction was significantly reduced, and it was abolished completely in the family support reform of 1994 (see Table 8.1). At the same time universal child benefits were raised. Although the immediate purpose of reducing and then abolishing the childcare deduction was to cut public expenditure, the measure in effect also promoted economic gender equality.

Regarding municipal taxation, until 1993, families with children were granted child deductions separately for each child under the age of 17. After application of the child deduction, it was possible for very low-income earners and/or families with many children to become entitled to a basic subsistence deduction, which reduced their taxes even further. Those without any income at all, of course, did not benefit whatsoever. Due to the basic subsistence deduction, it was usually profitable for low-income earners and/or families with many children to transfer the child deductions to the wife, who usually had the lower income; in theory, therefore, the deduction did not hamper economic gender equality in policy formulation.

Table 8.1: The effects of legislative amendments to taxation on gender equality

	Finland		Sweden
Childcare deduction (state taxation) – decrease 1993, abolition 1994	++	Spouse deduction – abolition 1991	++
Child deduction (municipal taxation) – abolition 1994	0	Deduction for reduced taxpaying ability – abolition 1992	–
Taxation increase for social benefits 1997	–	Deduction for paid maintenance – abolition 1991	–
Total	+		0

Note: 0 = no effect; – = negative effect; + = positive effect.

The single-parent deduction, granted until 1993, was similar to the childcare deduction; it applied only to municipal taxation. Unlike the child deduction, however, the single-parent deduction was applied only once, regardless of the number of dependants. Due to low incomes, however, relatively more single parents than two-provider families (approximately 6,000 single parents in 1989) could not benefit at all from this latter deduction (Perheturvan Rakennetyöryhmä Muistio, 1991, p 21).

Therefore, in the family support reform of 1994 the single-parent deduction was abolished, and replaced by special increased child benefits for single parents. This increase compensated for 86% of the tax benefit received by middle-income single parents with one child; for those with good incomes, the loss was somewhat greater (Hiilamo, 2002). Single parents with two or more children benefited from the reform, however, since the cash child benefit – unlike the single-parent deduction – was tied to the number of children. However, the clear majority of single parents in Finland have just one child. Moreover, in contrast to the procedure for the universal child benefits, single parents had to apply separately for the increased cash child benefits. Since most single parents are women with one child, the abolition of the deduction increased gender inequality. The prime losers with this revision were single parents cohabiting in a new common-law marriage who lost the single-parent deductions, but who – because of their common-law marriage – were not eligible for the special cash child benefits that replaced the abolished deduction (see also Skevik, this volume). This change thus increased the financial dependence of single parents living in common-law marriage on their partners.

In 1967 at the instigation of the Incentive Trap Committee (Kannustinloukkutyöryhmän... , 1996), the municipal earned-income deduction improved considerably, but at the same time, the deduction was abolished for taxable income transfers. The aim of this measure was to ease the taxation of those with low incomes and to overcome 'income traps', or in other words to increase the incentive to work. Thus, the taxation of families receiving maternity and parental per diem allowances, sickness allowances, and child home care allowances actually went up. The change enhanced gender inequality: it is usually mothers who receive the parental per diem allowances and child home care allowances.

Sweden

In the Swedish tax system after 1948, however, some features connected to the number of children in the family remained. In 1990, the Swedish tax system still had four tax deductions related to family policy: the deduction for a spouse (deduction from tax), the deduction for reduced taxpaying ability on the basis of the number of children in the family (deduction from income), the tax deduction of the person liable to provide maintenance (deduction from income), and the tax deduction of single parents (deduction from tax).

As a part of the major tax reform in Sweden, the tax deduction for single parents was abolished at the beginning of 1991 but was compensated for by introducing in May 1992 a temporary special allowance for single parents (SOU, 1995: 26, p 61). These special tax-free allowances were paid retroactively from the beginning of 1991 to the end of June 1993. Thereafter, social support to single parents was to be provided through housing allowances, but in practice, this compensation for the loss of the tax deduction remained only temporary.

In principle the most important family policy tax deduction was the spouse deduction (*hemmamakereduktion*), which was not directly related to children, but to the spouse. This deduction, made directly from tax, was granted to couples where only one of the spouses had earned income. The deduction was abolished, without any compensation, in the major tax reform of 1991 (Troedsson, 1999, pp 62-3). The abolition of the spouse deduction clearly promoted economic equality between spouses, as it abolished the last remnants of joint taxation and made labour force participation by both spouses a more profitable alternative. Note that it also reduced lifestyle choices.

The other remaining deduction was the deduction for reduced taxpaying ability (where the sum remaining after taxes was not enough for the minimum livelihood of the family). The deduction was also abolished in the 1991 tax reform, on the grounds that such families still had the possibility of applying for social assistance to pay taxes (Troedsson, 1999, pp 63-4). In the same reform, the tax deduction for maintenance payments (alimony, and so on) was also abolished. This was compensated for by reducing certain maintenance liabilities (SOU, 1995: 26, p 57). The abolition of the deduction for reduced taxpaying ability had a negative effect on economic gender equality, since single parenthood was one of the bases for entitlement to the deduction, and the overwhelming majority of single parents are women. The abolition of the deduction for maintenance liability weakened economic gender equality as maintenance liabilities were lowered and the recipients of maintenance are most often women.

Universal child benefits

Both quantitatively and in principle, universal child benefits are a very important element of family policy in Sweden and Finland; indeed, they constitute the backbone of the whole system (SOU, 2001: 24, p 115). The tax deductions, directed to spouses according to choice, are a family-oriented benefit, whereas cash child benefits, especially in the Nordic countries, are characteristically an individual benefit, usually paid to the child's mother on a universal basis (Wennemo, 1994). Child benefits promote economic gender equality, since the allowance is normally paid to the mother of the family, and the value of the allowance does not depend on the mother's position in the labour market. This increases the mother's economic independence and emphasises the nature of the allowances as an income to be used for the benefit of the child, not the family. Being tax-free the cash child benefits profit those with a low income more, because they form a larger proportion of the total income of low-income families than of those with a middle or good income. They constitute an important part of the income packages of, for example, single parents.

As the most visible form of family support, child benefits have been a very sensitive issue politically, probably because many voters' families receive cash child benefits and they are therefore every month aware of their direct impact on the finances of the family (Korpi, 1983; Kangas, 1994). This is reflected in the fact that all over the world the nominal level of child benefits has very seldom been cut (Wennemo, 1994). Of the variety of cuts made in benefits in Sweden and in Finland during the depression of the 1990s, it was probably the cuts in the universal child benefits implemented in both countries after the mid-1990s, that gave rise to most debate.

Table 8.2: The effects of legislative amendments to cash child benefits on gender equality

	Finland		Sweden
Increases in cash child benefits 1990 (two times)	+	Increase in cash child benefits 1990	+
Increase in cash child benefits 1991	+	Increase in cash child benefits 1991	+
Improvements in cash child benefits as compensation for deductions 1994	+++	Cut in large-family supplement 1994 and 1995	0
Cut in cash child benefits 1995	– – –	Cut in cash child benefits 1996	– –
Index adjustments discontinued starting from 1996	– –	Increase in cash child benefits 1998 (restoration of the 1996 cut)	++
Total	0		++

Note: 0 = no effect; – = negative effect; + = positive effect.

No major changes in principle occurred in the cash benefits system of either country during the first 40 years of the system, and no such changes took place in the 1990s either, although at that time – as Table 8.2 shows – legislation on child benefits underwent numerous minor amendments in both countries.

Increases in child benefits promoted economic gender equality in the early 1990s in both countries. Cuts in these benefits in July 1995 in Finland, and the abandonment of index adjustments to them, however, weakened it in the late 1990s, as did the cut in Sweden in 1996. However, another turning point for Sweden was in 1998, when cuts in child benefits were restored.

Paid parental leave in the 1990s

The rapid development of paid parental leave in Sweden and Finland (and Norway) from the early 1970s onwards distinguished these countries from the rest of the Western world (Gauthier, 1996; Lammi-Taskula, this volume).

Parental leave allowances are closely related to economic gender equality, since the purpose of the whole system is to level the costs of reproduction. In Finland and Sweden the majority of recipients of maternity/parental allowances are mothers. The difference between genders becomes greater if the values of the per diem allowances paid are examined (Sainsbury, 2000, p 96; see also Lammi-Taskula; Haataja and Nyberg, this volume). Because the level and implementation of parental allowances were unevenly distributed between genders, changes in per diem allowances directly affected economic gender equality. However, a decrease in the compensation rates of per diem allowances levelled the differences in net per diem allowances between genders, since men have higher incomes than women. The effect caused by progressive taxation was, however, fairly small.

In Sweden childcare leave for a sick child was paid when a child fell ill, the child's nurse fell ill or the child attended a public hospital or similar institution. The benefit was part of paid parental leave. The corresponding benefit was markedly weaker in Finland. The law guaranteed childcare leave for a sick child for one of the parents for a maximum of four working days at a time, to care for a child under age 10 suddenly taken ill. There was no benefit attached to the leave, and the employer was not obliged – unless under a collective agreement or it had been otherwise agreed – to pay wages for that time.

In broad outline, the systems in the two countries in the early 1990s were largely similar (see Haataja and Nyberg, this volume). Both in Finland and Sweden, the size of parental allowances above the minimum level was determined on the same bases as sickness allowances, that is, determined on the basis of earned income. Progressive taxation to some extent increased the net compensation rate of per diem allowances. Per diem allowances gave a strong incentive to participate in the labour market, because without earlier income the applicants were granted only a low minimum rate. Between the two countries there were, however, many differences in the details concerning, for example, compensation levels of per diem allowances, the duration of the payment period, and its structure.

Finland

In Finland, parental benefits before the 1990s consisted of three different elements: *maternity allowances*, *paternity allowances* and *parental allowances* (see also Lammi-Taskula; Salmi; Haataja and Nyberg, this volume). The right to maternity allowances started 30 days before the estimated due date. Only mothers were entitled to maternity allowances, and their duration was 105 working days. Parental allowances were paid for the following 158 working days to the mother or, alternatively, to the father if he remained at home caring for the child. Altogether the period extended to 11 months. At the birth of the child, subject to the mother's consent, the father was entitled to a paternity allowance for six to 12 days. Paternity

Table 8.3: The effects of legislative amendments to parental benefits on gender equality

	Finland			Sweden
Extension of parental allowances period 1991	+	Extension of temporary parental allowances period 1990		+
Reduction of compensation level 1992 and 1993	− − −	Deteriorations of temporary parental allowances 1991 and 1993		−
Shortening of parental allowances period 1993	0	Abolition of extended parental allowances (rise in minimum level) 1994		+
Minimum daily allowances raised to level of child home care allowance 1994	+	Reinstitution of extended parental allowances (fall in minimum level) 1995		−
End of payment of child increments 1994	+	Introduction of daddy month 1995		+
Reduction of minimum per diem allowances 1996	− −	Reduction of compensation level 1996 and 1997		− − −
Change in compensation levels 1996	−	Rise in compensation level 1998	++	
Total	− − −			−

Note: 0 = no effect; − = negative effect; + = positive effect.

allowances shortened the parental allowances period correspondingly. In Finland, three income brackets were used in the early 1990s, according to which the level of compensation fell as income increased.

As can be seen from Table 8.3, parental benefits underwent extensive change in both countries. This was due to policies to cut public expenditures. The levels of earning-related parental allowances fell in Finland very rapidly from the beginning of 1992 until the beginning of 1993. With these benefits cuts, carried out in three different stages, the percentage value of per diem allowances was reduced for all income levels, and the income limits of per diem allowance rates were tightened. A child increment (for previous child/children) of parental allowance was granted only to the higher-earning spouse, whose per diem allowances were determined on the basis of earlier earned income. Thus, the abolition of child increments from parental allowances at the beginning of 1994 applied mainly to single parents and to men who took paternity leave. The cut in the parental allowances period by 12 working days from the beginning of 1993 was a loss only to one-parent families and families where the father did not have the full two-week paternity leave when the baby was born. In other families, the shortening of the per diem allowances period was compensated for by the fact that the paternity leave in connection with the baby's birth was no longer discounted from the period of parental allowances.

In Finland, recipients of minimum per diem allowances include women who have, after the birth of their previous child and before a new pregnancy, remained at home caring for their children while receiving the home care allowance. In this case, the benefits for the following maternity and parental leave are not based on earned income. In 1997, minimum benefits accounted for 28% of all parental benefits and about 29% of benefits paid to mothers (Kela, 1998). The number of minimum benefit recipients was highest in 1996, when they accounted for about 30% of all recipients of parental benefits. As a result of the depression of the 1990s, the proportion of women receiving minimum maternity and parental allowances increased dramatically at the time (Keinänen et al, 1999). Before 1993, only 6% of parental allowances were awarded at the minimum rate.

Extension of the parental allowances period in 1991 promoted economic gender equality, as did the increase in minimum per diem allowances in 1994. The positive effect was, however, neutralised by the fact that minimum per diem allowances were reduced in 1996. The ending of the payment of child increments can be interpreted as having promoted economic gender equality. The earlier practice discriminated against women, because the supplement was granted only to the higher-earning spouse (however, single parents also lost the increment). Shortening the parental allowances period did not affect economic gender equality. It weakened the situation of single parents, but on the other hand furthered shared parenthood by guaranteeing fathers in practice a paternity allowance period of three weeks. Cuts in compensation levels in 1996 reduced equality as it was mainly women who suffered from the cuts.

Sweden

In Sweden, too, parental leave benefits consisted of three different elements in the late 1980s: *parental allowances, leave to care for sick children* and *pregnancy allowances*. However, measured in terms of the level and the coverage of the benefits, parental benefits in Sweden were significantly higher than in Finland. Besides, the benefits were broader (for example including leave to care for sick children) and their payment more flexible. Parental allowances were granted for 450 days (about

15 months) to those who remained at home caring for the child. The days of parental allowances were divided equally between both parents, and could be transferred between the parents at their own discretion. Single parents had the right to use all the days themselves. Earnings-related parental allowances were paid as a fixed percentage of earlier income (see also Lammi-Taskula, this volume). The per diem allowances were linked to earnings to a high maximum level. Government revised the threshold level annually to match inflation.

The mother was allowed to start the paid leave 60 days before the estimated due date. It was possible to get the allowances until the child had turned eight or finished the first class at school. It was also possible to take paid leave full time or part time according to choice. The compensation for the first 360 days was tied to the income base for per diem sickness allowances. After 1974, the maximum level of compensation amounted to as much as 90% of the recipient's gross income. Compensation for the last three months or 90 days (extended parental allowances) was paid at flat-rate minimum benefit (*garantinivå*). In cases where a new child was born in the family within 24 months of the previous child, the per diem allowances were determined on the basis of earlier income, thus the loss of income due to the birth of a child did not reduce parental allowances. This was a kind of 'speed bonus' (*snabbhetspremie*) for child bearers (Hoem, 2000). Without earlier employment (and after 360 days), the parental allowances were paid at the minimum rate. In the early 1990s this minimum rate was somewhat lower in Sweden than in Finland.

Year 1990 was a time when parental leave benefits were still being improved. However, reforms were fairly modest. At the beginning of July 1990, the maximum duration of leave to care for sick children was extended by 30 days, to 120 days a year. Lowering the level of compensation of parental allowances started in 1991. However, the reductions were initially small. The most significant changes were carried out towards the end of the 1990s. From the beginning of 1996, the level of compensation of parental allowances was cut to 80% except for 60 days (one month for the mother and one month for the father), for which the compensation was 90%. However, it was an improvement that parental allowances now included a month of paternal benefit (*pappamånad*); in other words, it was possible to divide the parental allowances between the spouses acting as guardians, but at least 30 days belonged to each parent. A year later the compensation level was reduced to 75%. However, the cut was restored in 1998.

The extension of paid leave to care for sick children in 1990 improved economic gender equality, since leave to care for sick children supported women's employment and the participation of both spouses in childcare. In addition, women tend to claim leave to care for sick children more often than men do. Correspondingly, deteriorations in paid leave to care for sick children in 1991 and 1993 promoted – although only to some extent – economic gender inequality. Cuts in the compensation and minimum rate of parental allowances in 1995 had the reverse effect.

In 1997 as many as 69% of the recipients of parental allowances were women (Sainsbury, 2000, p 96), as were almost 62% of the recipients of leave to care for sick children. From 1990 to 1998, the proportion of male recipients of parental allowances increased from 26% to 32%, but the proportion of male recipients of leave to care for sick children fell from 41% to 39%. A study by the National Social Security Agency (Riksförsäkringsverket) found that it is not only the level of parental allowances, but also attitudes towards shared parental leave that affect the number of men receiving parental allowances (RFV Redovisar, 2000: 1).

On the other hand, better compensation for fathers encouraged them to use their per diem allowances and thus promoted economic gender equality (Sainsbury, 2000, p 99). Earlier, the 12-day paternity allowance period dedicated to fathers had only shortened the parental allowances period, that is, the period that is to be shared between the parents. The introduction of the daddy month in 1995 promoted equality, as it furthered the division of childcare between parents. There were thus more changes furthering equality than decreasing it.

The final result is that during the 1990s the earnings-related levels of parental benefits in Finland were cut from 80% to 70%, from 50% to 40%, and from 30% to 25%. Revised income limits between the levels compensated the fall in the value of money for the first income level, but not for rising incomes. For the second income level the increases did not compensate even for inflation. In other words, the real level of compensation of per diem allowances also fell through the application of income limits. In Sweden, during the 1990s the level of compensation was cut from 90% to 80%. It should also be noted that the maximum value of parental allowances remained significantly higher than the income threshold for the highest level of compensation in Finland. Thus, parental allowances in Sweden, especially in the higher income brackets, were tied more closely to previous income than in Finland.

Public provision of day care and home care allowance

Although the comprehensiveness and levels vary, all Western European countries have direct income transfers to families with children, but few countries have such extensive social services for families with children as do the Nordic countries (Kvist, 1998, p 169). Social services for families with children are even considered 'the key to the Nordic welfare model' (Sipilä, 1997). Extensive public day care systems favour mothers' labour market participation, and therefore, they are a major factor in the realisation of economic gender equality.

In Finland, in 1990, all children under three were granted the subjective right to day care, expanded in 1996 to all children of pre-school age. This meant that municipalities were obliged by law to provide day care for every child under school age. Finland was the first country in the world to implement such a subjective right, but Sweden very soon followed suit (Anttonen and Sipilä, 2000, pp 128-9). These reforms finally made day care services universal in the strict sense of the word, and they promoted formal economic gender equality significantly. It needs to be emphasised that day care in both countries is affordable: day care fees constitute only 10% to 15% of the overall costs of day care arrangements (Hiilamo, 2002).

What is most striking is that expansion of day care took place at a time of austerity, when cutbacks were implemented in many other areas of social support. However, in practice the number of places in day care in both countries almost met demand even before the reforms. The share of children below school age in public day care increased only modestly in both countries (see Figure 8.1; and Nyberg, 2004; Hiilamo, 2005). In spite of statutory reforms, public gross expenditure on day care fell in both countries during the 1990s (Hiilamo, 2002, pp 208-9). As a conclusion we may note that the availability of day care improved in both countries during the 1990s but parental fees increased (Bergqvist and Nyberg, 2001).

As regards the cost of day care for parents, it is difficult to make a comparison between Sweden and Finland due to administrative differences in the systems. In Sweden, the administration of day care has traditionally been the responsibility of municipalities, which have extensive freedom in the fees that they charge: they determine the principles, level, number of payment classes, and income limits. Practices differed significantly in different parts of the country (SOU, 2000: 3, pp 117-8). Very little information on day care fee systems is available for the country as a whole. In Finland, municipalities had only limited

Figure 8.1: The share of children below school age in public day care (%)

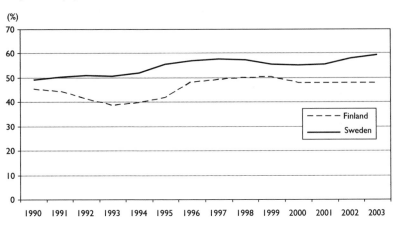

Source: Hiilamo (2005)

authority to make decisions on day care fees up to 1997. Since then, fees have been determined according to a national fee system.

Developments in the early 2000s

In the early 2000s the countries chose clearly different strategies with regard to family and parenthood policy. Sweden restored many of the benefits, and actually increased some of the others, for example universal child benefits. Meanwhile, Finland kept the cutbacks in force and allowed inflation to further erode the value of the family policy-related benefits (Hiilamo, 2004).

In 2000, the Swedish Parliament passed a resolution, which outlined that pre-school activity of at least three hours per day was to be organised for children of unemployed parents and the children of parents on parental leave (Timonen, 2003), extended parents' leave by one month and introduced a national day care fee table, which reduced fees considerably. Paid parental leave was extended to 460 days, 60 days of which are reserved for the mother and 60 days for the father (that is, cannot be used by the mother). In 2002, the minimum per diem allowance was doubled, and further increased in 2003 and 2004. The level of the universal child benefit was raised in 2000 and in 2002, and has since been higher in Sweden than in Finland.

The day care fee reform reduced parental fees to below the corresponding level in Finland (Hiilamo, 2004), and led to an improvement in the financial situation of most families with children (Persson, 2000, 2001; Ministry of Health and Social Affairs, 2002). The reform resulted in decreased marginal effects (work disincentives) for women with low incomes. It was expected that the reform would result in a 7% increase in labour market participation among women from low-income households (Government of Sweden, 2002, p 28).

In Finland a working group on universal child benefits called for extension of benefits to 17-year-olds in 2001 (Lapsilisätyöryhmän Muistio, 2001). The Ministry of Finance rejected the proposition, as it would have increased government expenditure. A minor increase in the child benefits was introduced in 2004. This did not compensate for the erosion of the benefits due to inflation from 1995 to 2004, let alone reverse the cut made in 1995.

After many years of stagnation, a minor increase in the minimum parental leave benefits was included in the budget for 2003. The minimum benefit remained below the nominal level in 1994 and 1995, and has since 2002 been at a lower level in Finland than in Sweden.

When it comes to housing benefits, it has to be noted that in Sweden individual income limits were introduced, replacing the previous reliance on joint gross family income in 1997. The means test was now to be administered individually, and families with large income disparities between spouses, for example families caring for a child at home, suffered from the reform particularly severely (Troedsson, 1999, p 99). The change improved economic gender equality, in that a higher income of one spouse no longer prevented the other spouse from receiving housing allowances. A similar reform was not discussed in Finland.

Conclusions

The cuts made during the depression of the 1990s did not lead to profound changes of direction in the family policy systems of either Finland or Sweden. The systems have retained their structural features, although they have become less generous. This holds true also as regards to economic gender equality. Paid parental leave suffered in both countries, hampering economic gender equality, while the abolition of tax deductions, and especially the expansion of day care services for children, promoted economic gender equality. The expansion of day care entailed a subjective right to day care; this meant that municipalities were obliged by law to provide day care for every child under school age, which in turn improved women's chances of combining work

Table 8.4: The combined effects of legislative amendments to family policy on gender equality

	Finland	Sweden
Tax supports	0	+
Cash child benefits	0	++
Parental benefits	– – –	–
Balance	– – –	++

Note: 0 = no effect; – = negative effect; + = positive effect.

and family life. Changes in universal child benefits, housing allowances and benefits for single parents had only minor effects on economic gender equality. It is possible to argue, however, that the general reductions in family benefits discouraged economic gender equality, since women are most often recipients of these benefits (Hiilamo, 2002, 2004).

If we compare the development in both countries it seems that there were more reforms that promoted economic gender equality in Sweden than in Finland (Table 8.4). This is mainly the result of more profound cuts in parental benefits in Finland. Some points of convergence are also visible, for example both countries gave up the last remnants of joint taxation. At the end of the 1990s Sweden was still ahead of Finland in parental leave benefits, while the universal child benefits were higher in Finland.

Again, it has to be noted that these results deal only with legislative amendments to family policy, and they do not concern gender outcomes. A challenge for further research is to contrast the changes in family policy institutions with family policy outcomes such as female labour force participation, fertility and poverty among single parents (Haataja, 2003, 2004).

In conclusion, we may note that economic gender equality, as an ideal goal for Nordic family policy, was not rejected either in Finland or in Sweden. However, the 1990s were a period of cuts more than of expansion. Compared with the 1970s and the 1980s there were only very few improvements. Individual taxation and the subjective right of children to day care (and individual income limits for the housing allowance in Sweden) make it easier for women to combine family life and paid employment.

In the early 2000s these two countries chose clearly different strategies with regard to family policy. Sweden restored many of the benefits, and actually increased some of the others. Meanwhile, Finland kept the cutbacks in force and allowed inflation to further

Table 8.5: Main family policy elements in Finland and Sweden (2004)

	Finland	Sweden
Tax supports/tax credits	none	none
Cash child benefits		
Amount of cash child benefit for the first child, euros per month	100	103
Extra benefit for single parent, euros per month	36.6	–
Paid parental leave		
Maximum number of weeks in which parental leave is payable	44	69
Replacement rate (%)	67	80
Minimum benefit, euros per month	275	548
Day care		
Entitlement	universal	universal
Maximum fee for first child, euros per month	200	137

erode existing benefits. The Finnish case could be labelled as 'permanent austerity' (Pierson, 1994), but that does not hold true for Sweden.

The different strategies may be partly explained by the fact that Sweden experienced a sharp fall in fertility in the mid–1990s (Hoem and Hoem, 1997). Declining fertility has been the strongest argument for developing family and parenthood policies through modern history (Gauthier, 1996). That was the case in Sweden as well (Hoem, 2002; Hiilamo, 2004). In Finland fertility remained at a comparatively high level through the 1990s. In the early 2000s the minor improvement in family benefits coincided with a renewed debate on long-run negative effects of below replacement rate fertility.

If we compare policy packages in Finland and Sweden in the early 2000s, Sweden proves a more woman-friendly country than Finland. More extensive paid parental leave arrangements and the lower cost of day care make it easier for Swedish mothers to participate in the labour market (Table 8.5). These changes in Sweden clearly promoted economic gender equality, and it seems that in comparison with Finland, Sweden is again the forerunner as it was in the 1970s.

References

Alestalo, M. and Kuhnle, S. (eds) (2000) *Survival of the Welfare State*, London: Routledge.

Anttonen, A. and Sipilä, J. (2000) *Suomalaista Sosiaalipolitiikkaa*, Tampere: Vastapaino.

Bergqvist, C. and Nyberg, A. (2001) 'Den svenska barnomsorgsmodelle – kontinuitet och förändring under 1990-talet', in Statens Offentliga Utredningar (2001: 52) *Välfärdtjänster i Omvandling*, Forskarantologi från Kommittén Välfärdsbokslut, Stockholm: Statens Offentliga Utredningar, pp 239-86.

Björnberg, U. (2002) 'Ideology and choice between work and care: Swedish family policy for working parents', *Critical Social Policy*, vol 22, no 1, pp 33-52.

Gähler, M. (2001) 'Bara en mor – ensamstående mödrars ekonomiska levnadsvillkor i 1990-talets Sverige. Ofärd i välfärden', in Statens Offentliga Utredningar (2000:1:54) *Forskarantologi från Kommittén Välfärdsbokslut*, Stockholm: Statens Offentliga Utredningar, pp 15-99.

Gauthier, A.H. (1995) 'Policies and the division of labour within families: the neglected link', in T. Willemsen, G. Frinking and R. Vogels (eds) *Work and Family in Europe: The Role of Policies*, Tilburg: Tilburg University Press, pp 243–65.

Gauthier, A.H. (1996) *The State and the Family: A Comparative Analysis of Family Policies in Industrialized Countries*, Oxford: Clarendon Press.

Government of Sweden (2002) *Sweden's Action Plan for Employment*, May, Stockholm: Ministry of Industry, Employment and Communications.

Haataja, A. (2003) 'How does motherhood and fatherhood 'pay' after the policy reforms of the 1990's in Finland?', Paper presented at 'Modelling our Future', International Microsimulation Conference on Population and Ageing, Canberra, 7-12 December.

Haataja, A. (2004) 'Pohjoismaiset vanhempainvapaat kahden lasta hoitavan vanhemman tukena', *Janus*, vol 12, no 1, pp 25-48.

Hernes, H.M. (1987) *Welfare State and Women Power: Essays in State Feminism*, Oslo: Norwegian University Press.

Hiilamo, H. (2002) *The Rise and Fall of Nordic Family Policy?: Historical Development and Changes during the 1990s in Sweden and Finland*, Helsinki: Stakes.

Hiilamo, H. (2004) 'Changing family policy in Sweden and Finland during the 1990s', *Social Policy and Administration*, vol 38, no 1, pp 21-40.

Hiilamo, H. (2005) 'Subjektiivisen päivähoito-oikeuden toteutuminen Ruotsissa ja Suomessa 1990-luvulla', in P. Takala (ed) *Onko Mmeillä Malttia Sijoittaa Lapsiin?*, Helsinki: Kelan tutkimusosasto, pp 58-79.

Hoem, B. (2000) 'Utan jobb – inga barn. Fruktsamhetsutvecklingen under 1990- talet. Välfärdens förutsättningar', in Statens Offentliga Utredningar (2000: 37), *Forskarvolym från Kommittén Välfärdsbokslut*, Stockholm: Statens Offentliga Utredningar, pp 119-43.

Hoem. B. and Hoem, J.M. (1997) *Sweden's Family Policies and Roller-coaster Fertility*, Stockholm Research Reports on Demography 115, Stockholm: Stockholm University.

Kalela, J., Kiander, J., Kivikuru, U., Loikkanen, H.A. and Simpura, J. (2001) *Down from Heavens, Up from the Ashes: The Finnish Economic Crisis of the 1990s in the Light of Economic and Social Research*, Helsinki: VATT.

Kamerman, S. and Kahn, A. (2001) 'Child and family policies in an era of policy retrenchment and restructuring', in K. Vleminckx and T. Smeeding (eds) *Child Well-Being, Child Poverty and Child Policy in Modern Nations: What Do We Know?*, Bristol: The Policy Press, pp 501–26.

Kangas, O. (1994) 'Tarveharkinta ja yhteiskuntaluokat – pohjoismaisen universalismin tausta', *Janus*, vol 2, no 1, pp 25-35.

Kannustinloukkutyöryhmän Loppuraportti (1996) *Kannustinloukkutyöryhmän Loppuraportti*, Helsinki: Valtioneuvoston kanslian julkaisuja.

Kaufmann, F.-X. (1993) *Familienpolitik in Europa: In 40 Jahre Familienpolitik in der Bundesrepublik Deutschland. Rückblick-Ausblick*, Neuwied: Luchterhand.

Kaurala, M. (1993) *Yksinhuoltajat ja Elatusvelvolliset – Taloudellinen Asema ja Tukivaihtoehdot*, Helsinki: Sosiaali – ja terveysministeriön monisteita.

Keinänen, P., Savola, L. and Sauli, H. (1999) 'Suhdanteet, sosiaalipolitiikka ja naisen paikka', *Hyvinvointikatsaus*, no 3, pp 34-36.

Kela (1998) *Kansaneläkelaitoksen Tilastollinen Vuosikirja 1997*, Kansaneläkelaitoksen Julkaisuja, Vammala: Kela.

Korpi, W. (1983) *The Democratic Class Struggle*, London: Routledge and Kegan Paul.

Korpi, W. (2000) 'Faces of inequity: gender, class and patterns of inequalities in different types of welfare states', *Social Politics*, vol 7, Summer, pp 127-91.

Kvist, J. (1998) *New Perspectives in Comparative Social Policy*, Odense: Odense University and The Danish National Institute of Social Research.

Lapsilisätyöryhmän Muistio (2001) *Lapsilisätyöryhmän Muistio*, Helsinki: STM Työryhmämuistioita (2000: 26).

Ministry of Health and Social Affairs (2002) *Swedish Family Policy: Fact Sheet no 5, April 2002*, Stockholm: Ministry of Health and Social Affairs.

Nyberg, A. (2002) 'Gender, (de)commodification, (in)dependence, and autonomous households: the case of Sweden', *Critical Social Policy*, vol 22, no 1, pp 72-95.

Nyberg, A. (2004) 'Parental insurance and childcare in Sweden', in Peer review programme of the European Employment Strategy, European Commission, DG Employment and Social Affairs (available at: www.almp.org/en).

OECD (Organisation for Economic Co-operation and Development) (2001) 'Balancing work and family life: helping parents into paid employment', in *Employment Outlook: June 2001*, Paris: OECD, pp 129-66.

Palme, J. (2000) 'Socialförsäkring och kontanta familjestöd', in Statens Offentliga Utredningar (2000: 40) *Välfärd och Försörjning, Antologi från Kommittén Välfärdsbokslut*, Stockholm: Statens Offentliga Utredningar, pp 61–86.

Perheturvan Rakennetyöryhmän Muistio (1991) *Perheturvan Rakennetyöryhmän Muistio*, Helsinki: Sosiaali – ja terveysministeriö työryhmämuistio (1991: 4).

Persson, G. (2000) 'Government policy 2000', Speech by the Prime Minister to the Parliament of Sweden, 19 September 2000 (unofficial translation).

Persson, G. (2001) 'Government policy 2001', Speech by the Prime Minister to the Parliament of Sweden, 18 September 2001 (unofficial translation).

Pfenning, A. and Bahle, T. (eds) (2000) *Families and Family Policies in Europe: Comparative Perspectives*, Frankfurt am Main: Peter Lang.

Pierson, P. (1994) *Dismantling the Welfare State?*, Cambridge: Cambridge University Press.

Popenoe, D. (1988) *Disturbing the Nest: Family Changes and Decline in Modern Societies*, New York, NY: Aldine de Gruyter.

RFV Redovisar (1995) *Bostadsbidrag till Barnfamiljer m fl*, Stockholm: Riksförsäkringsverket.

RFV Redovisar (2000:1) *Båda blir Bäst: Attityden till Delad Föräldraledighet*, Stockholm: Riksförsäkringsverket.

Sainsbury, D. (1994) 'Women's and men's social rights: gendering dimensions of welfare states', in D. Sainsbury (ed) *Gendering Welfare States*, London: Sage Publications, pp 150–69.

Sainsbury, D. (2000) 'Välfärdsutvecklingen för kvinnor och män på 1990-talet', in Statens Offentliga Utredningar (2000: 40) *Välfärd och Försörjning, Antologi från Kommittén Vältfärdsbokslut*, Stockholm: Statens Offentliga Utredningar.

Siaroff, A. (1994) 'Work, welfare and gender equality: a new typology', in D. Sainsbury (ed) *Gendering Welfare States*, London: Sage Publications, pp 82–100.

Sipilä, J. (ed) (1997) *Social Care Services: The Key to the Scandinavian Welfare Model*, Avebury. Aldershot.

SOU (1995: 26) *Underhållsbidrag och Bidragsförskott, Betänkande av Underhållsbidrags- och Bidragsförskottsutredningen −93*, Stockholm: Statens Offentliga Utredningar.

SOU (2000: 3) *Välfärd vid Vägskäl, Kommittén Välfärdsbokslut − Delbokslutet*, Stockholm: Statens Offentliga Utredningar.

SOU (2001: 24) *Ur Fattigdomsfällan, Slutbetänkande från Kommittén Familjeutredningen*, Stockholm: Statens Offentliga Utredningar.

Timonen, V. (2003) *Restructuring the Welfare State: Globalisation and Social Policy Reform in Finland and Sweden*, Cheltenham: Edward Elgar.

Troedsson, I. (1999) *Den Kommenderade Familjen: 30 år med Alva Myrdals Familjepolitik*, Stockholm: Timbro.

Wennemo, I. (1994) *Sharing the Cost of Children: Studies on the Development of Family Support in the OECD countries*, Edsbruk: Akademitryck.

Wolfe, A. (1989) *Whose Keeper? Social Science and Moral Obligation*, Berkeley, CA: University of California Press.

NINE

Working time and caring strategies: parenthood in different welfare states

Thomas P. Boje

Introduction

The aims of this chapter are to examine how parents manage their work and caring obligations, to identify which working and caring arrangements help parents balance their obligations, and how parents' strategies are influenced by welfare state policies. Of particular interest is the impact of flexible working time as well as different types of care policies in creating a more gender-balanced division of labour in families. It is widely recognised that mothers' involvement in employment and their caring obligations differ strongly, depending on norms and values as well as the profile of family and caring policies in different welfare states (Millar and Warman, 1996; Gornick et al, 1997; Leira, 2002; Brannen et al, 2004). Thus in order to understand mothers', and fathers', work and care practices it is necessary to examine gender-specific norms embedded in social structures and in women's and men's decisions related to employment and family.

Most of the literature dealing with the interface between work and family focuses on the state–labour market relationship and on how to integrate women into paid labour (Lewis 1992, 2002; Esping-Andersen, 1990, 1999; Lister, 2002). The weakness of the state–labour market approach, however, is that it primarily describes women's socioeconomic position and the impact of the welfare state policies on their employment conditions. It fails to explain why the gendered division of paid and unpaid work has been so persistent in all European countries (Ellingsæter, 1998; Pfau-Effinger, 1998). This chapter compares mothers' and fathers' participation in paid work and in care, and the work–family conflict they experience, in four countries, the two Nordic countries Denmark and Sweden, the Netherlands and the UK. The four countries represent three different social structures concerning norms and values for parenthood as well as in the profile of family and caring policies in Northern Europe (Perron et al, 1998; Esping-Andersen, 1990, 1999; Gallie and Paugam, 2000). Denmark and Sweden represent the Nordic welfare model. Both countries score high on equal opportunities and are characterised by working-time regimes with few disincentives against gender equality, and an active policy on reconciling work and family is pursued. However, there is also considerable variation among the countries, and within the countries among different groups of families.

Intra-Nordic comparisons reveal significant differences between Denmark and Sweden in the type of employment regulation, working-time regimes and policies such as the provision of childcare services, leave arrangements and cash transfers (see, for example, Leira, 1992; Anttonen and Sipilä, 1996; Ellingsæter, 1998; Leira, 2002; Abrahamson et al, 2005). Labour relations are highly regulated in both Scandinavian countries but in different ways. Employment protection and working hours are in Sweden regulated according to statute and in Denmark according to collective agreements. Looking at family policy models we also find marked differences between the two Scandinavian countries. The Swedish leave system has traditionally been more flexible in combining parental leave and gainful employment, the leave period is more extended in time, the period to be taken by the secondary carer − normally the father − is longer and the income compensation has been more generous than in the Danish system (Boje and Almqvist, 2000). The supply of day care services has been better in Denmark.

The Netherlands is characterised by a working-time regime that encourages individualised arrangements, but without a comprehensive childcare policy it has been impossible to achieve even a modest level of gender equity in terms of work and care. The Dutch social policy system is highly segmented with respect to both benefits and services. Services are organised according to religion. Often they are attached to one's job (Remery et al, 2002). Consequently, the Netherlands holds a position at the bottom among European countries on equal opportunities. The UK, on the other hand, scores medium on several employment indicators for women, but extremely low both on a consistent childcare policy and on a working-time regime favourable to women. It is a paradox that the UK, despite having a market-driven, highly expensive and individualised care system and until recently a meagre provision of paid parental leave, has a relatively high level of female employment. However, most women in the UK are employed on a part-time basis and in contingent jobs, which typically are low paid (Lewis, 1992; Plantenga and Hansen, 1999a; Warren, 2000).

The empirical data used in the comparison in this chapter derives partly from different Organisation for Economic Co-operation and Development (OECD) databases and partly from a large comparative data set collected within the 'Household, Work and Flexibility' (HWF) project (see Wallace, 2002, 2003b). The HWF survey used a common questionnaire on random samples in eight European Union and candidate countries. The interviews were carried out in spring 2001. The questionnaire was designed to cover the combination of paid and unpaid work among household members and map the strategies pursued by the household members in dealing with work as well as family responsibilities. Here I have used the data sets for the Netherlands, Sweden and the UK. In Sweden 1,287 households were interviewed, in the Netherlands 1,008 households and in the UK 945 households. In Denmark a similar survey was completed in the autumn of 2004, with 1,408 households interviewed.

The chapter takes the following form. First the level of employment and working-time strategies among mothers and fathers are examined. A main point is to explore social differences among groups of women and how different types of care obligation influence their working time. The second part discusses how the chosen work–care strategies can be explained by the different childcare policies developed in the four countries. How parents themselves experience work–family conflicts, and discrepancies between actual and preferred working time are discussed in the third part. Finally, the implications for gender equality of different strategies in organising working time and care are elaborated.

Working time – differentiation and polarisation

Changes in women's employment pattern have been conceptualised in terms of integration, differentiation and polarisation. The increasing integration of women into the labour market has been analysed in a large number of comparative studies and will not be the main objective of this chapter. Instead, I want to focus on processes of differentiation and polarisation in the conditions under which households are managing work and care obligations within different welfare systems. These processes are most evident at the household level with a growing polarisation in employment relations, income and social inclusion between 'work-rich/high-income' households and a continuing

Table 9.1: Women's employment rates and the gender employment gap by presence of children (2000), for women aged 25-54 (%)

	No children		One child		Two or more children	
	Employment rate	Gender gap	Employment rate	Gender gap	Employment rate	Gender gap
Denmark	78.5	7.7	88.1	3.5	77.2	12.9
Netherlands	75.3	5.6	69.9	24.3	63.3	30.8
Sweden	81.9	– 0.4	80.6	9.8	81.8	9.4
UK	79.9	5.4	72.9	17.1	62.3	28.2
Variation between countries	6.6	16.0	18.2	20.8	19.5	21.4

Source: OECD (2002, p 77, table 9.1)

significant proportion of 'work-poor/low-income' households (see, for example, Brannen, 1998). Polarisation in women's and men's labour market affiliation is thus unfolding along many different dimensions and here I shall focus on family status, employment conditions, working time and level of education.

Employment rates for mothers and fathers

Table 9.1 shows the employment rates for women with and without children below the age of 15 in the four countries.

Having responsibility for small children in Denmark and Sweden does not mean that women are forced to give up employment. In Denmark the rate of employment even increases among mothers with one child compared to non-mothers but falls again for mothers with two or more children. Among Swedish women the rates of employment are nearly constant whether they have children or not. Both Denmark and Sweden have significantly higher rates of employment for mothers and lower gender employment gaps between mothers and fathers than all other European countries. Other studies have reached a similar conclusion: becoming a mother has little impact on women's overall employment rate and may even increase the rate of employment for some groups of women in Denmark and Sweden (Rubery et al, 1999). However, for Sweden a significant proportion of the mothers maintain their labour market affiliation by reduced working hours while their children are young (see Table 9.2).

In most other European countries becoming a mother means

that women leave the labour market in large numbers because of difficulties in reconciling work and caring for small children, and as a consequence of the prevailing division of labour within families. A majority of both UK and Dutch mothers who remain in the labour market have significantly reduced their weekly working hours. In both countries, women's employment rates thus decline markedly when becoming mothers, and the difference between women's and men's rates of employment – the gender gap – increases when they become parents. A polarisation takes place both between mothers and non-mothers, and between fathers and mothers, when women have to combine work with caring for small children.

Fathers, on the other hand, seem to be more strongly involved in the labour market than non-fathers (Rubery et al, 1999, pp 106-7). In all four countries fathers have rates of employment of more than 90% irrespective of the number of children and this is significantly higher than among non-fathers in all countries.

The polarisation in women's labour market position takes place not only within the countries, but also between them. According to a study by Jacobs and Gornick (2001) based on Luxembourg Income Study (LIS) data, the large majority of Scandinavian couples are dual-earner couples while this is only the case for about half of the couples in the Netherlands and the UK. Similarly, for Dutch and UK couples, having children below the age of 15 results in a significant reduction in women's labour market participation, while women's status in Scandinavia is almost unchanged. For men, the presence of children in the family increases the level of labour market participation in all four countries.

The increased polarisation between mothers and non-mothers in their labour market affiliation took place during the 1990s when the level of employment increased for nearly all groups of women in Europe. The growth in female rates of employment is more pronounced for mothers living in couples than for lone parents – who primarily are lone mothers (OECD, 2001). The increase in women's employment rates is especially remarkable for the Netherlands. For Dutch women the rate of employment has nearly doubled, although from a low level in 1989 compared with the other three countries. In Sweden, on the other hand, the economy experienced a downturn and the overall rate of employment fell significantly in the early 1990s (see Haataja and Nyberg, this volume). This applied particularly to mothers, and a polarisation was found between different groups of mothers.

The fall in the rate of employment was markedly more dramatic for lone mothers than for mothers living in couples. Lone mothers together with low-educated immigrants are the two social groups for which the labour market conditions have been deteriorating continuously in Sweden ever since the late 1980s (see Åberg et al, 1997). In Denmark also, mothers – and especially lone mothers – experienced a marked fall in employment during the early 1990s in combination with the economic recession, but rates of employment for Danish mothers have recovered during the late 1990s. Today, Danish mothers as a group have about the same level of employment as in the late 1980s, while lone mothers are still some percentage points behind (see also Plantenga and Hansen, 1999b; Rubery, Grimshaw and Smith, 2001).

Level of education is another dimension that differentiates between mothers and non-mothers. Level of education seems thus to be crucial for their possibilities of obtaining employment when they have caring obligations, as well as for their abilities to reconcile work and family obligations (OECD, 2002, p 80). Looking at the effects of the presence of children on mothers' employment, the OECD finds that mothers with low education are more often out of employment and less often in full-time jobs than non-mothers. Both concerning motherhood and education, the differences are more pronounced in the Netherlands and the UK than in the Scandinavian countries. In both Denmark and Sweden the policies of parenthood have been more comprehensive than in the Netherlands and the UK and this has to some extent reduced the effects of motherhood on labour market involvement for women with higher education (OECD, 2002, p 81).

In all four countries mothers with high education have higher employment rates than those with lower education. But probably more important is that the involvement in full-time work increases more sharply than for part-time employment with level of education for all countries except the Netherlands, where the overwhelming majority of women work part time (see Rubery et al, 1999, p 109; Visser, 2000). For mothers with low education the rate of employment is stagnating, and in the UK and the Netherlands even falling, resulting in a polarisation both between mothers and non-mothers, as well as within the group of mothers (OECD, 2001, p 133).

Flexibility in employment and working time by gender

Transformation of the industrial structure as well as work organisation has changed the employment conditions for large groups of the labour force. This development has caused a strong pressure for more flexible use of labour and a more flexible organisation of firms (Sennett, 1998). Castells concludes his comprehensive analysis of flexibility by saying that the traditional form of work based on full-time employment and long tenure has been slowly eroded, and instead different types of non-standard employment contracts have been introduced (Castells, 1996, p 268). The 'non-standard' employment contract is characterised by lack of continuous employment and variability in work schedule (Boje and Grönlund, 2003, p 188). It is primarily men's employment conditions that have changed. According to Dex and McCulloch (1997), women have always been in the majority in the so-called 'non-standard' types of employment, and they have learned to cope with the insecure and tenuous employment conditions.

'Non-standard' types of employment and flexibilisation in general are gendered. The definition of 'non-standard' employment contracts is closely related to flexible employment and includes typically temporary work, contract work, part-time employment, certain categories of self-employed persons, sub-contracted work and work at home (see Dex and McCulloch, 1997; Purcell et al, 1999). The level of flexibility accomplished by introducing these new types of employment contracts varies, however, tremendously, depending upon which measure of flexibility is being used, and takes different forms depending on the system of employment regulation. Self-employment is primarily male-dominated and part-time employment is overwhelmingly a female type of employment while temporary employment seems to be more gender-balanced at least in the two Scandinavian countries (European Commission, 2002, pp 173-80). Here I will not go into a more detailed discussion of flexibilisation and its impact on the working conditions of men and women, as the focus will be on working time and continuity in employment and how these two dimensions of flexibility influence the conditions of parenthood in different welfare systems.

On the one hand, standardisation of working time has strengthened the workers in their fight for a regulated and normal working day but, on the other hand, it has been argued that the criteria for regulating working hours have been settled based on norms prevailing in the Fordist type of production – male, skilled full-time workers in manufacturing (Hinrichs et al, 1991). With growth in service sector employment and still more women in gainful employment, working-time preferences have generally become more diverse (Meulders et al, 1997). We know from our studies – both national and comparative –

that women want to work even if the return is low but they also want flexible work schedules and comprehensive periods with leave for care in addition to high-quality childcare (Wallace, 2002, 2003b).

Flexibility in work organisation and in working-time schedules is often seen as an opportunity for both women and men to handle the conflicts between work, care and family obligations, but this is only the case if flexibility is controlled by the employees and not imposed by the firms. Asking employees who makes the decisions on the number of hours they work it is clear that a larger proportion of men than women in all four countries decide themselves the length of working hours and how they are scheduled (Wallace, 2003b, pp 190-1). A recent Swedish study of flexibility and gender based on detailed interviewing of both employers and employees confirms this result: it is primarily the male-dominated types of flexibility that are controlled by the employees, and not the female-dominated types of flexibility (Grönlund, 2004).

Variability in working time is considered as an important type of flexibility. The use of part-time workers as well as overtime and long hours as a 'buffer' when demand for products and services changes and the fact that part-time schedules can more easily be changed than full-time schedules are important elements of flexibility. The pattern of working time is highly gendered in all labour markets. Only a small proportion of men work less than full time, whereas the proportion of women working part time is large (see Table 9.2).

The overwhelming majority of men in all countries, except Denmark, work 40 hours or more. In the UK, a significant group of about 30% works even more than 50 hours per week, while it is the case for about 20% in both Sweden and the Netherlands (see Visser, 2000; den Dulk, 2001). In Denmark the average weekly working time is lower for men – and for women – than in the other three countries. Among men working 50 hours or more we find surprisingly only small differences between numbers of fathers and non-fathers. In both the Netherlands and the UK the proportion of fathers working long weekly hours is even higher than for non-fathers.

The pattern of women's working time differs strongly between on the one hand the Netherlands and the UK and on the other hand the Scandinavian countries. In both the UK and the Netherlands the large majority of mothers work part time. According to a recent OECD study the proportion of mothers with two children below the age of 15 working part time in the Netherlands and the UK is 83% and 63%, respectively, but also among non-mothers in these two countries working part time is widespread. In

Table 9.2: Working-time patterns of men and women with and without children in Denmark, the Netherlands, Sweden and the UK (2001)

Country	Family status	Hours of work per week				
		1-19	20-29	30-39	40-49	50+
Denmark	Fathers	1	2	60	25	12
	Non-fathers	3	2	64	20	11
	Mothers	3	15	68	11	3
	Non-mothers	7	15	68	8	2
Netherlands	Fathers	1	1	26	50	22
	Non-fathers	2	6	33	41	17
	Mothers	39	41	15	5	1
	Non-mothers	20	19	36	20	4
Sweden	Fathers	1	1	13	69	17
	Non-fathers	2	3	12	63	19
	Mothers	4	11	34	47	5
	Non-mothers	2	9	26	54	9
UK	Fathers	2	4	18	43	32
	Non-fathers	7	5	22	36	27
	Mothers	31	27	29	9	4
	Non-mothers	17	13	33	26	5

Sources: HWF survey 2001 and the Danish survey 2004 – unified international data collection: Cousins and Tang (2003); Wallace (2003b)

Denmark and Sweden most women – mothers as well as non-mothers – work full time, which is 37 hours in Denmark and 40 hours in Sweden. The proportion of part-timers among mothers with two children in Denmark and Sweden are 16% and 22%, respectively, and thus remarkably lower than in the other countries (OECD, 2002). In Denmark the proportion of mothers working part time is the same or even lower than for non-mothers. In total the proportion of Scandinavian women working part time has declined over time from about 40% in the late 1980s to less than 20% in 2002 (Wallace, 2003a). The dual-earner couple characterised by two full-time jobs thus prevails in Scandinavia, while most couples in the Netherlands and the UK are one-and-a-half earner or solo male breadwinner families.

Labour market flexibility is often considered as closely combined with shorter job tenure and employment instability. This does not seem to be correct on a general level. In all four countries the average tenure of both men and women has increased during recent decades (Boje and Grönlund, 2003). On the other hand, instability in employment conditions might be a consequence of the demand for flexibility among vulnerable groups of employees – low education, heavy caring obligations, and so on. Furthermore there is a risk that employees working irregular hours – especially women working in unskilled service jobs – may be trapped in insecure and low-paid part-time jobs.

A recent OECD study looked at the effects of gender, presence of children and educational level on continuity in employment status over a five-year period. This study found that, regardless of gender and presence of children, individuals with low education are less likely to be in continuous employment than those with higher education (OECD, 2002, p 84). Continuity in full-time employment is less likely for women with low education than among highly educated mothers *and* non-mothers. A higher share of men with children than childless men are continuously employed, while the pattern is more mixed for women. Children have, as mentioned previously, generally a negative impact on low-educated women's possibilities of remaining in continuous employment in all four countries. Among the highly educated women the impact of children differs depending on country. In Denmark and Sweden continuous employment is higher among well-educated mothers than non-mothers, and the large majority of both groups are in full-time employment (Boje, 2003). In the Netherlands and the UK the proportion of highly educated women in continuous employment declines with the presence of children, and a significant number of these women take up part-time employment. In both countries the difficulties in practising parenthood are tougher than in Scandinavia because care obligations are primarily a private concern in the Netherlands and the UK and only partly coordinated with the parents' working obligations.

Policies supporting working parents

Caring obligations are defined differently in Europe. In some countries the welfare state provides services and social transfers to the family when provision of care is at issue. What were formerly defined as family obligations have been redefined as the responsibility of the state and local government – for example, in Scandinavia. In other countries social rights are highly individualised either as an entire family obligation or as provided for by paying through private non-profit institutions or on pure market conditions – for example, in the Netherlands and the UK. In this section I am looking at differences in the provision of care for children – paid leave or childcare facilities – and who takes up childcare in the family.

The intervention of the welfare state in areas traditionally considered as belonging to the private domain is particularly well demonstrated in social care policies. One of the distinctive features of the Nordic welfare states lies in the fact that care of children as well as 'dependent' adults has become a core element in welfare policies. The exercising of parenthood has increasingly become a public concern. To a larger extent than in other European welfare states the opportunity for the giving and receiving of care has been transformed into social rights of citizens, and the welfare state has expanded as a social service state (Leira and Saraceno, 2002). A look at the organisation of the family policy towards small children illustrates clearly the remarkable differences between caring regimes among our four countries (see OECD, 2001; Plantenga and Hansen, 1999a; Jacobs and Gornick, 2001).

In both Denmark and Sweden the public sector runs the major part of childcare and nearly all privately organised childcare institutions are heavily subsidised by the welfare state. The lower level of childcare coverage for children aged 0 to three in Sweden can be explained by a longer period with highly paid parental leave in Sweden. The coverage for Swedish children aged one to three is thus about 80% (Boje and Almqvist, 2000). In both countries institutional childcare is provided on a full-day basis, making it possible for both parents to take up full-time jobs.

In the more restricted and market-oriented welfare states like the UK, substantial parts of the care work are provided in individual households; the major responsibility for care work falls on women and is unpaid – in spite of their growing involvement in paid work. In the 1990s a large number of childcare institutions were established but most of them are private and often highly expensive. In the Netherlands caring for small children is the concern of the family, while children from the age of three are cared for primarily in public day care centres, as is the case in all four countries. Furthermore, in both the Netherlands and the UK the availability of institutional childcare is typically on a half-day basis, which makes it nearly impossible for both parents to take up full-time jobs.

An alternative to formal childcare is paid or unpaid leave, which is primarily taken by the mothers in all four countries. Only in Sweden are fathers substantially involved in caring for small children. In the late 1990s Sweden had the most generous leave system among the four countries with the longest period of paid leave. The UK has the most restricted system, where only a shorter period of maternity leave is well paid, while parental leave is an unpaid right. The Dutch and Danish systems were placed in between these two

Table 9.3: Who takes the responsibility for childcare in families with children under the age of 15 (2001) (% by gender in Denmark, the Netherlands, Sweden and the UK)

	Denmark		Netherlands		Sweden		UK	
	Man	Woman	Man	Woman	Man	Woman	Man	Woman
Respondent	4	18	7	60	10	51	10	77
Partner	19	5	31	1	34	1	56	2
Other family members	3	6	2	1	-	-	4	2
Shared equally	49	47	22	20	53	45	27	19

Note: The table does not include answers such as 'other situation', 'not applicable' or 'don't know'.

Sources: HWF survey, 2001, and the Danish survey, 2004 – unified international data collection: Cousins and Tang (2003, p 219); Wallace (2003b)

extremes. From the beginning of 2002, however, the Danish leave system was changed. The time period with a high level of income compensation has been extended to 52 weeks but the special quota for men was abolished (see Borchorst, this volume).

The Swedish system for combining work and family life seems more gender-balanced than the system in other European Union countries. Fathers' rate of take-up of parental leave is higher in Sweden than elsewhere and a period of parental leave of 60 days has to be taken by the secondary carer – normally the father. Furthermore, it is possible in the Swedish system to combine parental leave and work – both on a part-time basis – which typically makes it easier for fathers to be involved in caring responsibilities (Näsmann, 1999; Boje and Almqvist, 2000, see also Lammi-Taskula, this volume).

Even if mothers in all four countries have taken up employment in large numbers, the traditionally gendered pattern of responsibility for childcare remains in the large majority of families (see Table 9.3). Denmark and Sweden seem to have the most equal division of caring responsibilities among the four countries. However, a larger number of Danish than Swedish parents find caring alternatives outside the core family – family members not living in the household or paid private childcare. In Sweden the strong political commitment to gender equality has not fundamentally changed the gendered division of childcare. The traditional gendered norms about how to divide the responsibility for childcare prevail in all four countries, and 'people's choice in these circumstances further naturalizes the image of women as carers and men as market laborers'

(Olson, 2002, p 393). Progressive and women-friendly policies concerning work and family might modify the prevailing gender order but more profound changes can only be accomplished through comprehensive changes in norms and values concerning gender roles. Therefore, 'in a pervasively gendered society … the welfare state is only one structuring influence among many. Reforming welfare tears out one root of the current gender order, leaving many more' (Olson, 2002, p 394). Through an increasing politicising of parenthood based on equal division of labour in paid work and unpaid work as well as care, it might be possible slowly to change norms and values concerning gender roles in society (Leira, 2002; Lister, 2002).

Gender equality – division of work and care responsibilities

As shown in the previous sections the gendered division of labour has been changed in relation to paid work but in the division of caring obligations progress towards a universal caregiver model has been minimal and the gender norms of a male-breadwinner society are prevailing. Thus, in promoting equal opportunities and gender equality the division of both paid and unpaid work becomes crucial. The gender division in paid labour has, as mentioned above, declined because a substantial number of women have entered the labour market. However, this development has not led to decisive changes in the gender division of unpaid work – that is, domestic work and caring (Gershuny, 2000; Bonke, 2002). According to a European Union study carried out by Plantenga and Hansen (1999a), an equitable division of both paid and unpaid work is a long way off. In all four countries included in this comparison as well as in the European Union as a whole we find higher equality in the labour market between men and women than in the gender distribution of paid and unpaid work. On average, women in European Union countries spend about four times as much time as men on unpaid work and caring tasks. Denmark and Sweden hold a front position, with the UK in a middle position, and the Netherlands at the bottom among the European Union countries. Equal opportunities have been on the agenda for a longer time in Scandinavia, and the welfare state has taken a more 'woman-friendly' approach than in any other country in Europe. As a consequence, the rates of employment for parents are similar to the rates for non-parents, the gender gap is lower and the families have accomplished more progress in the sharing of the household's unpaid work – caring and domestic work.

However, despite some obvious progress in Scandinavia concerning the integration of women in the labour market we find still significant barriers concerning equal pay and in women's access to highly ranked and well-paid job positions (OECD, 2002). An important dimension in explaining both the occupational segregation and the gender pay gap is normally conceptualised as women's larger responsibilities for raising children and performing domestic tasks compared to men. On the other hand, recent data on career progress for women and men show only a minor effect of motherhood on women's career mobility when comparing career mobility among fathers and mothers with overall differences in career mobility between men and women. In Scandinavia, but also in countries like the UK, France and Spain, well-educated mothers who are in gainful employment seem able to overcome at least partly the motherhood effect, which is clearly not the case in the Netherlands, where the large majority of mothers work part time (see OECD, 2002, p 96).

We find another indication of the troubles families have in reconciling work and families when asking parents and non-parents how they experience the conflicts in combining work and family responsibilities. According to Table 9.4, both mothers and fathers in all four countries clearly experience more conflicts in combining work and family responsibilities than non-parents. Parents' constraints compared with those of non-parents were most obvious in Sweden, both for fathers and mothers, while the differences between parents and non-parents were relatively modest in the Netherlands.

Both Swedish mothers and fathers express greater difficulties in reconciling work and family than parents in the other three countries. This might be a surprising result considering that the Swedish caring system for children is more comprehensive than in the other countries but, on the other hand, Swedish mothers are also more often in gainful employment and work longer weekly hours than at least most Dutch and UK mothers (Tables 9.1 and 9.2; and Jacobs and Gornick, 2001). Furthermore, the Swedish norms for good parenthood might also be more demanding than at least those of the Netherlands and the UK. Next to the Swedish parents in experiencing work–family conflicts come Danish mothers, who are also gainfully employed in large numbers and are also expected to be strongly committed to being good mothers.

In addition to Scandinavian mothers it is fathers in the UK who experience the highest level of conflict in reconciling work and

Table 9.4: Work–family conflicts as experienced by working men and women with and without children in Denmark, the Netherlands, Sweden and the UK (2001) (% saying sometimes, often or always)

Country	Work–family conflicts	Non-fathers	Fathers	Non-mothers	Mothers
Denmark	Work makes it difficult for me to do household tasks	37	51	35	57
	Work makes it difficult for me to fulfil family responsibilities	20	40	20	40
	Family responsibilities prevent me from working adequately	6	11	6	17
	I have to take work from my employment home to finish	26	31	17	28
	I prefer to spend more time at work than to spend more time at home	6	4	8	6
Netherlands	Work makes it difficult for me to do household tasks	39	55	42	42
	Work makes it difficult for me to fulfil family responsibilities	20	42	28	30
	Family responsibilities prevent me from working adequately	7	14	7	15
	I have to take work from my employment home to finish	30	31	19	23
	I prefer to spend more time at work than to spend more time at home	13	11	16	11
Sweden	Work makes it difficult for me to do household tasks	38	57	44	60
	Work makes it difficult for me to fulfil family responsibilities	30	50	39	52
	Family responsibilities prevent me from working adequately	7	15	8	18
	I have to take work from my employment home to finish	28	41	26	31
	I prefer to spend more time at work than to spend more time at home	9	9	7	6
United Kingdom	Work makes it difficult for me to do household tasks	33	55	24	36
	Work makes it difficult for me to fulfil family responsibilities	18	46	15	29
	Family responsibilities prevent me from working adequately	15	28	8	17
	I have to take work from my employment home to finish	11	25	16	14
	I prefer to spend more time at work than to spend more time at home	6	8	5	6

Sources: HWF survey, 2001, and the Danish survey, 2004 – unified international data collection: Cousins and Tang (2003); Wallace (2003b)

family obligations. This is definitely not surprising considering the extremely long weekly hours they are working. The group with the lowest level of work–family conflicts is the UK women. This is again understandable given that they have reduced their working hours significantly or are completely leaving the labour market when becoming mothers. A relatively low level of work–family conflicts is also found among the Dutch mothers and Danish fathers. Given the high proportion of women working short weekly hours and a widespread tradition for male breadwinner families in the Netherlands, the low level of work–family conflicts among Dutch women might be expected. For Danish fathers the result is more surprising but a combination of lower average working hours (Table 9.2) and a low involvement in childcaring (Table 9.3) might explain the lower level of work–family conflicts among Danish fathers compared with other fathers.

In all four countries it is the work conditions that create problems in the work–family relations rather than the family responsibilities. Only a small minority of the respondents want to spend more time at work compared with the time spent at home. Highly educated women generally have better possibilities for combining work and caring obligations and they seem to prefer reducing their working time instead of exiting employment. Similarly, women living in countries with a comprehensive family policy and work–family-friendly labour market regulation tend to prefer full-time work irrespectively of caring obligations. In a survey carried out by the European Foundation in Dublin, families were asked which kind of employment pattern they preferred (see Table 9.5).

Table 9.5: Actual and preferred employment pattern, by full-time and part-time working couples with a child below six years of age (1998) (%)

	Man full time/ woman full time	Man full time/ woman part time	Man full time/ woman not employed	Other	Total
Sweden					
Actual	51.1	13.3	24.9	10.7	100.0
Preferred	66.8	22.2	6.6	4.4	100.0
Netherlands					
Actual	4.8	54.8	33.7	6.7	100.0
Preferred	5.6	69.9	10.7	13.8	100.0
UK					
Actual	24.9	31.9	32.8	10.4	100.0
Preferred	21.3	41.8	13.3	23.6	100.0

Source: OECD (2001, p 136)

Swedish families' preferred choice is full-time employment for both partners, followed by a combination of full-time employment for men and part-time employment for women as the second preference. A striking contrast is that nearly one fourth of Swedish households has an actual work pattern characterised by the man in full-time employment and the woman not employed. This phenomenon can be explained by the large number of Swedish women who are on extended parental leave or on leave for caring for a sick child or for an educational purpose. These women consider themselves as out of employment despite the fact that the large majority on leave are registered as employed in the official employment statistics. On the other hand, a large majority of women on full-time leave seem to prefer a labour market solution that combines part-time leave and part-time employment instead of being on full-time leave. The preferences are different for Dutch and UK families. Here the dominant pattern is a combination of part-time employment for women and full-time employment for men. In both countries we find a significantly higher proportion of families who want this combination than those practising it, while the combination of the man in full-time employment and the woman not employed is less preferred than the actual pattern. Furthermore, among UK families we find a higher proportion preferring full-time employment for both partners than among Dutch families, indicating a more work-oriented family culture in the UK than in the Netherlands where the traditional breadwinner family model still prevails strongly.

Gender equality for all parents

Parents' working time and caring strategies and the policies supporting work–life balance differ between the four countries compared in this chapter. To sum up, in Denmark and Sweden the employment rates of mothers are high and the great majority are working full time. This is combined with a generous parental leave system for mothers – and potentially also for fathers – with small children, and a high coverage of relatively inexpensive public full-time day care. In the Netherlands nearly all mothers in employment work part time and often with short weekly hours, while among UK mothers we find huge differences in working-time patterns. However, in both the UK and the Netherlands a large proportion of mothers with small children have to leave the labour market for caring obligations, because of a lack of, or extremely expensive, childcaring facilities.

In all four countries, work–family conflicts were clearly more widespread among parents than non-parents, and were especially pronounced among Swedish parents. Furthermore, it is work demands and not family responsibilities that make family life difficult. Turning to the preferred working-time pattern it is clear that the large majority of Dutch and UK couples want the 'one-and-a-half adult worker' model, while the Scandinavian couples go for the 'individualised adult worker' model with both father and mother in full-time employment. These results can be explained by considering the prevailing family/caring policies and working-time regimes in the four countries.

During the last decades, all couples in the Scandinavian countries – and more generally in Europe for highly educated couples – have experienced a profound redistribution of paid work from a male-breadwinner model to a 'one-and-a-half-earner' or a 'dual-earner' model. This change in labour market status in the families is not reflected in any redistribution of the unpaid work and in the division of caring obligations among parents.

The social roles defined through the prevailing practices of parenthood in all four countries have a strong impact on the organisation of employment relations. The male-breadwinner model assumes that men will follow a pattern of continuous, full-time employment, while mothers are expected to balance their labour market involvement with extensive family responsibilities characterised by reduced working hours in combination with comprehensive caring obligations. The effect of motherhood on employment relations and working time has to some extent been modified in Denmark and Sweden through the family/caring policies, but definitely not in the Netherlands and the UK. The male-breadwinner model still prevails among families with small children in the Netherlands. In the UK the pattern is more differentiated between the highly educated and well-paid mothers, who work full time and organise costly private care for the children, and mothers with low education and badly paid part-time jobs, who leave the labour market in the period with small children.

Despite a growing involvement of women in gainful employment and still more women working full time, the family obligations are thus highly gendered with women doing the major part of caring and domestic work. Arlie Hochschild (1989) describes the lack of changes in the household division of labour in US households in the early 1980s, when women had entered paid labour in large numbers, as 'lagged adaptation'. She found a marked contradiction between the attitudes and actions among both the men and women in the families. This has been confirmed in several more recent studies, but some also report a slow progress towards a more equal division of labour in the families (see, for example, Gershuny, 2000; Bonke, 2002; Hantrais, 2004).

A decisive question is thus how best to facilitate the process of equalising working and caring parenthood, and how greater equality in attitudes towards work–family relations can be implemented through measures in the workplace and/or through family policies related to childcare and parental leave. A variety of economic, social and cultural conditions under which work and care are undertaken have to be taken into consideration. Social citizenship in all four countries is still strongly connected to paid work, meaning that social rights are differentiated according to valuation of and access to paid work. As long as paid work is gendered, the condition for exercising parenthood will therefore be gendered. A gender-balanced solution in practising parenthood can only be implemented through 'politicising' a gender-inclusive citizen–worker–carer model that promotes an equal distribution of paid and unpaid work and care (see, for example, Lister, 1997, 2002; Lewis, 2001; Leira, 2002). This will only be the case if care and unpaid work are recognised as equally important for social participation as paid work, and thereby being an integrated part of the individual's rights and obligations as a citizen.

References

Åberg, R., Strandh, M., Nordenmark, M. and Bolinder, M. (1997) 'Massearbetslösheten på 90-tallet', in J.Vogel and L. Häll (eds) *Välfärd och Ojämlikhet i 20 års Perspektiv 1975-1995*, Report 91, Örebro: Statistics Sweden.

Abrahamson, P., Boje, T.P. and Greve, B. (2005) *Families and Welfare in Europe*, Aldershot: Ashgate.

Anttonen, A. and Sipilä, J. (1996) 'European social care services: is it possible to identify models?', *Journal of European Social Policy*, vol 6 no 2, pp 87-100.

Boje, T.P. (2003) 'Towards a post-industrial service society', in T.P. Boje and B. Furåker (eds) *Post-industrial Labour Markets*, London and New York, NY: Routledge, pp 124–46.

Boje, T.P. and Almqvist, A.-L. (2000) 'Citizenship, family policy and women's patterns of employment', in T.P. Boje and A. Leira (eds) *Gender, Welfare State and the Market*, London and New York, NY: Routledge, pp 41–70.

Boje, T.P. and Grönlund, A. (2003) 'Flexibility and employment insecurity', in T.P. Boje and B. Furåker (eds) *Post-industrial Labour Markets*, London and New York, NY: Routledge.

Bonke, J. (2002) *Tid og Velfærd*, Copenhagen: Socialforskningsinstituttet.

Borchorst, A. (1999) 'Ligestillingslovgivningen', in L. Bergqvist and A. Borchorst (eds) *Likestilte Demokratier?*, Oslo: Unioversitetsforlaget, pp 176-91.

Brannen, J. (1998) 'Employment and family lives: equalities and inequalities', in E. Drew, R. Emerek and E. Mahon (eds) *Women, Work and the Family in Europe*, London: Routledge, pp 76–86.

Brannen, J., Moss, P. and Mooney, A. (2004) *Working and Caring over the Twentieth Century*, London: Palgrave MacMillan.

Castells, M. (1996) *The Information Age: Economy, Society and Culture*, Oxford: Blackwell.

Cousins, C. and Tang, N. (2003) *Working Time Flexibility and Family Life*, Thematic Paper, London: HWF-project.

Dex, S. and McCulloch, A. (1997) *Flexible Employment: The Future of Britain's Job*, Basingstoke: MacMillan Press.

Dulk, L. den (2001) *Work-family Arrangements in Organisations: A Cross-national Study in the Netherlands, Italy, the United Kingdom and Sweden*, Amsterdam: Rozenberg.

Ellingsæter, A.L. (1998) 'Dual breadwinner societies: provider models in the Scandinavian welfare states', *Acta Sociologica*, vol 41, no 1, pp 59-73.

Esping-Andersen, G. (1990) *The Three Worlds of Welfare Capitalism*, Cambridge: Polity Press.

Esping-Andersen, G. (1999) *Social Foundations of Postindustrial Economies*, Oxford: Oxford University Press.

European Commission (2002) *Employment in Europe 2002*, Luxembourg: Office for Official Publications of the European Communities.

Gallie, D. and Paugam, S. (eds) (2000) *Welfare Regimes and the Experience of Unemployment in Europe*, New York, NY, and Oxford: Oxford University Press.

Gershuny, J. (2000) *Changing Times: Work and Leisure in Post-industrial Society*, Oxford: Oxford University Press.

Gornick, J.C., Meyers, M.K. and Roos, K.E. (1997) 'Supporting the employment of mothers: policy variation across fourteen welfare states', *Journal of European Social Policy*, vol 7, no 1, pp 45-70.

Grönlund, A. (2004) *Flexibilitetens Gränser*, Umeå: Borea Förlag.

Hantrais, L. (2004) *Family Policy Matters: Responding to Family Change in Europe*, Bristol: The Policy Press.

Hinrichs, K., Roche, W. and Sirianni, C. (1991) 'From standardization to flexibility: changes in the political economy of working time', in K. Hinrichs, W. Roche and C. Sirianni (eds) *Working Time in Transition*, Philadelphia, PA: Temple University Press.

Hochschild, A. (1989) *The Second Shift: Working Parents and the Revolution at Home*, New York, NY: Viking Press.

Jacobs, J.A. and Gornick, J.C. (2001) 'Hours of paid work in dual-earner couples', Keynote Address at the North Central Sociological Society meeting, Philadelphia, March 2001.

Leira, A. (1992) *Welfare States and Working Mothers*, Cambridge: Cambridge University Press.

Leira, A. (2002) *Working Parents and the Welfare State*, Cambridge: Cambridge University Press.

Leira, A. and Saraceno, C. (2002) 'Care: actors, relationships, contexts', in B. Hobson, J. Lewis and B. Siim (eds) *Contested Concepts in Gender and Social Politics*, Cheltenham: Edward Elgar.

Lewis, J. (1992) 'Gender and the development of welfare regimes', *Journal of European Social Policy*, vol 2, no 3, pp 159-73.

Lewis, J. (2001) 'The decline of the male breadwinner model: implications for work and care', *Social Politics*, vol 8, no 2, pp 152-69.

Lewis, J. (2002) 'Gender and welfare state change', *European Societies*, vol 4, no 4, pp 331-57.

Lister, R. (1997) *Citizenship: Feminist Perspectives*, London: MacMillan.

Lister, R. (2002) 'The dilemmas of pendulum politics: balancing paid work, care and citizenship', *Economy and Society*, vol 31, no 4, pp 520-32.

Meulders, D., Plasman, O. and Plasman, R. (1997) *Atypical Employment in the EC*, Aldershot: Dartmouth.

Millar, J. and Warman, A. (1996) *Family Obligations in Europe*, London: Family Policy Studies Centre.

Näsman, E. (1999) 'Sweden and the reconciliation of work and family life', in L. den Dulk, A. van Doorne-Huiskes and J. Schippers (eds) *Work–Family Arrangements in Europe*, Amsterdam: Thela-Thesis, pp 131–51.

OECD (Organisation for Economic Co-operation and Development) (1999) *Employment Outlook, 1999*, Paris: OECD.

OECD (2001) *Employment Outlook, 2001*, Paris: OECD.

OECD (2002) *Employment Outlook, 2002*, Paris: OECD.

Olsen, B.M. (2000) *Nye Fædre på Orlov: En Analyse af de Kønsmæssige Aspekter ved Forældreorlovsordninger*, København: Sociologisk Institut.

Olson, K. (2002) 'Recognizing gender, redistributing labor', *Social Politics*, vol 9, Autumn, pp 380-410.

Perron, D. (1998) *Flexible Working and the Reconciliation of Work and Family Life: A New Form of Precariousness*, Luxembourg: European Commission, DG Employment and Social Affairs.

Pfau-Effinger, B. (1998) 'Gender culture and gender arrangement – a theoretical framework for cross-national gender research', *Innovation*, vol 11, no 2, pp 147-66.

Plantenga, J. and Hansen, J. (1999a) 'Assessing equal opportunities in the European Union', *International Labour Review*, vol 138, no 4, pp 351–379.

Plantenga, J. and Hansen, J. (1999b) *Benchmarking Equal Opportunities in the European Union: Synthesis Report based on Eight European Countries*, Utrecht: Equal Opportunities Unit DGV, Utrecht University.

Purcell, K., Hogarth, T. and Simm, C. (1999) *Whose Flexibility? The Costs and Benefits of Non-standard Working Arrangements and Contractual Relations*, York: Joseph Rowntree Foundation.

Remery, C., van Doorne-Huiskes, A. and Schippers, A. (2002) 'Labour market flexibility in the Netherlands: looking for winners and losers', *Work, Employment and Society*, vol 16, no 3, pp 477-95.

Rubery, J., Grimshaw, D. and Smith, M. (2001) *Gender Equality and the European Employment Strategy: An Evaluation of the National Action Plans for Employment 2000*, Manchester: EWERC, Manchester School of Management, UMIST.

Rubery, J., Smith, M. and Fagan, C. (1999) *Women's Employment in Europe: Trends and Prospects*, London: Routledge.

Sennett, R. (1998) *The Corrosion of Character*, New York, NY, and London: W.W. Norton.

Visser, J. (2000) *The First Part-Time Economy in the World: Does it Work*, Amsterdam: AIAS.

Wallace, C. (ed) (2002) *Critical Review of Literature and Discourses about Flexibility*, HWF Research report 1, Vienna: IHS.

Wallace, C. (ed) (2003a) *Country Contextual Reports: Demographic Trends, Labour Market and Social Policies*, HWF Research Report 2, Vienna: IHS.

Wallace, C. (ed) (2003b) *Comparative Report. Volume 2: Thematic Reports Vienna*, HWF Research Report 4, Vienna: IHS.

Warren, T. (2000) 'Diverse breadwinner models: a couple-based analysis of gendered working time in Britain and Denmark', *Journal of European Social Policy*, vol 10, no 4, pp 349-71.

TEN

Diverging paths? The dual-earner/ dual-carer model in Finland and Sweden in the 1990s

Anita Haataja and Anita Nyberg

Introduction

In much feminist comparative research on welfare state policies, Finland and Sweden are seen as similar cases. Both countries have for a long time supported gender equality by policies encouraging employment for mothers and childcare for fathers. Both are welfare states that have moved away from the male breadwinner model and towards a dual-earner/dual-carer model. This is confirmed in a recently conducted state-of-the-art review of welfare states and motherhood, where the two nations were classified in the same category in all 13 studies that included both countries (European Commission, 2002). There are also, however, researchers who oppose the idea of Finland and Sweden supporting the same kind of model. Mahon (2002) argues, for example, that since the 1990s, the two states have promoted different models. In her terminology, parenthood policies in Sweden continue to be committed to strengthening the *egalitarian* model, while the more recent development in Finland reflects a move towards *neofamilialism*.

This means, according to Mahon, that in Finland the development is moving towards a model that encourages parents to stay at home for long periods after the birth of a child, and thus departs from the basis of institutionalised childcare as a right of social citizenship. This model emphasises choice between a (temporary) homemaker role and paid employment. In Sweden, on the other hand, the development exhibits a continued commitment to and strengthening of the egalitarian model. This has been pursued through a dramatic expansion of publicly financed childcare – even in the 1990s, in spite of the economic recession – and the introduction of the 'daddy quota' in the parental leave, which offers incentives for parents to share infant care. The parental leave is short enough to limit adverse effects on women's income and situation in the labour market, and the supply of public childcare is large enough to cover demand.

We believe that any analysis of change in policy models and their outcomes needs to be interpreted in relation to labour market developments and macro-economic conditions more generally. These are important premises for parents' opportunities of choice. It is sometimes assumed that policies furthering women's position and gender equality are prone to retrogression and to cutbacks in times of economic recession. In such an economic situation women might increasingly be defined through motherhood, while men are increasingly defined as workers and earners. The 1990s are particularly interesting in this respect, since economic growth was negative at the beginning of the 1990s, budget deficits grew enormously, unemployment rose dramatically, and employment rates fell (Kautto, 2000; Hiilamo, this volume).

In this chapter, our examination of the concept 'politicising parenthood' includes a short discussion of the public motivation, the legislation and enactment of reform policies of parenthood, and the parental response to policy interventions. The policies examined are paid parental leave, home care allowance and publicly financed day care services. The parents' use of these facilities is also briefly discussed. However, parental response to or effects of policy interventions in combination with economic development are mainly analysed in terms of changes in mothers' and fathers' employment, unemployment and incomes. Our point of departure is that politicising parenthood, motherhood and fatherhood concerns earning as well as caring. We examine the period from the end of the 1980s to the beginning of the 2000s. We shall argue, as others have also done, that in conceptualising developments in the policies of parenthood, the distinction between policies for children below the age of three versus those for older children is crucial (for example, Kamerman and Kahn, 1991; Daune-Richard, 2005). It is also important to analyse partnered and lone mothers separately since parental response to and/or effects of the policies and economic development might differ between the two categories (for lone mothers see also Skevik, this volume).

The 'male-breadwinner model' and the 'dual-breadwinner model' are the regular concepts used. However, we believe these concepts to be problematic. In the first concept only men are visible, while women are invisible. In the second concept only paid work is visible, while unpaid work is invisible, and women only enter the model when they enter the labour market. In this chapter, we use the concept dual-earner/dual-carer model. This is done in order that both women and men and unpaid and paid work are visible, but also, and more importantly, because the process towards a dual-earner/ dual-carer model includes both a stronger situation for women in the labour market and men's greater responsibility for children and domestic work.

Policies of parenthood in Finland and Sweden

Parenthood policies consist in both countries of parental leave with benefits and publicly financed childcare. In addition, there is a cash grant for childcare for children below three years of age in Finland. In both Finland and Sweden the parental leave benefit is linked to earlier wage income. This encourages women to establish themselves in the labour market before they have children and it facilitates their return to the labour market, especially in combination with publicly financed childcare (Ruhm, 1998; Leira, 2002; Jansson et al, 2003). Paid parental leave may also encourage fathers' participation in care and create more flexibility for mothers to choose between childcare and employment. Parental leave and publicly financed childcare thereby further the dual-earner/dual-carer model. However, although this is true for shorter leaves, the effects of longer parental and/or childcare leaves are much more complex. If mothers opt for very long leaves and/or part-time work, it may solidify gender differences in childcare and domestic work and aggravate gender inequality in the labour market, employers might be reluctant to hire and promote women, and women's economic dependence on men increases (Sipilä and Korpinen, 1998; Bruning and Plantenga, 1999; Moss and Deven, 1999; Salmi, 2000; Anttonen, 2001; Leira, 2002). Research from Norway, which also has a cash benefit for childcare for children one to two years old, shows that mothers' employment rates have been stable in the years since the reform, but one study attempting to estimate what would have happened if the benefit had not been introduced suggests that both employment levels and working hours would have been increasing significantly (Rønsen, 2005; see also Ellingsæter, this volume).

Fathers' incentives to use various leaves increase when fathers' rights are granted on an individual basis, and the rights cannot be transferred to the mother (Ellingsæter, 1999). In this connection we would also like to point out that the concepts 'parental leave' and 'paternity leave' are not the same kinds of leaves in terms of encouraging fathers to share childcare. Paternity leave is short and must be used in connection with the birth of the child, and at the same time as the mother is on leave. Thus, paternity leave might be considered as more of a help to mothers than expecting fathers to take the main responsibility for childcare. In this respect, Finnish fathers have been treated more as 'junior' carers than Swedish fathers (see also Lammi-Taskula, this volume).

In Sweden, the development of fathers' right to leave to care for children was introduced when parental leave replaced maternity leave in 1974. Paternity leave – 'daddy days' – was introduced later, in 1980. Parental leave was an equal and individual right – even though transferable – for both parents. In 1995 fathers' rights were further developed by introducing a one-month non-transferable fathers' (and mothers') quota of the parental leave (Nyberg, 2004). In the 1990s, the Swedish parental leave consisted of 15 months, three months of which were compensated for with a flat-rate benefit.

In Finland, paternity leave was first introduced in 1978, and then parental leave came two years later. The father's use of leaves, however, depended on the mother's consent until 1991, and until 1993 paternity leave, if used, reduced the parental leave days. In the early 1990s, paternity leave was lengthened from two to three weeks (Haataja, 2004; Lammi-Taskula, this volume). The parental leave period was a full 10 months in the 1990s, of which four months were reserved for the mother, one to two months to be used before the child's birth. The last six months can be shared between the parents.

In the beginning of the 2000s, both countries introduced further steps in order to promote fathers' participation. Sweden extended parental leave by one month up to 16 months in 2002, and reserved two months of the total period as a non-transferable right for fathers (and mothers). In 2005, increasing the length of the quotas has been proposed, as well as improvements in the earnings-related benefit (SOU, 2005:73). In Finland, a two-week daddy quota was introduced in 2003. These are called 'bonus weeks', since the father must 'earn' them by using at least the last two weeks of the ordinary parental leave (Takala, 2003). The reform has not been successful, and in 2005 proposals were presented to increase compensation levels and make the bonus weeks more flexible (Lammi-Taskula, this volume; Perhevapaasäännösten ..., 2005).

After the parental leave, the families are supported by public childcare in both countries. At that time Finnish children are around nine months old, depending on how the mother has used her leave and whether the father has used paternity leave or not. Swedish children are 15 to 16 months old, if leave has been taken continuously since the birth of the child. Public childcare was expanding in both countries in the early 1970s (see Hiilamo; Leira, this volume). However, during the 1970s and 1980s the queues for places were very long. This problem was solved differently in Finland and Sweden.

In Finland, a compromise between parties to the left and to the centre-right (Bergqvist et al, 1999) involved a cash-for-care provision alongside public childcare. Since 1990, all parents with children below the age of three have a right to choose between a child home care allowance and a place in publicly financed childcare services. The level of the child home care allowance and fee policies in childcare varied in the 1990s according to the composition of the government (Haataja, 2005). In the beginning of the 1990s, during the recession, the amount of child home care allowance was increased, and was higher than the basic unemployment benefit. In the latter part of the decade benefits were again cut. Since the child home care allowance is part of the municipal childcare provision, there might also be economic incentives for the municipalities to increase the statutory child home care allowance in order to restrain demand for childcare. The right to publicly financed childcare was extended to cover all children of pre-school age in 1996. The childcare fees varied a lot in the first part of the decade (Forssén, 1998), but were harmonised in the latter part of the 1990s. At the same time, a cash benefit for private extra-parental childcare was introduced. Thus, during the first part of the 1990s parental care was encouraged, while during the latter part the emphasis was more on non-parental care. However, the role of the child home care allowance has not been questioned, and the policies have aimed at compensating for the cuts in the allowance in the late 1990s.

A cash benefit for childcare was also introduced in Sweden. This was done in 1994 by a non-social democratic government, which also launched the 'daddy month'. When the Social Democrats came back into power in the autumn of 1994 they abolished the cash grant for childcare, but kept the daddy month. In Sweden, children of employed or studying parents had the right to a place in publicly financed childcare, but it was not until the end of the 1990s that children could get a place in pre-school within a reasonable time (three to four months) (Nyberg, 2004). At the beginning of the 2000s, the right to publicly financed childcare was extended to cover children of the unemployed, children with a parent on parental leave with another child and all four- to five-year-olds, and, in 2002, a maximum childcare fee was introduced, which meant that a ceiling was set on the fees payable by parents for childcare.

Parents' response to parenthood policies

Finnish as well as Swedish fathers use paternity leave to a great extent. There was a large increase among Finnish fathers using paternity leave in the 1990s, and in 2000 the shares of fathers using paternity leave were of about the same magnitude in the two countries. On the other hand, Finnish fathers use the parental leave to a very small extent, and take-up rates even decreased in the 1990s. Of 100 completed parental leaves, fathers were involved in three (Haataja, 2004). The share of fathers who use any parental leave in Sweden before the child turns four years of age, amounts to 75%, and fathers' compensated days increased from 7% to 19% between 1990 and 2004 (SOU, 2005: 73, p 123).

The proportion of mothers in Finland who started a period with a child home care allowance after the parental leave amounted to 78% in 2001. Of those, 22% received a child home care allowance for six months or less, 40% for seven to 24 months, and the remaining 37% for more than 24 months (Social Insurance Institution).[1] As a comparison it can be mentioned that, in Sweden, the length of the parental leave for almost all children was between 12 and 19 months, for 6% to 7% the parental leave was longer than two years, and around 12% of the children were at home for less than a year (SOU, 2005: 73, p 143). The reason for the variation in the length of the parental leave in Sweden is that it is possible to spread out the use of the paid leave until the child is eight years old.

In spite of earlier subjective rights for public childcare, the share of children in public childcare decreased in Finland, while it increased in Sweden. In 1990, more one- and two-year-olds were in publicly financed childcare in Finland than in Sweden (NOSOSCO, 2001: 16, table 4:12). In 2003, the situation was reversed; 36% of the Finnish children and 65% of the Swedish were then in publicly financed childcare. Even among older children – three- to five-year-olds – the share of children in childcare in 2003 was higher in Sweden (94%) than in Finland (68%) (NOSOSCO, 2005: 26, table 4:12). The principal reason for this is that Finnish mothers take care of their children at home longer than they did previously, and longer than Swedish mothers. Often they also take care of the newborn child's older siblings.

It can also be pointed out that almost half of the Swedish children whose parents were on parental leave with another child were in public childcare (Skolverket, 2003, table 2:2). This is unusual in Finland; of all children in full-time (at least 25 hours) public childcare, 2.9% had a parent on parental or child home care leave, and if in part-time care, 1.7% (Väinälä, 2004).

———

Fathers in both countries, but more so in Sweden than in Finland, participate more in childcare today than previously, but their share of total leave days is still low. The lack of job opportunities for mothers restricts their choices between work and childcare and thus also negatively affects fathers' possibilities to share the transferable parental leave. To conclude, a majority of Finnish mothers were absent from the labour market for longer periods of time than Swedish mothers in the 1990s. Thus, we might expect the labour market and earnings potential of Finnish mothers to be more negatively affected than those of Swedish mothers in the 1990s.

Mothers' and fathers' employment and unemployment

Policies of parental leave and public childcare are usually seen as encouraging the dual-earner/dual-carer model, while many researchers see cash benefits for childcare as supporting a traditional gender division of labour. This is true, to different degrees, also of Finnish researchers. However, in general, they seem to doubt that Finnish women will change from being full-time working mothers to full-time homemakers for any length of time.[2] It could furthermore be argued that since women in Finland, including mothers, typically work full time, while mothers in Sweden often work part time, the employment situation might be more precarious for Swedish than for Finnish women, especially in an economic recession.

Below we compare the employment rates of lone and partnered mothers and fathers with children in different age groups in the years 1989 and 2002 in Finland and in Sweden. The economic status of lone mothers is an important litmus test for the fallback position of partnered mothers and the extent to which mothers can form autonomous households independent of men (Orloff, 1993; see also Skevik, this volume).[3]

At the beginning of the 1990s, employment rates fell and unemployment rates increased in all categories in the labour market, and the changes were greater in Finland than in Sweden. Towards the end of the 1990s, the situation became brighter. The employment rate was higher and the unemployment rate lower in 2002 than in the years between 1989 and 2002 (see also Hiilamo, this volume).

As can be seen in Figure 10.1, in 1989, with the exception of lone mothers with children of 0 to six years of age, the employment rate was slightly higher in Sweden in all categories. In 2002, the employment rate was higher in all categories in Sweden compared with Finland, but lower in both Sweden and Finland in all categories compared with 1989. The drop is most pronounced among lone mothers with small children in Finland – from 85% to 53%. However, also, lone mothers in Sweden and lone mothers with school children in both countries have been harder hit than partnered mothers and fathers (see also Nyberg, 2005; Skevik, this volume).

The employment rate, however, overestimates women's involvement in wage work since many women work part time. If we define full time as 35 hours or more per week and part time as 34 hours or less, and investigate mothers' working time, the share of Finnish mothers working part time has increased from 17% in 1989 to 25% in 2002 when the youngest child is below seven years of age, and from 15% to 17% if the child is older. The corresponding proportions of Swedish mothers working part time decreased from 55% to 41% and from 45% to 34%, respectively (AKU, Statistics Sweden; Haataja, 2005b).

Women who work part time are on average more dependent on the income of their husband and do more domestic work than women working full time (Nyberg, 1995). We might therefore conclude that the increase in part-time work in Finland indicates a move in the direction of a more traditional gender model, while in Sweden women are moving in the direction of the dual-earner

Figure 10.1: Employment rate, lone and partnered mothers and fathers with children 0 to six years of age and seven to 16/17 years of age, Finland and Sweden (1989 and 2002) (%)[a]

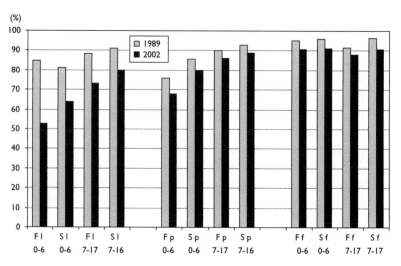

Note: [a] F=Finland, S=Sweden, l=lone, p=partnered, f=fathers.
Sources: Finland: Haataja (2005b); Sweden: AKU, Statistics Sweden

model. However, to what extent part-time work is voluntary is hard to say, as we will see below.

Let us also look at the development of the unemployment rate for the different categories (see Figure 10.2). In 1989, the unemployment rate was higher in Finland in all categories, with the exception of lone mothers with small children, where unemployment was higher in Sweden than in Finland. In 2002, the unemployment rate was higher in all groups than in 1989. This is especially true for lone mothers in both countries, but it is also true for partnered mothers in Finland compared to fathers, while the difference between partnered mothers and fathers in Sweden was very small. The unemployment rate in 2002 was higher in Finland than in Sweden and the variation between the categories was greater.

Women's unemployment is, however, underestimated. Since women often work part time, the incidence of part-time unemployment is higher among women than among men, but part-time unemployment is not measured and data are not published in the same way as is the case with full-time unemployment (Nyberg, 2003). Of the mothers working part time in Finland, the share doing so involuntarily because of lack of full-time work increased from 37% to about 50% in 2002 (Haataja, 2005b). In Sweden part-time work among mothers has been very common, but also among

Figure 10.2: Unemployment rate, lone and partnered mothers and fathers with children 0 to six years of age and seven to 16/17 years of age, Finland and Sweden (1989 and 2002) (%)[a]

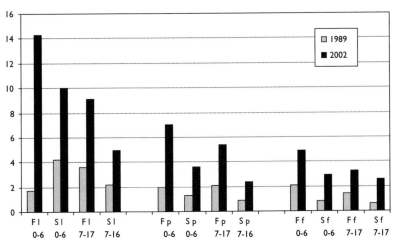

Note: [a] F=Finland, S=Sweden, l=lone, p=partnered, f=fathers.

Source: Finland: Haataja (2005b); Sweden: AKU, Statistics Sweden

Swedish mothers a relatively large share (20%) are working part time involuntarily (Nyberg, 2005).

It could also be pointed out that in Finland long-term unemployment is highest among mothers with children aged three to six years of age, that is, after the child home care leave (Haataja, 2005). One important reason for this is probably the growth of temporary work among women. Temporary work contracts increased among Finnish mothers of pre-school children from 16% to 20% of all contracts between 1989 and 2002 (Haataja, 2005b). Mothers might be on long full-time child home care leave instead of being unemployed. In the latter part of the 1990s the share of mothers who were unemployed before the child's birth and received a child home care allowance started to increase (see for example, Salmi, 2000, p 194). Recent studies indicate that 40% to 50% of the mothers receiving a child home care allowance have no real choice between paid and unpaid work, because they have no job to return to (Hämäläinen, 2005). In Sweden, temporary work contracts are rarer than in Finland, especially among mothers with pre-school children. The share of temporary contracts has, however, increased from 11% to almost 15% between 1989 and 2000 in this category (AKU, Statistics Sweden).

When comparing mothers in the two countries, we find that lone mothers have been hit harder than other groups in both countries, but more so in Finland than in Sweden. Their employment rate is much lower and their unemployment rate much higher today than at the end of the 1980s. The unemployment rate has increased more for Finnish mothers than for Swedish mothers, which can partly be explained by the generally higher unemployment rate in Finland than in Sweden. But if this is taken into consideration, by comparing the labour market situation of partnered mothers to partnered fathers, we find that Finnish mothers have been doing less well than Swedish mothers. The changes in the employment rate and in the unemployment rate are very small when partnered mothers and fathers in Sweden are compared, and not always in the fathers' favour.

Mothers' and fathers' earnings

Earlier studies of women's and men's earnings and incomes have shown similarities between Finland and Sweden. One study including nine countries concludes that mothers' and lone mothers' poverty ratios are the lowest in Sweden and Finland and that 'in these nations, it appears that women are most able to form autonomous, non-poor households independent of men' (Christopher, 2001, p 12). Other studies reveal that even though Finland and Sweden are similar, there are also differences. Finnish women, for example, appear to be less economically dependent on their spouses than Swedish women (Huber et al, 2001, table 3; Sørensen, 2001, table 5.3).

Compared with a decade ago, Finnish mothers are on average absent from the labour market for longer periods and work shorter hours, while Swedish mothers are absent for slightly shorter periods and work longer hours. We can therefore assume that Finnish mothers have become more economically dependent on men and Swedish mothers less dependent on men than before. However, it might also be the case that the proportion of dual-earner families has decreased in both countries since employment rates are lower and unemployment rates are higher today than previously. From the labour market data, we would also suspect that lone mothers have a harder time supporting themselves and their children on their earnings.

Whether these assumptions are correct or not is analysed using data from the Luxembourg Income Survey (LIS) (see www.lisproject.org). We use the LIS survey waves, which represent the total household population, of 1987 and 2000, in both countries.[4]

When we use earnings as a measure of the prevalence of the dual-earner model, we have taken into account three different considerations: first, the proportion of couples with two earners, second, mothers' earnings as a percentage of fathers' earnings in dual-earner families, and third, the share of fathers' and mothers' earnings of family income. The more common it is to have couples with two earners, the more equal mothers' earnings are to fathers' earnings, and the bigger the share mothers contribute to the family income, the stronger the dual-earner model is considered to be. We are well aware that there are several objections to this way of measuring the dual-earner model. One is that a couple is considered to consist of dual earners if both have earnings, however small. Another is that we do not take into consideration transfer incomes, which mothers of small children especially have from paid leave and child home care allowance. A majority of these mothers are on temporary leave from employment, even though the leaves can be rather long. We therefore underestimate women's incomes. However, the data do not allow us to distinguish these transfers on an individual level.

Figure 10.3 shows that the proportion of dual-earner couples has decreased in all categories and in both countries. The change is dramatic in Finland when the child is 0 to two years of age. In 2000

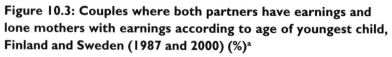

Figure 10.3: Couples where both partners have earnings and lone mothers with earnings according to age of youngest child, Finland and Sweden (1987 and 2000) (%)[a]

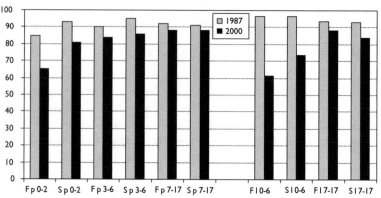

Note: [a] F=Finland, S=Sweden, l=lone, p=partnered.
Source: Calculated from data from the Luxembourg Income Study

only 65% of the couples in Finland had two earners, compared with 85% in 1987. In Sweden the corresponding shares dropped from 93% to 81%. When the child is older the differences are small between Finland and Sweden in 2000.

The tendency is the same for lone mothers. The proportion of lone mothers with pre-school children who have no earnings decreased from 96%-97% in both countries in 1987 to 61% in Finland and 74% in Sweden, while the development among lone mothers with school children is the same as for partnered mothers. The share has fallen slightly from over 90% to 88% in Finland, and to 80% in Sweden.

In all categories, except families with children 0 to two years of age in Finland, the proportion of dual-earner families is currently between 84% and 88%. The rest mainly consist of male-earner/female-carer families, but there are also some female-earner families. In families with children aged seven to 17, female-earner families are as common as male-earner families in both countries (around 5% in 2000). Most common is the male-earner/female-homemaker family in Finnish families with children 0 to two years of age (27% in 2000).

Now we turn to investigating the development of mothers' earnings compared to their spouses' in the dual-earner families. In Figure 10.4 we see that, on average, Finnish mothers contribute more than Swedish mothers. This mirrors the fact that it is more

Figure 10.4: Lone and partnered mothers' share in relation to fathers' yearly earnings in dual-earner families, according to age of youngest child, Finland and Sweden (1987 and 2000) (%)[a]

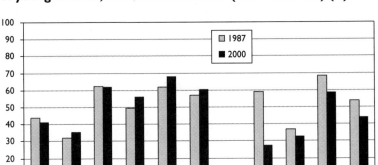

Note: [a] F=Finland, S=Sweden, l=lone, p=partnered. Partnered mothers' earnings are compared with their spouses', and lone mothers' earnings (where they have earnings) with dual-earner couples' fathers' average earnings in the same age groups of children.

Source: Calculated from data from the Luxembourg Income Study

common for Swedish mothers to work part time; that is, Swedish mothers are to a greater extent than Finnish mothers 'junior providers' (Ellingsæter, 1998). If we compare 1987 and 2000, we find that partnered mothers' earnings vary according to the age of the youngest child and that, in most cases, their earnings have increased slightly. When the child is under three in Finland, the earnings have decreased from 44% to 41%, while in Sweden they have increased from 32% to 35%. When the child gets older, Finnish women's earnings reach about two thirds of their husbands' earnings, and Swedish women's earnings reach 50% to 60% of their husbands'.

Mothers who have earnings earn more in comparison to the fathers in dual-earner families than in 1987, while mainly the opposite is true for lone mothers with earnings. They earn less, and again this is especially so for mothers of pre-school children in Finland. Swedish lone mothers with pre-school children, however, make an exception – their earnings level has risen.

A larger proportion of the Finnish mothers have indeed become homemakers, but, at least until now, this does seem to be temporary in the sense that women with small children are affected, but not partnered women earners with older children. Finnish mothers of children aged three or older actually (still) contribute to the family's income to a greater extent than Swedish mothers, whose position as 'junior providers' is more prevalent. Lone mothers have lost the most. Their possibilities of supporting themselves and their children on their earnings are much smaller today than previously, and especially so if they have pre-school children.

Mothers' contribution to household income

For assessing mothers' contribution to yearly gross household income we have to use both individual- and household-level incomes. Individual incomes consist of earnings, unemployment benefits and pensions, which we call 'work incomes'.[5] Parental leave benefits, child home care allowance, child allowances, alimony and maintenance allowance for lone parents are available only at household level and are called 'incomes for children and childcare' here. In spite of child allowances and lone parents' maintenance allowances, most of these incomes are concentrated in families with children below three years of age. The benefits are mainly paid to the mother, but not always (Haataja and Nyberg, 2005). The remaining household income we call 'other incomes', which is the difference between the above-mentioned incomes and household gross income.

Two-parent families

The development of mothers' work income as a share of households' gross income can be seen as an index of women's general integration into the labour market and the economy. It mirrors differences between women and men as far as employment, yearly and daily working time, and wage level are concerned. It gives us a measurement that combines different aspects of gender equality and the dual-earner model.

In two-parent families in Finland, spouses' combined work income, as well as fathers' work income, as a share of gross income decreased between 1987 and 2000 (see Table 10.1). This is not the case in Sweden, where no clear tendency can be seen. Mothers' work income as a share of gross income in families with pre-school children shows different tendencies in Finland and Sweden. In Finland, mothers' work income contributes a smaller share of gross income in 2000 than at the end of the 1980s. This is especially the case when the child is under three years of age. The tendency is

Table 10.1: Spouses' individual work income, income for children and childcare and other incomes as a share of the household gross income, in two-parent families, according to age of youngest child, Finland and Sweden (1987-2000) (%)

	Finland				Sweden			
Youngest child 0-2 years	1987	1991	1995	2000	1987	1992	1995	2000
Spouses' work income	81	76	71	75	72	68	71	77
Fathers	58	56	52	57	55	51	53	58
Mothers	23	20	19	18	17	17	18	19
Income for children and childcare	14	18	21	17	18	21	20	16
Other incomes	5	6	8	7	10	10	9	7
Gross income	100	100	100	100	100	100	100	100
Youngest child 3-6 years	1987	1991	1995	2000	1987	1992	1995	2000
Spouses' work income	92	89	85	86	85	83	84	85
Fathers	58	55	52	55	57	53	54	54
Mothers	34	34	33	31	28	30	30	31
Income for children	3	5	9	7	7	8	7	6
Other incomes	5	6	6	7	8	9	9	9
Gross income	100	100	100	100	100	100	100	100
Youngest child 7-17 years	1987	1991	1995	2000	1987	1992	1995	2000
Spouses' work income	90	90	87	85	88	88	88	85
Fathers	56	54	52	50	57	56	55	54
Mothers	34	36	35	35	31	33	33	31
Income for children	2	2	5	4	4	4	4	3
Other incomes	8	8	8	11	8	8	8	12
Gross income	100	100	100	100	100	100	100	100

Source: Calculated from data from the Luxembourg Income Study

similar, but weaker, when the youngest child is three to six years of age. In Sweden, the tendency is the opposite. Women in different categories contribute a larger share of gross income than they did earlier.

The tendency which can be observed in families with pre-school children does not seem to have influenced the share among women with school children. In this category, women's contribution to gross income is relatively stable in both countries. The temporary increase in women's share between 1991 and 1995 was a result not of an increase in women's income, but of a decrease in men's because of their higher unemployment rate at that time.

Families in Finland did receive a larger share of gross income in 2000 than in 1987 from incomes related to children and childcare and a smaller share from work income. This was not the case in

Sweden. The increase in transfers for children and childcare in families with older children during the second half of the 1990s in Finland can partly be explained by the fact that tax reductions were compensated for by a higher level of child allowance in 1994. But, as can be seen in Table 10.1, the share of gross income of income related to children and childcare is of about the same size and as substantial in both countries, and especially in families with children below three years of age.

Lone mothers

Among lone mothers with pre-school children, work income as a share of gross income decreased dramatically in Finland, but the decline is considerable also among mothers with school children in both countries (see Table 10.2). Swedish mothers with pre-school children did not lose as much, but, on the other hand, they started from a low level.

In Finland, income for children and childcare received from the welfare state as a share of gross income increased, partly because of the tax reduction reform of 1994, and partly because of changes in lone mothers' economic status. They more often took care of children at home when the child was 0 to six years of age in 2000 than was the case towards the end of the 1980s. In Sweden, the

Table 10.2: Lone mothers' work income, income for children and childcare and other incomes as a share of gross income, according to age of youngest child, Finland and Sweden (1987-2000)

	Finland				Sweden			
Youngest child 0-6 years	1987	1991	1995	2000	1987	1992	1995	2000
Mothers' work income	68	57	35	40	47	40	37	44
Income for children and childcare	16	22	33	30	31	33	28	25
Other incomes	16	21	32	29	22	27	35	31
Gross income	100	100	100	100	100	100	100	100
Youngest child 7-17 years	1987	1991	1995	2000	1987	1992	1995	2000
Mothers' work income	72	73	60	65	63	59	54	56
Income for children and childcare	7	9	14	14	16	14	13	14
Other incomes	20	18	26	21	20	27	32	30
Gross income	100	100	100	100	100	100	100	100

Source: Calculated from data from the Luxembourg Income Study

share of income for children and childcare decreased. The increase in other incomes has increased dramatically in both countries and, in Sweden, even among lone mothers with school children. Other incomes among lone mothers mainly consist of income-tested allowances such as housing and social allowance, and so on.

The work income of lone mothers as a share of gross income has decreased in both countries and in both age categories. The result is in line with the development of earnings in Figure 10.4, and indicates that it is much harder today for lone mothers to support themselves and their children on wage income, and that they are much more dependent on other income sources.

Towards temporary homemakers, or a more robust dual-earner/dual-carer model?

Many researchers conclude that Finland and Sweden have moved away from the male breadwinner to the dual-earner/dual-carer model. Mahon (2002) contends, however, that the parenthood policies have differentiated between the countries in the 1990s and that the dual-earner/dual-carer model has been weakened in Finland, while it has been strengthened in Sweden. We argue that the tendency is less unambiguous than both the majority of researchers and Mahon suggest. Finland and Sweden are moving in different directions, yet also in the same direction. To recognise how and why this is so, it is important to differentiate between policies and practices and the age of the youngest child, but also to realise that the policies seem to have a more pronounced effect on lone mothers' labour market situation and incomes than partnered mothers'. The paradox is that the weakening of the dual-earner model both as a result of changes in the parenthood policies and in the economic situation hit lone-mother families harder than partnered parents. Lone mothers' possibilities of maintaining themselves and their families by participating in the labour market are nowadays smaller than for partnered mothers in both countries. If employment remains low and unemployment high also in the future, and lone parents' situation is not taken seriously at the political level (see Skevik, this volume), it can be asked whether there is a risk that a new category of 'welfare mothers', like in other countries, will also appear in Finland and Sweden.

The age of the youngest child divides families into different categories of childcare needs and responsibilities, and regulates what kind of public childcare provisions the parents are entitled to, and what kinds of choices between childcare and employment they are able to make. It is at the age of below three where Finnish and Swedish parenthood policies and responses differ. That, in part, affects how older siblings are cared for and how care is divided between parents.

As far as parental leaves are concerned, the policies in both Finland and Sweden have strengthened the dual-earner/dual-carer model, by introducing individual rights for fathers. The use of the parental leaves, however, is much more gendered than what follows from the contents of the policies in both countries. Both at the policy level and in practice, the mother of small children in Finland is basically perceived as the primary carer and the father as a helper of the mother. Mothers take maternity leave and parental leave and, on top of that, they use the child home care allowance, while the fathers use the daddy days. Leave policies in Sweden address both parents, and the involvement of fathers as carers is stressed. The introduction of the daddy quota increased fathers' use of parental leave, but mothers still use an overwhelmingly large proportion of the total parental leave.

In the area of public childcare services, Finland introduced a subjective right of children to use public childcare services before Sweden did, which contradicts Mahon's conclusion concerning the policies on this account (2002, p 350). At the same time, however, and consistent with Mahon's analysis, the use of childcare actually decreased for small children in Finland, while it increased extensively in Sweden. The decline in the use of public childcare in Finland is related to the child home care allowance, which is an alternative care provision to a place in public childcare. However, the childcare allowance is also related to increased unemployment and temporary work contracts, which have affected the possibilities of especially younger and less educated mothers to choose between employment and childcare. Therefore, in spite of the early introduction of publicly financed childcare in Finland, a policy which supported the dual-earner/dual-carer model, practices are more in line with the dual-earner/dual-carer model in Sweden.

In spite of the partly different roads taken in the two countries as far as policies of childcare leaves are concerned, the empirical analyses of the dual-earner part of the model indicate both growing differences and an increasing convergence between Finland and Sweden. The cash benefit allowance acts as a watershed here and mainly affects families with children under three years of age. Growing differences can be seen in both policies and practices of families with children under the age of three. The policies in Finland are more in line with recognising and rewarding women's care-giving in the home, and the practice of Finnish families can here be seen to move in the direction of the male-earner/temporary female-homemaker model. In Sweden, the policies have focused primarily on a more equal division of care work, and parents' practices are also moving, although slowly, in the same direction as the intention of the policies. Both policies and practices indicate, although with some qualification, that Sweden and Finland are today moving in different directions for these families.

On the other hand, for mothers with children of three years and older, labour market participation is encouraged in both countries through the supply of affordable publicly financed childcare. As far as partnered parents are concerned, the dual-earner part of the model has not weakened. Employment, the share of dual-earner families, and mothers' contribution to family earnings were more similar in the two countries around 2000 than towards the end of the 1980s. The difference in the proportion of dual-earner families is about the same, while Finnish women contribute more to family earnings. Furthermore, if paid work was measured in full-time equivalents, Finnish women would probably be ahead of Swedish women, although women are still 'junior' earners and 'senior' carers in both countries.

Notes

[1] Fathers' share of benefits has been a small percentage in the 1990s except for the recession years 1992-95, when it was possible to transfer the allowance to the working parent if the other was unemployed at home (Haataja, 2005a).

[2] Sipilä and Korpinen (1998); Salmi (2000) and this volume; Korpinen (2000); Rissanen and Knudsen (2001).

[3] For the situation of lone mothers, see also Skevik, this volume.

[4] We have in fact used the four latest LIS survey waves, 1987, 1991/92, 1995 and 2000, but we only show 1987 and 2000 in this chapter. See Haataja and Nyberg, 2005.

[5] Families with self-employment income are excluded due to lack of individual information. See Haataja and Nyberg, 2005.

References

AKU Arbetskraftsundersökningarna (Labour Force Surveys), Statistics Sweden.

Anttonen, A. (2001) 'The female working citizen: social rights, work and motherhood in Finland', *Kvinder, Køn & Forskning*, no 2, pp 33-44.

Bergqvist, C., Kuusipalo, J. and Styrkársdóttir, A. (1999) 'The debate on childcare policies', in C. Bergqvist, A. Borchorst, A.-D. Christensen, V. Ramstedt-Silén, N.C. Raaum and A. Styrkársdóttir (eds) *Equal Democracies? Gender and Politics in the Nordic Countries*, Oslo: Scandinavian University Press, pp 137-57.

Bruning, G. and Plantenga, J. (1999) 'Parental leave and equal opportunities: experiences in eight European countries', *Journal of European Social Policy*, vol 9, no 3, pp 195-209.

Christopher, K. (2001) *Caregiving, Welfare States and Mothers' Poverty*, Luxembourg Income Study Working Paper No 287 (available at: www.lisproject.org/publications/wpapers.htm).

Daune-Richard, A.-M. (2005) 'Women's work between family and welfare state: part-time work and childcare in France and Sweden', in B. Pfau-Effinger and B. Geissler (eds) *Care and Social Integration in European Societies*, Bristol: The Policy Press, pp 215-33.

Ellingsæter, A.L. (1998) 'Dual breadwinner societies: provider models in the Scandinavian welfare states', *Acta Sociologica*, vol 41, no 1, pp 59-73.

Ellingsæter, A.L. (1999) 'Dual breadwinners between state and market', in R. Crompton (ed) *Restructuring Gender Relations and Employment: The Decline of the Male Breadwinner*, Oxford: Oxford University Press, pp 40–59.

European Commission (2002) *The Rationale of Motherhood Choices: Influence of Employment Conditions and of Public Policies*, Community Research, State of the Art, EUR 20792 (available at: www.ulb.ac.be/soco/mocho/reports.htm).

Forssén, K. (1998) 'Decentralisation of decision-making: the case of payment policies for children's daycare', in K. Forssén (ed) *Children, Families and the Welfare States: Studies on the Outcomes of the Finnish Family Policy*, Research Report 92, Helsinki: National Research and Development Centre for Welfare and Health (STAKES), pp 73–93.

Haataja, A. (2004) 'Pohjoismaiset vanhempainvapaat kahden lasta hoitavan vanhemman tukena', *Janus*, vol 12, no 1, pp 25-48.

Haataja, A. (2005a) 'Outcomes of the two family policy reforms at the turn of the 2000s in Finland', *Yearbook 2005 of Population Research in Finland 41*, pp 5–28.

Haataja, A. (2005b) *Äidit ja isät työmarkkinoilla 1989-2002/2003*, Selvityksiä 29, Helsinki: Ministry of Social Affairs (also available at: www.stm.fi.).

Haataja, A. and Nyberg, A. (2005) *Did the Dual-Earner Model Become Stronger or Weaker in Finland and Sweden in the 1990s?*, Luxembourg Income Study Working Paper No 415, available at: www.lisproject.org

Hämäläinen, U. (2005) 'Perhevapaiden aikaiset tulot ja toimeentulo', in P. Takala (ed) *Onko Meillä Malttia Sijoittaa Lapsiin*, Kelan tutkimusosasto, Helsinki: Kela, pp 126–47.

Huber, E., Stephens, J.D., Bradley, D., Moller, S. and Nielsen, F. (2001) *The Welfare State and Gender Equality*, Luxembourg Income Study Working Paper No 279, available at: www.lisproject.org/publications/wpapers.htm

Jansson, F., Pylkkänen, E. and Valck, L. (2003) *En jämställd försäkring?: Bilaga 12 till Långtidsutredningen 2003* (SOU 2003:36), Stockholm: Fritzes.

Kamerman, S.B. and Kahn, A.J. (eds) (1991) *Childcare, Parental Leave, and the Under 3s: Policy Innovation in Europe*, New York, NY: Auburn House.

Kautto, M. (2000) *Two of a Kind?: Economic Crisis, Policy Responses and Well-Being During the 1990s in Sweden and Finland* (SOU 2000: 83), Stockholm: Fritzes.

Korpinen, J. (2000) 'Child Home Care Allowance: Framing the Finnish Experience', in L. Kalliomaa-Puha (ed) *Perspectives on Equality: Work, Women and Family in the Nordic Countries and EU*, Nord 5, Copenhagen: Nordic Council of Ministers, pp 174–86.

Leira, A. (2002) *Working Parents and the Welfare State: Family Change and Policy Reform in Scandinavia*, Cambridge: Cambridge University Press.

Mahon, R. (2002) 'Childcare: toward what kind of 'Social Europe'?', *Social Politics: International Studies in Gender, State and Society*, vol 9, no 3, Autumn, pp 343–79.

Moss, P. and Deven, F. (eds) (1999) *Parental Leave: Progress or Pitfall?*, Volume 35, The Hague/Brussels: NIDI/CBGS Publications.

NOSOSCO (Nordic Social Statistical Committee) (2001: 16) *Social Protection in the Nordic Countries 1999*, Copenhagen: NOSOSCO.

NOSOSCO (2005: 26) *Social Protection in the Nordic Countries 2003*, Copenhagen: NOSOSCO.

Nyberg, A. (1995) *Hemarbetets volym och värde*, Tema-T Arbetsnotat, Linköping: Linköpings Universitet.

Nyberg, A. (2003) *Deltidsarbete och Deltidsarbetslöshet: En uppföljning av DELTA-utredningen* (SOU 1999: 27), Stockholm: Arbetslivsinstitutet.

Nyberg, A. (2004) *Parental Insurance and Childcare in Sweden*, Peer review programme of the European Employment Strategy, European Commission, DG Employment and Social Affairs (available at: www.peerreview-employment.org).

Nyberg, A. (2005) 'Har den ekonomiska jämställdheten ökat sedan början av 1990-talet?' In *Forskarrapporter till Jämställdhetspolitiska Utredningen* (SOU 2005:66), Stockholm: Fritzes.

OECD (Organisation for Economic Co-operation and Development) (1995) 'Long-term leave for parents in OECD countries', *Employment Outlook*, Paris: OECD.

Orloff, A.S. (1993) 'Gender and the social right of citizenship: the comparative analysis of gender relations and welfare states', *American Sociological Review*, vol 58, no 3, pp 303-28.

Perhevapaasäännösten Toimivuus (2005) *Perhevapaasäännösten Toimivuutta Arvioineen Työryhmän Raportti*, Työhallinnon Julkaisu 358, Helsinki: Työministeriö.

Rissanen, T. and Knudsen, C. (2001) *The Child Home Care Allowance and Women's Labour Force Participation in Finland, 1985-1998*, Oslo: Norwegian Social Research.

Rønsen, M. (2005) *Kontantstøttens langsiktige effekter på mødres og fedres arbetidstilbud*, Statistisk Sentralbyrå, Olso: Kongsvinger.

Ruhm, C. (1998) 'The economic consequences of parental leaves mandates: lessons from Europe', *The Quarterly Journal of Economics*, vol 113, no 1, pp 285-317.

Salmi, M. (2000) 'Analysing the Finnish homecare allowance system: challenges to research and problems of interpretations', in L. Kalliomaa-Puha (ed) *Perspectives of Equality: Work, Women and Family in the Nordic Countries and EU*, Copenhagen: Nordic Council of Ministers, pp 187-205.

Sipilä, J. and Korpinen, J. (1998) 'Cash versus child care services in Finland', *Social Policy and Administration*, vol 32, no 3, pp 263-77.

Skolverket (2003) *Uppföljning av reformen maxtaxa, allmän förskola m.m*, Skolverkets Rapport No 231, Stockholm: Skolverket.

SOU (Statens Offentliga Utredningar) (2005: 73) *Reformerad föräldraförsäkring – Kärlek, Omvårdnad, Trygghet*, Stockholm: Fritzes.

Sørensen, A. (2001) *Gender Equality in Earnings at Work and Home*, Luxembourg Working Paper No 251, Luxembourg (available at: www.lisproject.org/publications/wpapers.htm).

Takala, P. (2003) 'Ny pappaledighet biter inte', FPA-bladet, no 3, pp 4-5.

Väinälä, A. (2004) *Selvitys Kotona Olevien Vanhempien Lasten Päivähoitotilanteesta, Syyskuu 2004*, Selvityshenkilön raportti, ensipainos, Sosiaali – ja terveysministeriön työryhmämuistioita 16, Helsinki: Sosiaali – ja terveysministeriö.

ELEVEN

Lone motherhood in the Nordic countries: sole providers in dual-breadwinner regimes

Anne Skevik

Introduction

Lone motherhood is a key issue when exploring the politicisation of parenthood. The meaning of lone motherhood has changed quite radically from the early days of the welfare state. Two or three generations ago, lone mothers made up a small group of women surrounded by stable two-parent families provided for by the male breadwinner. As we enter the 2000s, high proportions of women pass through a stage as a lone mother, and the ideal of lifelong partnerships between male breadwinners and female homemakers has lost considerable normative power. This presents policy-makers with new challenges. The challenges are particularly acute in the Nordic countries, with their high rates of parental break-ups and strong traditions for female employment. Should lone mothers still be understood as a group with special needs in this situation? What is the proper conception of public and private responsibilities towards lone mothers and their children? How should lone mothers be expected to juggle their earning and caring responsibilities at different stages in their children's lives?

Lone mothers are women living with children, but without men. From Biblical times, the high poverty risk of this group has been recognised. Traditional responses to the poverty problem among lone mothers have typically been mixed. Poor relief has existed in many countries, but payouts from the public purse have been strictly tested against other possible sources of provisions: the mother's own capacity to work, and the existence of a potential private breadwinner. As welfare states developed in Europe, these criteria have been applied less rigorously. It became less common to insist that a mother should take up employment while she had young children, the obligations on biological fathers were negotiated and codified, and it was no longer to be assumed that any new boyfriend was a potential family provider. Since the mid-1990s, however, we may be witnessing a new gradual shift: increasing numbers of countries place stronger emphasis on employment, and use this as an argument to withdraw or reshape benefits for lone mothers (Millar and Rowlingson, 2001). Simultaneously, given more unstable partnerships and increasing numbers of couples cohabiting, policy-makers have to address again the question of what sort of obligations should follow from different forms of private relationships. Married couples are legally obliged to provide for each other, but what are the obligations of cohabiting partners? And where should benefit authorities draw the line between a lone-mother family and a cohabiting couple – how many nights, for how long a period, can a new boyfriend spend with a lone mother before the right to benefits as a lone parent is lost? Two old demarcation lines for public support have thus reappeared on the political agenda in a new shape: the demarcation against mothers' employment, and the boundary between lone parenthood and cohabitation. Both boundaries are drawn by political decision-making – there is not one obvious set of answers to the dilemmas involved that is true in all contexts at all times.

This chapter deals with the politics of lone parenthood in three Nordic countries[1] in the 1990s – Norway, Sweden and Finland. Denmark is not included, mainly due to the lack of data on lone parents' situation in this country. The aim is to explore the emerging policy agenda in three countries that have arguably moved well beyond the male-breadwinner model of the family. How was the state/family or the state/employment boundary redrawn in this period of economic recession, unstable parental partnerships and new policy influences? The answer to this question is essentially descriptive, and it requires an overview of what actually happened to lone mothers' labour market participation in this turbulent period. The next question asked is more analytical: has the (potential) problem of poverty and/or social exclusion in lone-parent families been solved in these countries, or are they merely emerging in a new form? The normative issue underlying both these questions is whether welfare states should support lone mothers as workers, or carers, or both.

The focus is on tax and benefit policies that target lone parents especially, as these bring out the underlying 'policy logics' regarding this group most clearly (Lewis and Hobson, 1997). Although lone parents obviously benefit from high coverage of public day care services (see Leira; Haataja and Nyberg, this volume) as well as relatively generous benefit schemes for all families with children, and may also be eligible for comprehensive schemes targeted at unemployed and disabled people, these benefits are not discussed here.

Data on lone mothers' participation and unemployment rates come from national sources. They are based on the Survey of Level of Living in Sweden, the Labour Force Survey in Finland, and the Survey of Income and Wealth in Norway, and have been made available in English through the project 'Welfare policies and employment in the context of family change'.[2] Informants have been asked to present data following the 'standard definition' of lone parenthood: a lone parent is a parent who has at least one child under 18, who is not living with a partner but who may or may not be living in a household with others. Considerable effort has been made to make sure the data are accurate and comparable. However, since we only have macro-level data on participation rates and unemployment rates, there is a limit to what kinds of questions can be answered. Issues relating to working hours and periods on leave are thus not discussed here. The data relate only to lone mothers; the small groups of lone fathers are excluded from the analysis. Many of the arguments nevertheless apply equally to lone fathers. When discussing the general issues I use gender-neutral language; the evidence is, however, presented gender-specifically.

In what follows, I will first outline the issues of the two demarcation lines in more depth. Has the politicisation of lone parenthood entailed an increasing emphasis on family support, public transfers, or a stronger promotion of labour market participation for all mothers? Then I will give an overview of developments in the three countries, with an emphasis on macro-economic developments and policy responses. While the late 1980/early 1990 recession is seen as a main explanatory factor for developments in Sweden and Finland (see also Haataja and Nyberg; Hiilamo, this volume), the Norwegian changes are explained in terms of the rapid expansions of family policies in this country since the mid-1980s. Although policies and economies obviously interacted in all countries, this is broadly in accordance with how national analysts tend to tell the story of their countries (Björnberg, 1997a, 1997b; Forssén, 1998; Gähler, 2001; Kjeldstad and Rønsen, 2002). Having done this, I will return to the question of the relationship between state support, family support and labour market provision: to sum up how, if at all, the balance between the three changed in all three countries in the 1990s.

Lone parents: the welfare state, labour market and family support

In the international literature, it is generally assumed that lone parenthood does not pose a problem in the Nordic countries: 'In most Nordic countries, lone-parent families are not singled out in relation to 'the family', as in Britain, but are seen as a part of all families,' asserted Miri Song in 1996 (p 377). Or in the words of Jane Lewis and Barbara Hobson (1997, p 10), 'The Scandinavian countries have moved furthest away from the male breadwinner model towards an assumption that all adults, male and female, will be in the labour market, which means that lone mothers per se are not conceptualised as a problem'. The background for these claims was both demographic and political: the Nordic countries all have relatively high proportions of lone parents, and there has at no point been a moral panic regarding this fact. Moreover, given the high rates of female employment in the Nordic countries, it is no longer the disaster it used to be for a woman to lack a male provider. Poverty rates for children living in one-parent families are also generally low in the Nordic countries (Bradbury and Jäntti, 2001), compared with most other European countries. It is not unusual, it is argued, for a woman to support a family, and a lone mother needs only the same support as mothers living in partnerships: high-quality childcare and sufficient leave arrangements. In each respect, the Scandinavian countries lead the way.

In questioning this rosy picture, it may be useful to remind ourselves of why lone mothers were singled out as a problem group in the first place. There are three key reasons for this, as outlined by Annemette Sørensen (1994): first, women's income from waged work is typically lower than that of men. Second, lone parents do not benefit from the economies of scale that families with two or more adults do. Third, they do not have access to a partner's income, and are solely responsible for bringing money into the household. They will in many cases receive child support, sometimes also alimony, but in the vast majority of cases these payments are too low to compensate for the income of a resident partner. The second and third points apply relatively independently of national context, in that they follow directly from the situation a lone mother finds herself in. The first point, women's lower wages, occurs for a series of reasons: first, women are less likely to be in employment than men, second, employed women typically work shorter hours than employed men, and third, women are typically paid less even when they work the same hours as men (Sørensen, 1994). Gendered wage differences are typically small in Scandinavia, but the points about women's lower labour force participation and higher propensity to work part time apply in all the countries discussed here – although less in Finland than in Norway and Sweden (Sørensen, 2001; OECD, 2003).

Sweden, and to some extent Finland, have been hailed as the countries that have come furthest in leaving behind the male-breadwinner model in favour of the dual-breadwinner model – a welfare state model in which both mothers and fathers are seen as workers and providers (Sainsbury, 1996). However, critical voices have also been raised towards this policy approach. Consider, for instance, Jessica Lindvert's (2002) criticism of Swedish gender equality policies, which she describes as a 'working mothers' policy' with little attention to other aspects of gender policy, and with very little attention paid to the downside to this approach in the public debate. 'Even though recent reports indicate that Swedish mothers are overwhelmed by guilt for not coping well with the burden of combining their career with motherhood, few alternative feminist approaches have gained serious attention' (Lindvert, 2002, p 100). Duncan and Edwards (1999) have documented how lone mothers, also in Sweden, hold very complex and refined notions regarding their roles as mothers/carers and workers/providers that may at times be out of phase with the assumptions and norms that guide public policies towards them. Similar points have been made with regard to Norway (Syltevik, 1996; Duncan and Strell, 2004).

With increasing diversity of family forms, the category 'lone mother' in itself becomes increasingly hard to define. Both entry into, and exit from, the category have become increasingly fuzzy. For instance, it is commonly argued that cohabitation solves two of the three essential problems of lone motherhood (see Sørensen, 1994): by adding another adult to the household, the (former) lone parent can benefit from the economies of scale, and the presence of a cohabiting partner gives her access to a second income. Yet both these assumptions are questionable: living with friends or family also increases economies of scale, yet lone parents living in such households are still counted as 'lone'. And it is not given that cohabitation implies intra-household distribution of resources, as some qualitative studies have pointed out (Syltevik and Wærness, 2004). The basic assumption behind this argument, then, to put it bluntly, is that a man with whom a woman has sexual relations is also ready and able to be a provider for her and her children. This assumption is a remnant of male-breadwinner ideology. Faced with macro-economic problems and increasing unemployment, could politicians be tempted to try to reintroduce the male-breadwinner model 'by the back door' for lone mothers, by placing more emphasis on new partners' duty to provide for them and their children?

To these principled considerations comes a practical concern: it can be difficult to determine when a benefit recipient has actually taken up cohabitation. This has been a major issue in situations where benefit entitlements have depended on the woman's status as single. Intrusive controls of the recipient's private life are obviously highly unwelcome, and can in some cases deter the parent from seeking lone-parent benefits in the first place. To the extent that more emphasis has been placed on the private duty to maintain one's household members financially, did this also increase social control of recipients of lone-parent benefits? These are issues to keep in mind when studying policy changes.

The 1990s: a tale of three countries

A brief overview of the basic outlines of the benefit systems may be useful before moving on to a more detailed examination of each country. These basics changed little, if at all, in the course of the 1990s. In all the Nordic countries, local authorities provide social assistance schemes that cater to the needs of people who are outside the labour force, and who are not entitled to any social security benefits (Bradshaw and Terum, 1997). In Sweden and Finland, this is where lone parents turn if they are unable to support themselves through employment. In Norway, lone parents in addition have separate entitlements through National Insurance. All three countries pay universal child benefits, and in Norway this is paid at a higher rate to lone parents (Skevik, 2001a). At the beginning of the 1990s, separate tax deductions for lone parents existed in all countries. Forwarded child maintenance also exists in all countries, although with slightly different designs. This payment is available to all lone parents (except widows), but also to parents who have set up new partnerships: the condition for receiving this payment is that there is a child in the household who does not live with both biological parents, not whether or not there is a new partner/step-parent in the household. In Finland, however, up to 1999, forwarded maintenance was paid at a lower rate to parents who cohabited (Hiilamo, 2002, p 277).

The state-guaranteed transfers targeted especially at parents living apart were thus limited to forwarded maintenance in Sweden and Finland. In addition, lone parents could benefit from certain special tax deductions. Those who could not cope would seek social assistance.

In Norway, a far more comprehensive arrangement existed, including forwarded maintenance, extra child benefit, tax deductions, and separate benefits under National Insurance that included a subsistence-level benefit (transitional allowance), childcare benefit and education benefit (Skevik, 2001a).

Recession and recovery I: Sweden

Sweden was hard hit by economic recession in the early 1990s. Between 1990 and 1993, the number of people in employment fell by more than half a million, Gross Domestic Product (GDP) fell for three years running and state finances showed a considerable deficit. The unemployment rate increased from 1.6% to 8.1% in the same period (Hiilamo, this volume). The impact of these macro-economic changes led to a new research interest in lone parenthood in Sweden. Quantitative studies showed that lone mothers had fewer financial resources than other groups even before the recession (Gähler, 2001). Their average income per consumption unit was lower than for other families with children, and they were more likely to report problems with everyday living expenses and that they lacked a cash margin. Their disadvantage increased in the course of the 1990s. Lone parents were not the only ones who fared worse in the mid-1990s than at the beginning of the decade, but their disadvantage seemed to continue well after the worst crisis was over. In 1997, lone parents had the lowest income per consumption unit of all family forms (Gähler, 2001; Haataja and Nyberg, this volume). Also, the proportion who struggled with living expenses and lacked a cash margin continued to increase.

Not only were lone mothers more vulnerable to poverty than other categories, analyses of large-scale surveys showed that they were also more likely than partnered mothers to lose their foothold in the labour market in the 1990s (Björnberg, 1996, 1997a, 1997b). The development of participation and unemployment rates for married/cohabiting mothers and lone mothers in Sweden is shown in Figure 11.1. The figure shows, first, that married/cohabiting mothers have higher labour market participation rates, and lower unemployment rates, than lone mothers. Mothers living in partnerships are thus both more likely to be economically active and more likely to succeed in finding and keeping a job than mothers living alone. Second, the figure shows how lone mothers were far harder hit by the economic recession in the early 1990s than partnered mothers were. Unemployment rates for lone mothers were higher than for married/cohabiting mothers even before the

Figure 11.1: Labour market participation rates and unemployment rates for lone mothers and mothers in two-parent families, Sweden (1990-2001) (%)

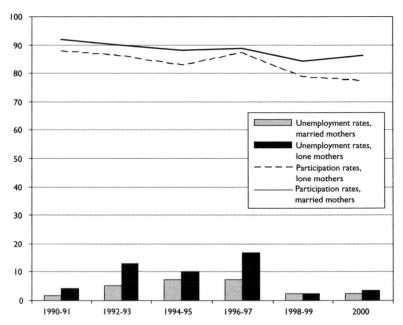

Note: Data from Undersökningar av Levnadsförhållanden (ULF) (Survey of Level of Living)
Source: Björnberg and Dahlgren (2003)

recession (1990-91), but increased far more strongly. Moreover, while the unemployment rates for married/cohabiting women stabilised, then fell, after 1994/95, unemployment rates for lone mothers continued to increase until 1996/97.

By 1998-99, Figure 11.1 shows that unemployment rates had returned to their 'normal' low level of 2% to 3% for both married/cohabiting and lone mothers. The fall is particularly dramatic for lone mothers: from over 17% to just above 2%. Apparently, the crisis was finally over, for lone mothers too. The labour market participation rates, however, continued to fall: lower unemployment rates did not translate into higher employment rates as much as into higher proportions being outside the labour market altogether. Björnberg and Dahlgren (2003) warn against taking the lower unemployment rates at face value, and point out that Sweden has a 'hidden' unemployment rate. First, there is quite a large discrepancy between the official unemployment rates and the proportions looking for work. More lone parents than mothers and fathers in two-parent families were looking for work throughout the 1990s (Björnberg and Dahlgren, 2003, p 11ff). Second, unemployment is 'disguised' in the unemployment programmes, since participants in such programmes are not counted among the unemployed. There was a strong increase in the proportion taking part in unemployment programmes in the 1990s, but no data on gender and family status are available. Finally, lone parents were far more likely to hold temporary work contracts than mothers and fathers in two-parent families throughout the 1990s. This is another indication of lone parents' more precarious relationship with the labour market, which becomes far more visible in times of recession.

At the beginning of the 2000s, the vulnerability of lone mothers in Swedish society was well documented. This has, however, not led to new policy initiatives to improve lone mothers' situation. There have been no activation measures targeted at this group, no initiatives to confront any special problems they may face as employees, and certainly no targeted benefits. One might say, rather, that what happened in the early 1990s was the opposite: as mentioned, lone parents in Sweden were entitled to a special tax allowance. This was discontinued in 1992, as part of the 'crisis package' introduced to tackle the consequences of the international recession (Hiilamo, 2002, and this volume). To (partly) compensate for the additional tax load, a special allowance for lone parents was introduced later the same year. In 1993, however, this temporary allowance was abolished. With these moves, all preferential treatment of lone parents in statutory tax and benefit schemes was abolished in Sweden. This also solved the question of drawing a demarcation line for support for lone parents against those in cohabiting relationships: after 1993, all benefits that took the living arrangement of the recipient into consideration had been abolished, and cohabitation was no longer an issue in this respect.

Recession and recovery II: Finland

Finland was the only Organisation for Economic Co-operation and Development (OECD) country in which the recession of the late 1980s/early 1990s was more severe than the crisis in the 1930s. 1990 was a year of zero growth, followed by three years of negative growth and a 13% GDP decline. Unemployment rates increased from under 4% to 17-18% in the same period (all figures: Heikkilä and Uusitalo, 1997; see also Hiilamo, this volume). This development simultaneously

Figure 11.2: Labour market participation rates and unemployment rates for lone mothers and mothers in two-parent families, Finland (1990-2000) (%)

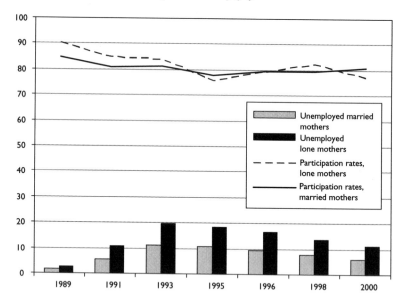

Note: Data from the Labour Force Survey, TASTY database.
Source: NOSOSCO (2004)

led to a considerable loss in revenue and increased needs for public transfers in the population. Families with children experienced cutbacks in the form of increased municipal taxes and service fees, reduced health, maternity and parental benefits, and tighter eligibility conditions for housing support (Forssén, 1998, p 138ff; Hiilamo, 2002; Forssén et al, 2003). Like in Sweden, mothers in Finland were strongly affected by the economic recession in the early 1990s, and lone mothers even more so than married mothers.

An analysis of developments in disposable incomes for different family types revealed a trend similar to that in Sweden: all family types experienced a sharp drop in incomes at the onset of the recession, that is, from 1991 to 1992. From 1992 to 1993, disposable equalised incomes remained fairly stable for all family forms except lone parents, who experienced a new decrease almost as strong as the first. The recovery for lone parents only seemed to happen between 1994 and 1995, when disposable incomes crept back to the level they had been around 1989 (Uusitalo, 1997, figure 8). Forssén (1998, p 141) has showed that the proportion of lone parents in the lowest income decile increased significantly between 1990 and 1994, while the corresponding increase for two-parent families was much smaller. Also, the poverty rate of lone parents increased from 2% in 1990 to over 7% in 1994. This was more than three times higher than the poverty rate for two-parent families. Using receipt of social assistance as an indication of poverty, a similar pattern is found (Forssén, 1998, figure 5.5).

As Figure 11.2 shows, lone mothers had very high labour market participation rates in Finland in 1990 – higher than those of mothers living in two-parent families. By 1995 the participation rates of lone mothers had fallen below those of married mothers, and have since been fairly similar. Unemployment rates remained high in Finland throughout the decade, and have been consistently higher for lone mothers than for mothers in two-parent families: even in 2000, unemployment was almost twice as high for lone as for married/cohabiting mothers (see also Haataja and Nyberg, this volume). The dramatic differences in unemployment rates together with the similarity of labour market participation rates – a pattern unlike that of the other countries studied here – may have to do with how Finnish mothers define their situation when out of employment: given the strong tradition for female employment in Finland, Finnish mothers may be more reluctant to define themselves as outside the labour force, and more likely to think of themselves as unemployed. In any case, the pattern is clearly that lone mothers are less likely to actually be in employment than partnered mothers, also in Finland.

Like in Sweden, lone mothers thus lost out on two (interlinked) accounts during the crisis years: their poverty rates increased, and their labour market participation decreased. In particular, their unemployment rates were at times extremely high, reaching 20% in 1993. Research seemed to suggest that lone mothers were definitely among the vulnerable groups in Finnish society during the crisis. Did this prompt Finnish politicians to create some special form of support for lone mothers? The crisis implied a considerable strain on Finnish public resources, which meant that there was little room for political innovation. No measures were implemented that specifically addressed the problems of lone mothers. Similar to what Sweden did in 1992, Finland discontinued its special tax allowance for lone parents in 1994, and replaced it with an increase in child allowances for the former beneficiaries (Hiilamo, 2002, and this volume). This allowance still exists. However, not all former beneficiaries of the special tax allowance were awarded increased child allowances: as part of the reform, entitlements were restricted to the parents who actually lived alone. A clearer line was thus drawn between lone parents living alone, and parents who cohabited with new partners. But the practice of separating lone parents from those who cohabited with a new partner was already established in Finland: as mentioned, forwarded child maintenance was paid at a lower rate to cohabiting couples. This practice of lowering rates of forwarded maintenance to cohabiting partners was ended in 1999, with an interesting argument: it was seen as too difficult to determine precisely when the conditions for reducing the payment (or reversing it to the non-reduced) had been met. Hiilamo (2002, p 279) describes this as a victory for citizens' rights organisations, who had raised this point on several occasions. Finnish policies by the late 1990s thus came across as rather Janus-faced (Leira, 1992) in this respect: the problems with determining when a lone parent had actually taken up cohabitation were acknowledged, but this argument did not weigh strongly enough to stop politicians from withdrawing the right to extended child benefit on these grounds.[3]

Lone parents as targets of activation policies: Norway

Norway, as seen above, is the only Nordic country that has implemented a separate benefit arrangement for lone parents. This has been highlighted as one example of how male-breadwinner assumptions are built into the Norwegian social security system in a way they are not in the other Nordic countries (Leira, 1992; Sainsbury, 1999). Before the reform in 1998, lone parents could in principle stay out of the labour force for as long as they had children under 10 years of age. Only then would the transitional allowance, which was the main benefit for lone parents with very low incomes, be withdrawn. Lone parents who were unable to support themselves after this point, could apply for social assistance. The benefit system was, however, not all geared towards home-based care for young children: two benefits existed specifically for lone parents to ease their transition into employment – education benefit could be awarded towards the costs of necessary education, and childcare benefit to offset the costs of childcare (Skevik, 2001a, 2001b). Both these benefits were introduced in the 1960s, thus they existed well before the international turn towards activation.

The Labour government elected in 1985 demonstrated a clear commitment to gender equality policies, and measures designed to help parents reconcile work and employment were expanded considerably in the latter half of the 1980s (see Kjeldstad and Skevik, 2004). In the early 1990s, this approach also caught up with the support arrangements for lone parents. The 1994 budget insisted: 'When society invests such considerable resources in easing the situation for families with young children, resources that also benefit lone parents, one can ask if lone parents *should* not also utilise this offer from society' (St. prp. no 1,1993/94, p 85; emphasis in original). Day care coverage and parental leave arrangements had been considerably expanded, thereby undermining the traditional arguments for lone-parent benefits: lone parents now had a different form of 'offer' from society. While the economic recession determined the agenda in Sweden and Finland, the backdrop for debates on policies towards lone parents in Norway was essentially political: policies for lone parenthood met the international trend of concern for activation of vulnerable groups more generally. Lone parents' economic problems were to be solved via labour market participation.

The time had come for a thorough review of the benefit arrangement for lone parents. The process culminated with the 1998 reform of the National Insurance Act (Skevik, 2001a), when the maximum period for receipt of transitional allowance was reduced to three years after the birth of the youngest child or the parental break-up, whichever happened later. All three years on allowance had to be taken before the child turned eight. Moreover, lone parents who did not have children under three were required to work at least part time, take up education, or actively seek employment in order to be eligible for the benefit. The only exception applied to the first year after the break-up, during which the parent could receive transitional allowance provided she had at least one child under 10. For lone parents who had children under three, benefits were increased slightly. Combined with the cash benefit for childcare, which was introduced in the autumn of 1998 (Ellingsæter, 2003), lone parents with children under three could receive quite considerable non-work incomes. Lone parents whose youngest child was older than three, on the other hand, faced relatively strict work requirements.

What, then, did the labour market participation of lone parents in Norway look like in the 1990s? Figure 11.3 shows the development of participation rates and unemployment rates for mothers in Norway 1990-99 (data from 2000 are not available). The figure shows increasing labour market participation rates for both married/cohabiting and lone mothers between 1990 and 1999. Norway felt the consequences of the international recession in the late 1980s to early 1990s, but far less severely than Sweden and

Figure 11.3: Labour market participation rates and unemployment rates for lone mothers and mothers in two-parent families, Norway (1990-99) (%)

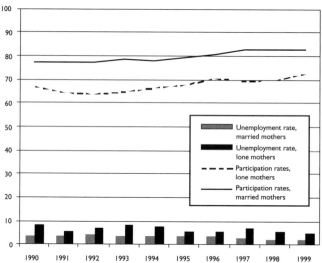

Note: Survey of Income and Wealth, various years.
Source: Kjeldstad and Rønsen (2002)

Finland: this is visible in the small decrease in participation rates for lone mothers between 1990 and 1992. Since 1992, however, participation rates have increased steadily, and in a very similar pattern for the two groups of mothers. On the other hand, there are clear differences in the unemployment rates of the two groups of mothers, with rates being consistently higher for lone mothers than for mothers in two-parent families. For both married/cohabiting mothers and lone mothers, however, unemployment rates fell in the course of the 1990s. The much-trumpeted 1998 reform of the benefit system for lone parents is invisible in Figure 11.3. Since we only have data up to 1999, the real effects of the reform might not show yet.

Given that Norway has a far more comprehensive benefit system for lone parents than Sweden and Finland, it is hardly surprising that the issue of cohabitation has been much harder to handle in this country. Whether or not lone-parent benefits should be withdrawn when the recipient moved in with a new partner was debated repeatedly: the centre-right parties feared for the incentive effects when people were 'penalised for getting married', while parties on the left argued that by ending entitlements the moment a recipient moved in with a partner, one risked taking benefits away from women who really needed them. In 1994, Norwegian family law adopted the principle that cohabiting couples with joint children were to be treated as a married couple in the benefit systems. This implied that the right to increased child benefit was lost to former lone parents who had a child by a new partner. Moreover, since 1999 all entitlements to benefits as a lone parent have been lost if the recipient has a child by a new cohabiting partner, or if the cohabiting relationship lasts for a year or more. The presence of joint children, and/or duration of the relationship for one year, are both taken as indicators that the relationship is 'stable and marriage-like', and therefore should be treated as a marriage for benefit purposes.

Welfare state, labour market, family – new boundaries?

To sum up: Sweden and Finland experienced severe economic depression in the 1990s, and neither country implemented any special policies to encourage (or maintain) lone mothers in the labour market. In both these countries, labour market participation rates for lone mothers fell during the decade, and more so than they did for mothers living in partnerships. Moreover, unemployment rates for lone mothers increased sharply, and well above the rates for married and cohabiting mothers. Norway was the only country in the Nordic cluster that implemented special activation measures for lone parents, and this happened against a backdrop of an economic boom and low and falling unemployment rates. In both Sweden and Finland, research into the consequences of the recession revealed that lone mothers made up one of the groups that were hardest hit. This did not, however, translate into political initiatives to improve their situation, or to address any special problems lone mothers might face in the labour market. During and immediately after the recession, there was no financial room for expanding social policies towards any group, and afterwards, this particular lesson from the crisis years has never been addressed. Lone parents' vulnerability might have become more visible, but they were still not seen as a distinct group that required political attention.

There are some points to be made regarding the demarcation line between family support (for new cohabiting partners) and state benefits. Can we interpret any of the changes in this respect as attempts to reintroduce the male breadwinner 'by the back door'? In Sweden, the question of household status is not relevant for any social insurance benefits. In Finland, the right to an extra transfer as a lone parent ceases when the parent moves in with a new partner.

The money lost is, however, only a small amount – so small, in fact, it can be argued that it makes up little more than compensation for the unfavourable economies of scale of living as a sole adult with a child. Taking economies of scale into consideration is different from assuming that need no longer exists because a male breadwinner has been reinstalled in the family. The Norwegian case is inherently more controversial, since there is more money at stake. The Norwegian solution must be seen as a compromise between, on the one hand, the wish to create a flexible system that does not discourage lone mothers from forming new relationships, and on the other hand, the fear of creating disincentives to marriage and fuelling resentment among married couples with children. The Norwegian solution, then, comes across as more pragmatic than as a covert attempt to reinstate the male breadwinner. Moreover, in both Norway and Finland, it is up to the benefit claimant herself to report any changes in her living arrangements. This amounts to only a minimal increase in social control.

Given what we have already mentioned about economies of scale, and also knowing that women generally bring home lower wages than men do, it is relatively easy to understand why lone mothers are still more vulnerable to poverty than people living in other family forms. A striking finding in the three country outlines above is, however, that lone mothers are also particularly vulnerable in the labour market – that they have lower participation rates and higher unemployment rates than mothers living in two-parent families. Why would this be? And to what extent could – or should – this disadvantage be countered by political intervention? The two latter questions are linked: types of policy interventions depend on the nature of the problem. In the final section of this chapter, I will outline five types of explanations for the patterns we have seen: choice/preferences, selection, stress/illness, inflexibility, and discrimination, and discuss what role policies may play in relation to each of these.

Why are lone mothers disadvantaged in the labour market?

The lower overall labour market participation rates among lone mothers can be explained by lone mothers' different *choices and preferences*. One obvious point, in the cases of Norway and Sweden, is that lone mothers are less inclined to take up part-time work. The high participation rates of married and cohabiting mothers in these countries are to a large extent made up of part-time workers, and in both countries lone mothers are more likely than married/ cohabiting mothers to work full time. This may also explain why participation rates of lone mothers are lower than those of partnered mothers in these countries, while the pattern is the reverse in many other countries (Bradshaw and Finch, 2002, p 31). The gender-segregated labour market with high incidence of part-time work among women may boost the participation rates of partnered mothers – who can rely on their partner to bring home the bigger income – while it does less to encourage work among lone parents who are solely responsible for the family economy. Another reason for the lower overall participation rates may have to do with different take-up in education: in all the Nordic countries we have information on, lone mothers are more likely than married/ cohabiting mothers to be in education (Gähler, 2001, table 4; Kjeldstad and Rønsen, 2002, p 86). Finally, it should be mentioned that lone mothers may actively choose home-based childcare in a transition period, to get some breathing space for themselves and their children while adapting to the radically new situation of living without a partner in the household (Duncan and Edwards, 1999; Syltevik, 1996).

Given the large proportions who pass through a period as a lone parent in the Nordic countries, the *selection* hypothesis is not immediately appealing. It gathers partial support in analyses undertaken in Norway (Kjeldstad and Rønsen, 2002, table 4.1) and Sweden (Nordenmark, 2000; Gähler, 2001), but has nevertheless failed to convince national analysts. Even though lone mothers, on average, are more likely to lack characteristics that make them attractive in the labour market, their unemployment rates are still higher than those of married/cohabiting mothers when such factors are controlled for. Negative selection to lone motherhood does not therefore seem to be a main factor causing disadvantage. There may, however, be factors related to the relationship break-up and transition period that influence the capacity to compete for work in strained labour markets. Lone parenthood itself tends to be a life phase of limited duration.[4] It follows that this category will at any point in time include a number of people in the midst of a dramatic transition, which can cause *stress and illness*. It is a known research finding that marital break-up increases the risks of health-related long-term absence from work and disability pensioning, and also often leads to lower concentration and less efficiency at work (for example, Eriksen et al, 1999). In Sweden, Nordenmark (2000, p 109) found that lone parents harbour greater worries for the future than any other group, that they far more often experience financial problems, and also that they far more often report general health problems (see also Gähler, 2001). Even if lone parents are not a select group of people lacking in resources, therefore, the stresses of becoming and being a lone parent may still take up a lot of energy and make lone parents vulnerable in turbulent periods.

Adding to this is the fact that lone parents are *less flexible* than workers with less comprehensive caring responsibilities. They have no partner to share responsibility with when the child is ill, who can stay at home with the children if they have to work late, or provide any of the practical help that is necessary for a flexible worker. It requires far more planning for them to maintain stable employment, especially if they are expected to work outside regular hours. They are also far more dependent on working in reasonable proximity to the home – long journeys to work may imply the child is left alone and unsupervised for hours after school. These factors are often emphasised by lone parents themselves in qualitative studies when employment is discussed (Syltevik, 1996; Duncan and Edwards, 1999; Morner, 2003). Since this lack of flexibility limits the range of jobs available to lone parents, it can account both for their lower participation rates and higher risk of unemployment. Another factor is that employers may be all too conscious of these limitations. National observers (Björnberg, 1997b; Kjeldstad and Rønsen, 2003; Ugreninov, 2003) have suggested that lone mothers may face *discrimination* in the labour market, although no studies have been done on this issue. Morner (2003, p 139ff) brought up the issue of employers' attitudes in her qualitative interviews with lone mothers in Sweden, and found that the responses carried a considerable ambivalence. Her respondents 'took for granted' that they would be judged by their capabilities rather than their family status, but on the other hand, they would avoid talking about the issue in job interviews, or they would go out of their way to convince employers that they would be good employees *despite* the fact they were lone mothers. The higher unemployment rates indicate that employers may be reluctant to hire a lone parent, but this is one area we still know too little about.

Each of these possible explanations for lone parents' different pattern of labour market participation suggests different policy responses. Lower labour market participation rates for lone mothers are not in themselves problematic, as long as they do not lead to poverty or permanent exclusion from paid employment. Indeed, the lower participation rates may be at least partly caused by the lone mothers' own preferences: they may reject the possibility of part-time work, want to go back to education, or be willing to pay the price for spending more time at home with the children. One can, however, think of measures to facilitate part-time work among lone mothers, to make it possible for them to integrate earning and caring responsibilities in the same way as so many mothers in couples do in the Nordic countries. Such measures would involve some form of wage subsidy, or special tax deductions. The problem with these kinds of strategies is of course the danger of creating a poverty trap, where the marginal tax rate on increasing incomes becomes extremely high.

The added challenges of being a lone parent in a strained labour market are not easily overcome. To the extent that negative selection is an issue, there is little public authorities can do about it. Physical and mental illness is a clear disadvantage in a workplace, and perhaps the best way of combating exclusion on these grounds is to work towards creating working environments that manage to include employees even in periods when their productivity is less than 100%. The inflexibility of lone parenthood can be alleviated, to some extent, through accessible childcare and frequent and reliable public transport. But a lone mothers will need a private support network with considerable resources if, for instance, she is to take up a job that includes frequent travels and overnight stays. There are certain limitations to this family situation that cannot be met by political interventions. Discrimination, on the other hand, is a political issue. All the Nordic countries employ anti-discriminatory policies in the workplace, with explicit policies against discrimination based on gender and ethnicity. More sensitivity to the possibility of discrimination on the basis of family situation may be a useful broadening of this perspective – although, it should be emphasised, we still lack solid information about if, or to what extent, such discrimination actually happens.

Conclusion

Sweden, Finland and Norway are all countries in which mothers are expected and encouraged to work outside the home. This policy also applies to lone mothers. Norway was the latecomer, but by the end of the 1990s there can be little doubt that 'employment' and 'activation' were the terms that most guided policies towards lone parents in this country. It is no longer argued that women need special support because they lack a man to provide for them –

rather, what women need are solid structures that help them reconcile their earning and caring responsibilities. Beyond the short-term transitional support available in Norway, none of the Nordic countries has a policy for 'unsupported mothers' in this day and age.

Solid evidence that lone mothers are still disadvantaged, particularly in times of recession, has done nothing to alter this policy approach. That there may be limitations to the strategy of treating lone mothers as (potential) workers – albeit workers with particular caring needs – jars with the ideology of gender equality that permeates the Nordic countries. The 'working mother's policy' (Lindvert, 2002) is still largely unchallenged. And it can easily be argued that to be included in the dual-earner/dual-carer state as working mothers is far preferable for lone mothers than to live on the margins of the male-breadwinner ideology and receive scattered support as unsupported mothers. But if the pitiful figure of the unsupported mother is gone, a new troubled woman (and a few men) may already be emerging to fill her place: the disadvantaged worker. Their flexibility is limited by their caring obligations, their energy to compete in the labour market may be drained by the stress and sadness of a relationship break-up, and they may face discrimination from prospective employers.

The vast majority of lone mothers in the Nordic countries are doing well, and available evidence, most importantly on child poverty, indicates that they do better than women in the same situation in most other countries. There is certainly no reason to argue that the working mothers approach has failed lone mothers. But as is often the case in social policy, measures that solve one set of problems have the tendency, over time, to create new ones. The very strong emphasis on employment may also have its costs, and these become particularly visible in times of recession. Strong belief in the merits of this approach is no reason not to consider potential downsides – not to turn back the clock, but to face the challenges of the present and the future as adequately as possible.

Notes

[1] For data on employment (short time series) and poverty, see, however, NOSOSCO (2004). For small-scale, qualitative studies of lone parenthood in Denmark, see Bak (1997); Juul Christensen (1999); Polakow et al (2001).

[2] The project was funded by the Nordic Council of Ministers and the Norwegian Research Council (for more information, see www.york.ac.uk/inst/spru/research/summs/welempfc.htm).

[3] Nevertheless, this brought Finnish policy principles in line with those of Norway and Sweden, where the status of the parent as single, married, or cohabiting never affected the right to forwarded child maintenance. Forwarded maintenance in these countries is seen as the child's right, and is not mediated by the parent's status as 'lone' or 'coupled' (see Skevik, 2001b, 2003).

[4] Research in Norway and Sweden indicates an average period of three to four years as a lone parent (Kjeldstad and Skevik, 2004).

References

Bak, M. (1997) *Enemorfamilien*, Copenhagen: Forlaget Sociologi.

Björnberg, U. (1996) 'Ensamstående mödrar i Sverige', in A.M. Berggren (ed) *Kvinnorna och Välfärden*, Stockholm: Forskningssamrådsnämden, pp 82-94.

Björnberg, U. (1997a) 'Single mothers in Sweden: supported workers who mother', in S. Duncan and R. Edwards (eds) *Single Mothers in an International Context: Mothers or Workers?*, London: UCL Press, pp 241-68.

Björnberg, U. (1997b) 'Mödrar på nittiotalets arbetsmarknad: en jämförelse mellan gifta och ensamstående', in I. Persson and E. Wadensjö (eds) *Glastak och Glasväggar? Den Könssegregerade Arbetsmarknaden* (SOU 1997:137), Stockholm: Fritzes, pp 213–28.

Björnberg, U. and Dahlgren, L. (2003) *Labour Supply: The Case of Sweden*, Report for the project 'Welfare policies and employment in the context of family change' (available at: www.york.ac.uk/inst/spru/research/summs/welempfc.htm).

Bradbury, B. and Jäntti, M. (2001) 'Child poverty across twenty-five countries', in B. Bradbury, S.P. Jenkins and J. Micklewright (eds) *The Dynamics of Child Poverty in Industrialized Countries*, Cambridge: Cambridge University Press, pp 62-91.

Bradshaw, J. and Finch, N. (2002) *A Comparison of Child Benefit Packages in 22 Countries*, Research Report 174, London: Department for Work and Pensions.

Bradshaw, J. and Terum, L.I. (1997) 'How Nordic is the Nordic Model?: Social assistance in a comparative perspective', *Scandinavian Journal of Social Welfare*, vol 6, no 4, pp 247-56.

Duncan, S. and Edwards, R. (1999) *Lone Mothers, Paid Work and Gendered Moral Rationalities*, Basingstoke: Macmillan.

Duncan, S. and Strell, M. (2004) 'Combining lone motherhood and paid work: the rationality mistake and Norwegian social policy', *Journal of European Social Policy*, vol 14, no 1, pp 41-54.

Ellingsæter, A.-L. (2003) 'The complexity of family policy reform', *European Societies*, vol 5, no 4, pp 419-43.

Eriksen, W., Natvig, B. and Bruusgaard, D. (1999) 'Marital disruption and long-term work disability – a four year prospective study', *Scandinavian Journal of Public Health*, vol 27, no 3, pp 196-202.

Forssén, K. (1998) *Children, Families and the Welfare State: Studies on the Outcomes of Finnish Family Policy*, Report Series No 92, Helsinki: STAKES.

Forssén, K., Laukkanen, A.-M. and Ritakallio, V.-M. (2003) *Labour Supply: The Case of Finland*, Report for the project 'Welfare policies and employment in the context of family change' (available at: www.york.ac.uk/inst/spru/research/summs/welempfc.htm).

Gähler, M. (2001) 'Bara en mor – ensamstående mödrars ekonomiska levnadsvillkor i 1990-talets Sverige', in A. Bergmark, O. Bäckman, M. Börjcson, P. Edin, F. Estrada, M. Gähler, A. Nilsson and O. Åslund (eds) *Ofärd i Välfärden: Kommittén Välfärdsbokslut* (SOU 2001:54), Stockholm: Fritzes, pp 15-99.

Heikkilä, M. and Uusitalo, H. (eds) (1997) *The Costs of Cuts: Studies on Cutbacks in Social Security and their Effects in the Finland of the 1990s*, Helsinki: STAKES.

Hiilamo, H. (2002) *The Rise and Fall of Nordic Family Policy: Historical Development and Changes During the 1990s in Sweden and in Finland*, Helsinki: STAKES.

Juul Kristensen, C. (1999) *Socialt Udsatte Enlige Mødre Med Flere Børn*, Frederikshavn: Dafolo.

Kjeldstad, R. and Rønsen, M. (2002) *Enslige Foreldre på Arbeidsmarkedet 1980-1999: En Sammenligning med Gifte mødre og Fedre*, Oslo: Statistics Norway.

Kjeldstad, R. and Rønsen, M. (2003) 'Lav sysselsetting blant enslige forsørgere: Arbeidsvegring eller utestengning?', *Søkelys på Arbeidsmarkedet*, vol 20, no 1, pp 37-43.

Kjeldstad, R. and Skevik, A. (2004) 'Enslige forsørgere: en sosialpolitisk kategori utgått på dato?', in A.-L. Ellingsæter and A. Leira (eds) *Velferdsstaten og Familien: Utfordringer og Dilemmaer*, Oslo: Gyldendal Akademisk, pp 231-60.

Leira, A. (1992) *Welfare States and Working Mothers*, Cambridge: Cambridge University Press.

Lewis, J. with Hobson, B. (1997) 'Introduction', in J. Lewis (ed) *Lone Mothers in European Welfare Regimes: Shifting Policy Logics*, London: Jessica Kingsley Publishers, pp 1-20.

Lindvert, J. (2002) 'A world apart: Swedish and Australian gender equality policy', *NORA – Nordic Journal of Women's Studies*, vol 10, no 2, pp 99-107.

Millar, J. and Rowlingson, K. (eds) (2001) *Lone Parents, Employment and Social Policy: Cross-national Comparisons*, Bristol: The Policy Press.

Morner, C.G. (2003) *Självständigt Beroende: Ensamstående Mammors Försörgningsstrategier*, Gothenburg: Gothenburg University.

Nordenmark, M. (2000) 'Familiesituasjon och arbetsmarknadsstatus: vad förklarar ensamstående fåoräldrars låga sannolikhet att erhålla ett arbete?', *Arbetsmarknad och Arbetsliv*, vol 6, no 2, pp 97-111.

NOSOSCO (Nordic Social Statistical Committee) (2004) *Single Parents in the Nordic Countries*, Report Series, Copenhagen: NOSOSCO.

OECD (Organisation for Economic Co-operation and Development) (2003) *Labour Force Statistics 1982-2002*, Paris: OECD.

Polakow, V., Halskov, T. and Scholtz Jørgensen, P. (2001) *Diminished Rights: Danish Lone Mother Families in International Context*, Bristol: The Policy Press.

Sainsbury, D. (1996) *Gender, Equality and Welfare States*, Cambridge: Cambridge University Press.

Sainsbury, D. (1999) 'Gender and social-democratic welfare states', in D. Sainsbury (ed) *Gender and Welfare State Regimes*, Oxford: Oxford University Press, pp 75-114.

Skevik, A. (2001a) 'Lone parents and employment in Norway', in J. Millar and K. Rowlingson (eds) *Lone Parents, Employment and Social Policy: Cross-national Comparison*, Bristol: The Policy Press, pp 87-105.

Skevik, A. (2001b) *Family Ideology and Social Policy: Policies toward Lone Parents in Norway and the UK*, Oslo: NOVA.

Skevik, A. (2003) 'Children of the welfare state: individuals with entitlements, or hidden in the family?', *Journal of Social Policy*, vol 32, no 3, pp 423-40.

Song, M. (1996) 'Changing conceptualisations of lone parenthood in Britain: lone parents or single mums', *The European Journal of Women's Studies*, vol 3, no 4, pp 377-97.

Sørensen, A.M. (1994) 'Women's economic risk and the economic position of single mothers', *European Sociological Review*, vol 10, no 2, pp 173-88.

Sørensen, A.M. (2001) 'Gender equality in earnings and at home', in M. Kautto, J. Fritzell, B. Hvinden, J. Kvist and H. Uusitalo (eds) *Nordic Welfare States in the European Context*, London: Routledge, pp 98-115.

St prp (Stortingsproposisjon) no 1 (1993/94) *Statsbudsjettet Medregnet Folketrygden for Budsjetterminen 1994*, Oslo: Statens forvaltningstjeneste.

Syltevik, L. (1996) *Fra Relasjonelt til Individualisert Alenemoderskap: En Studie av Alenemødre som Mødre, Lønnsarbeidere og Klienter i Velferdsstaten*, Bergen: Bergen University.

Syltevik, L. and Wærness, K. (2004) 'Det rasler i lenker – forsørgernormer i endring?', in A.-L. Ellingsæter and A. Leira (eds) *Velferdsstaten og Familien: Utfordringer og Dilemmaer*, Oslo: Gyldendal Akademisk, pp 100-27.

Ugreninov, E. (2003) 'Hvorfor jobber så få alenemødre?', *Samfunnsspeilet*, vol 17, no 6, pp 33-7.

Uusitalo, H. (1997) 'Four years of recession: what happened to income distribution?', in M. Heikkilä and H. Uusitalo (eds) *The Costs of Cuts: Studies on Cutbacks in Social Security and their Effects in the Finland of the 1990s*, Helsinki: STAKES.

TWELVE

Epilogue: Scandinavian policies of parenthood – a success story?

Anne Lise Ellingsæter and Arnlaug Leira

Since the early 1990s the Scandinavian welfare states have pursued wide-ranging parenthood policy reforms. Welfare state investment in the early childhood years, based on core programmes instituted in previous periods, has expanded in Denmark, Finland, Norway and Sweden, and public expenses for childcare have increased substantially. Policy innovations have been introduced; most notable are daddy quotas and more flexible uptake in parental leave arrangements. In general, childcare-related rights of parents and children have been strengthened (Leira, 2002). Paid parental leave has been prolonged. Cash grant schemes add to the entitlements of parents with young children in Finland and Norway. The Nordic countries are among those coming closest to meeting the European Union targets for childcare provision (European Communities, 2004). Childcare services are approaching universal coverage in Denmark and Sweden; the large majority of children under school age are enrolled in childcare institutions, including the under threes (Bergqvist and Nyberg, 2001; Borchorst, 2002; Leira, this volume). Despite considerable growth in coverage rates, in Norway demand still lags behind supply (Ellingsæter; Leira, this volume). In Finland all pre-school children have the right to attend state-sponsored childcare services, or alternatively, to receive a cash benefit for childcare (Salmi, this volume).

This study is set in a period that provided a new economic and cultural context for the Scandinavian welfare state model. Thus it is interesting to note that the expansion of parenthood policies took place during the troubled 1990s, a period of deep economic problems and labour market restructuring, and into the recovery of the early 2000s. In this period neoliberal currents, with particular emphasis on 'flexibility' and 'choice' got a stronger foothold in the welfare policy debate. In a period of economic austerity, as a main rule, work/family policy reform was not instituted to dismantle services or benefits. Welfare state approaches to families with young children show a remarkable continuity, although there were some cases of redesigning existing policy programmes, cuts in benefits, or slowing down of provision. However, in the few cases where benefits were not reduced, but abolished altogether, as happened to the cash grant for childcare in Sweden, and later, the daddy quota in Denmark, this was, arguably, due to a political shift in government, not a response to economic severity: a shift from a centre-right to a social democratic government in the first case, and the other way around in the latter. This may support Huber's and Stephens' (2001) interesting argument that partisan politics is the most important factor that has shaped welfare states. The varying strength of social democracy and the left has been vital for the continuation versus a weakening of the gender equality profile in parenthood policies. National differences are notable also in post-recession policies, in which the Swedish situation is back to 'normal' (Lindbom and Rothstein, 2004), recession policies representing a 'parenthesis' in the country's development (Hiilamo, this volume). Finland seems to be more deeply affected – and thus in line with the 'permanent austerity' diagnosis of welfare states suggested by some scholars (Pierson, 2001).

Parallel with the common conception and classification of the Scandinavian welfare states as fairly homogeneous, their differences have long been the subject of debate (for recent contributions, see Kautto et al, 1999, 2001). The Nordic similarities are most obvious when comparison is made with the welfare states of Southern and Continental Europe, where the private sector and the family play a much more significant role in providing social care and welfare (for example, Millar and Warman, 1996; Bettio and Prechal, 1998; Jenson and Sineau, 2003). Lately, the particular Scandinavian co-existence of high labour market participation among mothers and high fertility rates is often attributed to rather generous work/family policies. Certainly, welfare state policies play an important and necessary part, but are not sufficient as an explanation (Rønsen and Skrede, this volume).

Intra-Nordic comparisons reveal differences in mothers' employment patterns in the region. While the economic activity rate of mothers with children under the age of six was well above 70% in Sweden and Norway in 2000, the rate of Finnish mothers was significantly lower. The prevalence of women's part-time work has been quite different, with Norway at the high and Finland at the low end, although differences have been declining in recent years.

In the 1990s, as in previous decades, policies aimed at balancing jobs and childcare convey a picture of variation within relatively similar policy frameworks as witnessed in the provision of childcare services, leave arrangements and cash transfers (see, for example, Leira, 1992, 2002; Anttonen and Sipilä, 1996; Ellingsæter, 1998; Bergqvist et al, 1999). Nordic work/family policies reflect and support similar models of gender equality and family ideals. In various combinations, and to varying extents, the policies of the four countries all promote working motherhood and caring fatherhood. Throughout Scandinavia, state-sponsored childcare has been advocated as a means to further gender equality in employment, and as good for the children. Parental leave policies, in addition, are further committed to promoting equality between mothers and fathers, assuming that it is in the best interests of parents and children to equalise both the economic provider and carer aspects of parenthood. Still, important differences are visible. National particularities have long been noted. For example, main divergences between Finland and Sweden were demonstrated more than a decade ago in Kamerman and Kahn's (1991) study of European childcare, in the telling titles of the countries' respective contributions: 'Finland: Supporting Parental Choice' and 'Sweden: Supporting Work, Family, and Gender Equality'. Recent developments in parenthood policies indicate both converging trends, as well as continuing disparities. What this means is that all the four national models are more complex than the 'Scandinavian model' label indicates. National legacies and circumstances undoubtedly continue to shape work/family policies and their outcomes.

To sum up, in several respects, the policies of parenthood in Scandinavia are a success story, even if important criticisms are taken into account, such as shortages of services, reduction in standards, supply not meeting demands, eligibility criteria being too tight, and the setting up of schemes that are too rigid, and so on. Scandinavian policies facilitating work–life balance and gender equality in parents' practices are still ahead of other advanced industrial democracies. This is associated with the highest rates of labour market participation among mothers in the Western world, generating an increasing economic autonomy among women. Mothers' role as providers and as economic contributors, to both national and family economies, has been significantly strengthened over the period studied (for example, Haataja and Nyberg, this volume).

This is not to say that striving for gender equality is a thing of the past, nor is it neglecting the challenges facing Nordic family and gender equality policies in increasingly diversifying and multiethnic societies. The gender equality project is still unfinished. There are obvious limits to this success story when one asks in what directions are policies actually taking the gender relations of parenthood. The ideal of a combined dual-earner/dual-carer model, promoting gender equality in working life and in families, is only partially realised. Scandinavia is characterised by a situation of 'gender equality light' (Rønsen and Skrede, this volume). The gender division of labour is changing, most notably in the labour market, while unpaid family and domestic work is still rather unevenly divided. Hence, important questions concern the policy rationales behind the reforms instituted, and whose needs are being addressed – those of mothers, fathers or children? Are there any signs of shifts in 'childcare policy thinking'? There clearly are some influences in recent policy currents that may weaken the ambition of a more even distribution of paid and unpaid work among men and women (for example, Borchorst; Ellingsæter; Rønsen and Skrede; Salmi, this volume).

From welfare state crisis to internal 'enemies'

The crisis of the mature welfare state in advanced industrial democracies has been a recurring subject in welfare state analysis. Comparative studies have concluded that retrenchment was pervasive; almost all countries cut entitlements in some programmes (Huber and Stephens, 2001). Since the economic and employment crises of the 1990s, the economic and normative sustainability of the Nordic welfare state model has been repeatedly questioned. However, the Nordic economies have recovered, and the Nordic welfare states have been partially reformed but have proven remarkably resilient (Huber and Stephens, 2001, p xi). There is a growing consensus that economic, demographic and social pressures on the welfare state indeed exist, but rather than dismantling the welfare state, contemporary developments are characterised by welfare state redesign formed by national settings (for example, Pierson, 2001).

In this period, in which external pressures on the Nordic economies – small and open – have escalated, a consistent pattern in the work/family policy area is that policies to a considerable extent are patterned by national factors. This is in tune with the more general argument that the main challenge to the Nordic model is not necessarily an external 'enemy'; major threats of dismantling may come from within. The Scandinavian model is a political system that has grown over time through a cumulative process of adjustments and modifications (Barth et al, 2003). Whether this egalitarian, redistributive model will survive depends on its adjustment to a new situation of modern knowledge-based production, great affluence and a social structure with a dominant middle class (Barth et al, 2003).

Pressures for a shift in policy values and emphasis – from equality to choice – gained new momentum in the 1990s, triggered by ideological and social change. Parental choice was in tune with the individualism promoted in neoliberal policy and ideology, and found resonance in the increasing diversification of family forms and practices. General theories about increasing individualisation and new forms of individualisation have been highly influential in family studies (see, for example, Giddens, 1991; Baumann, 2000; Beck and Beck-Gernsheim, 2002). However, a wide range of empirical studies have questioned the notion of an excessive individualism that is disseminated in public debates and in research.

Parental 'choice' – confronting gender equality

As evidenced in several of the chapters in this volume, *parental choice* has become a highly influential family policy metaphor in the Nordic welfare state debates (see also Ellingsæter and Leira, 2004). Family policy metaphors have normative powers, political metaphors are part of the language of power, and may be more influential than metaphors within other social fields (Lakoff and Johnson, 1980). Arguments about individual and free choice are increasingly becoming relevant as policy rationales (Sipilä, 1995; Wærness, 2003). The opportunity of individuals to make choices about services or benefits is often presented as a welfare aim in its own right.

Parental choice is not a new idea, but its content and what it means have changed over time. Nordic parenthood legislation of the 1970s introduced parental choice in parental leave where parents were offered the choice of sharing the greater part of the leave period. At the time, legislation was commonly interpreted as an expression of the gender equality commitment of Nordic policies, inviting the fathers to become more equal partners in caring for very young children. Although politically 'correct', the sharing of caring did not strike home with parents. Recognising that the chances for obtaining greater equality in the labour market would be seriously undermined if gender equality stopped at home, in 2005 all the Nordic countries, except Denmark, add to the father's right to care by offering a daddy quota (Borchorst; Lammi-Taskula, this volume). The quota was welcomed by some as protecting the rights of fathers, but opposed by others because it interfered with the free choice of parents. Opportunities for parental choice were further expanded in Norway and Finland in the 1990s, when cash grants for parental childcare were instituted as an entitlement (Ellingsæter; Salmi, this volume).

Historically, a multitude of family forms is nothing new. Therborn (2004) argues that, since the 1970s, Western European families have returned to modern historical complexity. The 'recovered complexity' is likely to remain, generating contradictions and conflicts. What is new, Beck-Gernsheim (2002) points out, is that these forms are the result of more or less conscious *choices*. Individualisation has two components. While, on the one hand, many of the traditional social relations, bonds and belief systems that regulated people's lives have lost meaning, on the other hand the individual is regulated by the institutions of the modern society, such as the labour market, welfare state and educational systems, with all their rights and duties. This 'institutionalised individualism', a concept Beck and Beck-Gernsheim (2002) have derived from Talcott Parsons (1978), refers to regulations based on the individual's and not the family's rights and duties. Accordingly, the rights of the individual may collide with collective concerns, such as family concerns.

Different forms of detraditionalisation are clearly important in our understanding of family change. However, the individualised frame of interpretation of modern family life has raised critical questions. Individualisation is connected with a conception of autonomous actors who have to make choices in all life situations. This conceptualisation of the actor is too limited and needs to be supplemented with an understanding of the individual as anchored in different social relations, characterised by varying degrees of autonomy and dependence over the lifecourse (Syltevik and Wærness, 2004).

There is no disagreement about the fact that both mothers and fathers make real choices, and in that sense create their own individual life biographies. But the many normative and practical demands of parenthood challenge the exaggerated individualist thesis. In social tradition, family law and welfare legislation, parenthood involves long-lasting obligations. The choices made by parents are not independent of the family's economic and material resources and the opportunity structures mothers and fathers are facing. Market power is unequally distributed. Economic provider practices are not equal in most families. A considerable number of Scandinavian women do not have an income sufficient to provide for themselves and their children. Choices regarding number of children, childcare, consumption and paid work, or parental break-up for that matter, cannot be seen independently from the power relations within the family (Bourdieu, 1996; Jensen, 2004; Skevik, this volume). What 'parental choice' is about obviously varies between lone and partnered parents. Often overlooked in the parental choice discourse is the gendering of family and parental obligations, and the different moral worlds in which motherhood and fatherhood are embedded. The male-breadwinner norm is in decline, but not a thing of the past; the image of mother as primary childcarer is still brought to bear. What is first choice – wage work or care, and who chooses first – the mother or the father? Irrespective of how these processes of choice are decided, it is important to reflect over the long-term implications of choice especially with respect to gender equality in resources, opportunities and outcomes (Leira, 2002; Skrede, 2004).

As indicated in several contributions in this volume (for example, Ellingsæter; Lammi-Taskula), gender-neutral family policies advocating 'choice' with respect to care for children have gendered effects. In the everyday life of families with young children, 'choice' usually means *women* making the choices, that is, between paid employment and childcare. Men's choices between employment and children are seldom an issue, except in the case of father rights in relation to parental leave. In work/family policy studies, one main question is why parental choice results in reproducing gender inequality in the balancing of work and childcare.

In family and social care policies, choice is argued as a means by which to strengthen the consumer capabilities of families, as witnessed for example in the discussion of how demands for social care should be met, that is, with cash grants or the provision of care services. Choice is presented as a means by which to meet the diversifying needs of diversifying families. But in childcare, as in social care generally, choice of forms of care depends on alternatives to family-produced care services being available, at affordable cost, and on the individual being capable of making an informed choice.

The resources necessary for making a choice and the risks associated with it are, however, given little attention in public discourse. Baumann (2000, p 87) problematises this as: 'Not all choices on display are realistic; and the proportion of realistic choices is not the function of the number of items to choose from, but of the volume of resources at the disposal of the chooser'. Much more attention therefore has to be directed at people's *real* choices, the opportunities for choosing and the choices actually made. Mothers' employment rates cannot be read off as a function of public policies' treatment of families with children (Daly, 2000). Obviously, the context within which mothers are making their choices is fundamental for understanding the practices generated. In particular, the labour market situation cannot be overrated as a crucial prerequisite for mothers' (and fathers') employment patterns. Moreover, single mothers seem to be a group that is more sensitive to the labour market's ups and downs than other groups (Skevik, this volume).

Labour market restructuring and high unemployment rates in some of the countries mean that policy reforms and their reception were set in different contexts in the period examined. As shown in several of the contributions to this book, childcare policies are taken up and used in a variety of ways. Policies that look similar may differ with regard to motivation, context and effects on parents' practices, as is the case for the cash grant in Finland and Norway, and the daddy quota in Finland, Norway and Sweden. Legislation of cash grants for childcare was an expression of long-lasting political controversy over which family forms to support – families with employed or domesticated mothers. But, as demonstrated in a comparison of Finland and Norway, very high take-up rates of cash grants for childcare have different implications with regard to mothers' employment rates.

Policies for whose needs – mothers', fathers' or children's?

In answering the question about the direction in which policies are actually taking the gender relations of parenthood, it may be illuminating to ask a new question: what needs do Scandinavian parenthood policies address – those of mothers, fathers or children? In the late 1970s, discussing gender equality legislation, Scandinavian scholars pointed to possible conflicts of interests between women and men in families and between parents and children. However, mothers were not necessarily to shoulder alone the challenges posed by new family arrangements. Indeed, it was argued that it was worth considering 'whether the strengthening of women's position as mothers in the long run strengthen their position as women. A policy stimulating fathers to take care of their children might be more liberating to women' (Holter and Ve, 1979, p 209).

A common experience in the Nordic countries is that policies that familise or refamilise childcare, available for both parents, tend to be taken up by mothers. This is a general finding repeated over time, also in other countries. In the early 1990s this prompted Sheila Kamerman and Alfred Kahn (1991) to pose the fundamental question: 'Is there in fact a conflict between child policy and women's policy – between the interests of children and their mothers as individuals in their own right?' Their answer was 'no', based on the Swedish experiences so far.

Parental choice might appear as *the* policy response to the diversification of parents' work/family arrangements. However, in general, gender-neutral reforms that institute parental choice regarding childcare offer far more generous opportunities for fathercare and more equal sharing of childcare than is actually used. Take-up and use of gender-neutral reforms confirm mothers' position as the family's primary care person (Leira, 2002). Parental choice with respect to the balancing of work/family has not contributed impressively to the sharing of caring. However, more attention should be paid to the different formulations and regulations of the parental choice reforms, and whose needs are projected as the more important in political rhetoric, and whose needs are met under what circumstances. Is the take-up and use of parental choice reforms (parental leave and cash grants) evidence of the limits of policies in producing gender equality in parenthood? Why do some parents strive for equal sharing of earning and caring and some opt for more traditional approaches to parenthood? As demonstrated in several of the contributions, the questions might well be rephrased to ask under what conditions is 'parental choice' to succeed in providing greater equality of outcome.

Dismantling gender equality?

The role of policies in generating gender equality in the Nordic countries has been controversial and needs particular comment. The equal rights of women to engage in economic activity were, generally, accepted in the 1990s, although mothers' employment was still controversial in some parts of the population. Policies promoting gender equality within the private family sphere were, however, more controversial, and especially so in Denmark, where the daddy quota – promoting fathercare by 'gentle force', that is, with the earmarking of entitlements – was abolished after a short run.

How best to arrange children's care has remained a political hot topic throughout the period in question. Whether the state should fund defamilised childcare services or establish cash grants for parental childcare is one important question. More generally, which family forms should benefit from welfare state funding for care, for which forms of care and why, remain controversial topics. Should gender equality commitments give way to parental choice, or should the public purse be used purposefully for supporting the economic provider and carer responsibilities of both mothers and fathers? As formulated by Johanna Lammi-Taskula (this volume): 'can the welfare state change gender relations?'

In a situation of increasing emphasis not only on parental choice, but also on children's rights and welfare, work/care conflicts might well have to be put on the agenda again, and this time not as a female dilemma only.

In a wider perspective, the work/family policies and practices addressed in this book relate to the important debates about the future of the welfare state, and in particular the welfare states of the Nordic countries. The relationship between the welfare state and families is under continuous renegotiation regarding the distribution of responsibility and costs of welfare production and social care in society. An important question is which family patterns are targets of policy support, and which systems of income security and care provision the welfare state will guarantee for different families. While family patterns and parenthood are being transformed, it is important to acknowledge that the family institution is not only characterised by complexity and change, but also by considerable continuity.

Work/family policy analysis should focus not only on past policy patterns and the interest configurations associated with these, but also look into the emergence of new patterns (Michel and Mahon, 2002). While the crisis and predicted dismantling of the Nordic welfare state model seems to have been called off, at least temporarily, a critical question is whether we have come to a turning point with regard to the Nordic model of gender equality, in which reproductive policies have been so crucial. Are the Scandinavian welfare states facing the end of gender equality as a central aim of work/family policy?

In general, gender equality continues to be an important field of policy. Yet there are limitations and shortcomings. The degree of gender equality reflected in parents' practices shows that women continually spend less time in paid work, earn less and care more for their children than men do. There may be a case for particular concern regarding the childcare policy field, where there are signs of gender equality of outcome fading out as one of the central policy aims. The paradoxical reason for this may be that gender equality values are taken for granted, or alternatively that gender equality is considered as having gone too far, while pluralisation, individualisation and free choice are gaining ground ideologically and in practice.

The gains of policies aimed at equalising the opportunities and outcomes of women and men in the Nordic countries should not be underestimated. However, as is well known from Nordic research, gender equality concerns often come second to other considerations, and may have to give way (for example, Bergqvist et al, 1999; Skjeie and Teigen, 2003). The old question remains, however, as to what happens to gender equality in society at large if gender equality stops at the family front door? Under the redesign of the Scandinavian welfare states, also in work/family and care policies, questions about individual responsibility and the limits of solidarity are emerging. In light of current demographic trends and future labour shortages one might well ask how sustainable core elements of the current Nordic childcare policies are – long parental leaves and cash-for-care benefits. A mounting policy conflict between a 'care' line and a 'work line' might be on the horizon. A question pertaining to all European welfare states is to what extent it is advisable to develop/expand policies that are directed at keeping parents, in effect mainly mothers, out of the labour market for a substantial period of a work lifecourse that has been significantly shortened? However, the increasing involvement of fathers in the care of their children should not be overlooked, and the potential role of fathers in softening the work/care dilemma in Scandinavia should not be underestimated.

References

Anttonen, A. and Sipilä, J. (1996) 'European social care services: is it possible to identify models?', *Journal of European Social Policy*, vol 6, no 2, pp 87-100.

Barth, E., Moene, K. and Wallerstein, M. (2003*) Likhet under press: Utfordringer for den skandinaviske likhetsmodellen*, Oslo, Gyldendal Akademisk.

Baumann, Z. (2000) *Liquid Modernity*, Cambridge: Polity Press.

Beck, U. and Beck-Gernsheim, E. (2002) *Individualization*, London: Sage Publications.

Beck-Gernsheim, E. (2002) *Reinventing the Family*, Cambridge: Polity Press.

Bergqvist, C., Borchorst, A., Christensen, A.-D. Ramstedt-Silén, V., Raaum, N.C. and Styrkársdóttir, A. (eds) (1999) *Equal Democracies: Gender and Politics in the Nordic Countries*, Oslo: Aschehoug.

Bergqvist, C. and Nyberg, A. (2001) 'Den svenska barnomsorgsmodellen – kontinuitet och förändring under 1990-talet', in SOU 2001: 52, *Med välfärdsstaten som arbetsgivare*, Stockholm.

Bettio, F. and Prechal, S. (1998) *Care in Europe*, Joint report of the 'Gender and Employment' and the 'Gender and Law' Groups of Experts, Brussels, European Commission, DGV, Employment and Social Affairs.

Borchorst, A. (2002) 'Danish childcare policy: continuity rather than radical change', in S. Michel and R. Mahon (eds) *Childcare Policy at the Crossroads: Gender and Welfare State Restructuring*, New York, NY: Routledge, pp 267–85.

Bourdieu, P. (1996) 'On the Family as a Realized Category', *Theory, Culture and Society*, vol 13, no 3, pp 19–26.

Daly, M. (2000) 'A fine balance: women's labor market participation in international comparison', in F.W. Scharpf and V.A. Schmid (eds) *Welfare and Work in the Open Economy*, Volume II, Oxford: Oxford University Press, pp 467–510.

Ellingsæter, A.L. (1998) 'Dual breadwinner societies: provider models in the Scandinavian welfare states', *Acta Sociologica*, vol 41, no 1, pp 59–73.

Ellingsæter, A.L. and Leira, A. (2004) *Velferdsstaten og familien: Utfordringer og dilemmaer*, Oslo: Gyldendal Akademisk.

European Communities (2004) *Jobs, Jobs, Jobs: Creating More Employment in Europe*, Report of the Employment Taskforce chaired by Wim Kok, Luxembourg.

Giddens, A. (1991) *Modernity and Self-identity*, Cambridge: Polity Press.

Holter, H. and Ve, H.H. (1979) 'Social policy and the family in Norway', in J. Lipman-Blumen and J. Bernard (eds) *Sex Roles and Social Policy*, London: Sage Publications.

Huber, E. and Stephens J.D. (2001) *Development and Crisis of the Welfare State: Parties and Policies in Global Markets*, Chicago, IL: University of Chicago Press.

Jensen, A.M. (2004) 'Harde fakta om myke menn', in A.L. Ellingsæter and A. Leira (eds) *Velferdsstaten og familien: Utfordringer og dilemmaer*, Oslo: Gyldendal Akademisk, pp 201–30.

Jenson, J. and Sineau, M. (2003) (eds) *Who Cares? Women's Work, Childcare, and Welfare State Redesign*, Toronto, Buffalo, London: Toronto University Press.

Kamerman, S.B. and Kahn, A.J. (1991) *Child Care, Parental Leave, and the Under 3s: Policy Innovation in Europe*, New York, NY: Auburn House.

Kautto, M., Fritzell, J., Hvinden, B., Kvist, J. and Uusitalo, H. (2001) *Nordic Welfare States in the European Context*, London: Routledge.

Kautto, M., Heikkilä, M., Hvinden, B., Marklund, S. and Ploug, N. (1999) *Nordic Social Policy, Changing Welfare States*, London: Routledge.

Lakoff, G. and Johnson, M. (1980) *Metaphors We Live By*, Chicago, IL: University of Chicago Press.

Leira, A. (1992) *Welfare States and Working Mothers*, Cambridge: Cambridge University Press.

Leira, A. (2002) *Working Parents and the Welfare State*, Cambridge: Cambridge University Press.

Lindbom, A. and Rothstein, B. (2004) 'The mysterious survival of the Swedish welfare state', Paper for the Annual Meeting of the American Political Science Association, Chicago, 2-5 September.

Michel, S. and Mahon, R. (eds) (2002) *Childcare Policy at the Crossroads: Gender and Welfare State Restructuring*, New York, NY: Routledge.

Millar, J. and Warman, A. (1996) *Family Obligations in Europe*, London: Family Policy Studies Centre.

Parsons, T. (1978) *Action Theory and the Human Condition*, New York, NY: Free Press.

Pierson, P. (ed) (2001) *The New Politics of the Welfare State*, Oxford: Oxford University Press.

Sipilä, J. (1995) 'The right to choose: day care for children or money for parents', in J. Baldock (ed) *Social Policy Review* 7, pp 151-69.

Skjeie, H. and Teigen, M. (2003) *Menn i mellom*, Oslo: Gyldendal Akademisk.

Skrede, K. (2004) 'Familiepolitikkens grense – ved 'likestilling light'?', in A.L. Ellingsæter and A. Leira (eds) *Velferdsstaten og familien: Utfordringer og dilemmaer*, Oslo: Gyldendal Akademisk, pp 160-200.

Syltevik, L.J. and Wærness, K. (2004) 'Det rasler i lenker – forsørgernomer i endring?', in A.L. Ellingsæter and A.Leira (eds) *Velferdsstaten og familien: Utfordringer og dilemmaer*, Oslo: Gyldendal Akademisk, pp 100-27.

Therborn, G. (2004) *Between Sex and Power: Family in the World 1900-2000*, London and New York, NY: Routledge.

Wærness, K. (2003) 'Noen refleksjoner omkring det velgende individ, feministisk omsorgsetikk og den sosiologiske tradisjonen', *Sosiologisk Tidsskrift*, vol 11, no 1, pp 12-22.

Index